eBooked!

eBooked!

Integrating Free Online Book Sites into Your Library Collection

H. Anthony Bandy

LIBRARIES UNLIMITED

AN IMPRINT OF ABC-CLIO, LLC
Santa Barbara, California • Denver, Colorado • Oxford, England

Library of Congress Cataloging-in-Publication Data

Bandy, H. Anthony.
  eBooked! : integrating free online book sites into your library collection / H. Anthony Bandy.
    pages cm
  Includes bibliographical references and index.
  ISBN 978–1–59884–890–8 (pbk.) — ISBN 978–1–59884–891–5 (ebook) 1. Libraries—
Special collections—Electronic books. 2. Electronic books—Databases. 3. Books—Digitization. I. Title.
Z692.E4B36   2013
025.2′84—dc23   2013015533

ISBN: 978–1–59884–890–8
EISBN: 978–1–59884–891–5

17 16 15 14 13   1 2 3 4 5

This book is also available on the World Wide Web as an eBook.
Visit www.abc-clio.com for details.

Libraries Unlimited
An Imprint of ABC-CLIO, LLC

ABC-CLIO, LLC
130 Cremona Drive, P.O. Box 1911
Santa Barbara, California 93116-1911

This book is printed on acid-free paper ∞

Manufactured in the United States of America

Copyright Acknowledgments

Screenshots from DailyLit (www.dailylit.com), Google Books (books.google.com), HathiTrust (www.hathitrust.org), Ibiblio (www.ibiblio.org), Internet Archives (archive.org), Open Library (openlibrary.org), and Project Gutenberg (www.gutenberg.org), and others are all used with permission.

Contents

Acknowledgments

To my wife, Kelly and my kids, Brian, Kristin, and Matthew. Thanks for your help; I couldn't have done it without you!

To the staff and editors at ABC-CLIO, especially Barbara Ittner and Emma Bailey. Thank you for the opportunity as well as your patience as the book came together. Your knowledge and skills were invaluable in helping me tie all of these loose ends into something coherent!

A BIG thank you to the individuals, staff, and projects/websites who helped to answer all my myriad questions and comments, including DailyLit, the Internet Archive, HathiTrust, Google Books, the Open Library, ManyBooks, and Project Gutenberg. Thank you for your hard work in bringing your visions of knowledge and digital books so that everyone can share and learn together!

Introduction

I love being a librarian! There's something about libraries and books and helping patrons find the information they are looking for that makes it so satisfying as a profession. I also love books, either opening the latest shipment at the library or reading some of the volumes I have at home. There's just something about a physical book that's hard to completely describe. If you work in a library—either as staff, librarian, or administrator—then perhaps you feel the same way.

However, our world, our work, and our very definition of what a library is and does has completely changed in just the past few years. Cuts in both budgets and library funding have become the norm, while the Internet and easy digitization continue to transform our information exchanges. Our patrons are different as well—they expect more, both on a professional level as well as a resource level. From the librarian or staff perspective then, these transformations can make for challenging times.

No bigger adjustment can be seen than in the massive popularity and explosion of the digital book (or eBook, as its come to be known). Nothing is truly settled at this point—and we've only begun the transformation that has been led by publishers, authors, and the subject of this book: online digital book sites. With the arrival of the Google Books project, the continued popularity of HathiTrust, and a host of other online sites such as the Open Library, the Internet Archive, and even an old favorite, Project Gutenberg, our patrons and their eReaders—the iPads, the Nooks, the Kindles, and a host of cell phones and other portable devices—are demanding that we change.

As a profession, we're just now approaching this conundrum at somewhat full speed, discussing, Tweeting, and Facebooking all around. But the questions that arise are not simple to solve. For example, how do we train our staff on this digital revolution? What devices will our library support? Should our library just select a vendor and be done with the whole thing? Others in the profession are not asking questions at all and are instead secretly wishing their libraries, and librarianship, would return to the way things were. I have a message for those people: It's too late, the tide is rising, and you need to rapidly address this burgeoning issue.

Yet some questions now being asked go beyond our duties as librarians and staff. These questions address the whole issue of just what a library is and does. If we stop and consider this on a larger scale, how do changes such as these affect the library as an institution? How does your local community see your library? Is your library known for its forward thinking, or does your community see you as a relic of days gone by? From an internal standpoint, how does this digital revolution affect your budget? How about your technology plan? How about your strategic plan? From a staffing viewpoint, how do you get your staff quickly up to speed on such a shifting target?

These are just a few of the issues we've all heard raised and perhaps even considered ourselves. While we would all like a magic crystal ball to help us figure this out, and we would even settle for some form of standardization, there are really no hard and fast answers at this point. On the other hand, you have to do something. This book is based on the premise that we must go back to what has served us well since the early days of the Mosaic and Netscape web browsers: training and knowledge. Getting your staff up to speed with this digital revolution will go a long way toward helping to solve some of these essential questions we've been asking.

This book can be part of that approach. In this guide, you'll find information, you'll find knowledge, you'll find some questions, and you'll find some answers. So go ahead, highlight it, dog-ear it, and share it. Use this title as the springboard for getting yourself, your staff, and your library up to speed and knowledgeable about this new age and these digital book sites. Use this book as your analog companion, sitting by your keyboard or tablet as you surf. By taking a few moments and reading about each resource profiled here, you can get a better understanding of how these sites work, how to search them, and most importantly, how to use them in your everyday library workflow.

Structure

As you know, every book is different, both in teaching and approach. Some titles are academic in nature, helping readers understand relationships and principles. Others are practical, filled with examples, images, and answers. Which camp does this book fall in? While principles may be mentioned in passing, as you read the information in each chapter, my hope is that you will find this book to be an indispensable everyday resource. It is not theoretical; rather, it will help you understand and integrate this vital information as you work to serve your patrons.

The book begins by discussing problems many libraries are facing today, from budgets to staffing and more. Then it considers how digital book sites can address some of these issues and perhaps remove roadblocks that are impeding. From there, you'll move on to chapters about specific digital resource sites. What sort of digital resource sites will you explore? While there are many, in this book the list is condensed down to what I call the **Big Four,** plus a few others.

The **Big Four** consists of the following eBook sites:

- Google Books
- HathiTrust
- Internet Archive
- Open Library

There are other digital books sites that will be covered as well, although space constraints permit me to review only a few. Examples of these include Project Gutenberg, DailyLit, ManyBooks, and others. Some of these you may already be aware of, others perhaps not. As you learn about each one, take a look at its origins as well as the background information to understand what the site is intended for. Then move on to the discussion of how to use the resources on each site. You'll learn about searching and using results, along with various methods of integrating each resource into your library. This practical knowledge will go a long way toward helping you to remember specifics about each site as you work with your staff and patrons.

Illustrations and Screenshots

The old cliché "a picture is worth a thousand words" certainly holds true when referencing and teaching others about websites and computers. In my experience in training librarians on eBook technology and databases, I've found that presenting a dry topic mixed in with bullet points and statistics is a sure way to lose my audience and **not** get the message across. Knowing this to be a certainty, in this book I've tried to illustrate what the text is saying by including screenshots where applicable. In this way I hope to ease potential confusion or point out specific thoughts. As you work with each resource and then apply it to your own staff or patrons, you will hopefully remember the necessary information.

Other Resources

While most of the information you'll need is located in the chapters, you'll also find a small dictionary at the back of the book, as well as a bibliography section of sites and other articles. A vast amount of computer jargon is tossed around these days, and this dictionary will help you with specific definitions and abbreviations found in the book's chapters. The bibliography will help you find websites and other items used in researching this title and can provide more in-depth facts as needed.

Stories

Who doesn't love a story? If you've ever led storytime at the library or have experienced storytime as a patron at some point, then you know the fascination we all have with listening to the spoken word. Used to both illustrate and explain, stories can help get your point across in so many ways. In this same vein, this book presents scenarios, fictional libraries, and fictional librarians to illustrate both problems as well as potential solutions. In terms of budget wars, collection development, and even reference desks, hopefully you'll find these stories illustrative and helpful. You might have even experienced something similar to these stories yourself at some point!

Questions

As librarians or library staff, we're attuned to public service and are used to helping with myriads of questions from patrons of all types. From the mundane to the technically specific, we're all experts in one way or another on any number of topics. In this sense then, questions keep us sharp and knowledgeable both about our libraries' collections and our patrons' changing research and information needs.

Likewise, in this book you will find sample questions in each chapter. These reflect the chapter's contents and give you an opportunity to find the answers for yourself, learning more about each resource in the process. They can also be used in staff training. To help out, the answers are provided at the back of the book. However, try the questions first. As you answer, keep in mind that when all is said and done, there's really no right or wrong way. We all are wired differently and answer questions in different ways. So if my answer varies from yours, it's okay. The goal of learning more about the particular resource has been met!

Important Points to Remember

When working with new topics or techniques, sometimes there is just too much to remember. While it's certainly possible to take notes, often just going over the main topics is enough to help us remember what is important. So at the back of each chapter, you'll find a list of highlights and information—important points for you to remember about each site that has been discussed. These highlights consist of the main ideas from each resource and can serve as knowledge points when working with your staff or even when sharing with patrons.

Some Final Thoughts

So what is the purpose of this book? It is my hope that with this work, you can advocate better integration of these resources into your library. Technology is not a threat and neither are these sites. Rather, they are another set of tools that you can use as a librarian, both with your staff and your patrons, with the end goal being to illustrate to everyone that your library is a valuable resource, not something that can be easily replaced by a website, eBook, or computer file. Contrary to popular belief, I still believe libraries and librarians are relevant even in our current technological age.

Online digital book sites are rapidly changing libraries, and this book can help you and your staff stay informed and be knowledgeable about them. In addition, it provides help with developing the everyday skills needed to integrate these resources into your library work. Is this a perfect resource? Is it a finished resource? The answer is no on both counts, as in this digital age, there are always reinventions and reintroductions. But it is a great start to the ongoing digital adventure that our libraries have become.

I hope you enjoy this book and find it useful.

Chapter 1

Challenges, Issues and a Measure of Success

Millions of books and magazines! Free access to digital materials for your library and your patrons! No extra costs to your already pummeled materials budget! Who wouldn't enjoy access to resources such as this? But we all know this doesn't exist, right? **Wrong!** In reality, access to digital content just like this does exist and is growing at a stupendous rate. Yet, unfortunately, many libraries refuse to even acknowledge that these resources are available, or if they do, only use them to complement their current on-shelf collections and vendor-provided databases. *It doesn't have to be this way.*

Integrating free digital eBook sites such as Google Books, HathiTrust, and others into everyday library services is one of the best options currently available in solving some of the major challenges and issues currently threatening many of our institutions, and to a lesser extent, our library profession as a whole. In this chapter, you will take a look at this in detail, examining both the challenges and increased expectations of libraries, as well as how these sites can help. Along the way, you will look at a few of the digital book sites that will appear in the following chapters. For now, however, let's start with a story, one that might remind you of your library or another library you know.

Did You See Dos Passos?

Working at a small public library somewhere in the Midwest, John and Tracey are very much the typical "multi-hat" librarians. Besides reference, they share in storytime duties and circulation, and they even take a rotation or two in the bookmobile from time to time. While they like their jobs very much, they've started worrying about their library.

With severe budget issues as well as staffing changes and a recently failed local levy, things have become tense at work. While the library is doing well this year, future plans are currently on hold as the director struggles with the budget, the library's aging physical collection, and the continual technology changes and upgrades that cannot be avoided. While John and Tracey were on duty at the reference desk last week, all of these things seemingly came to a crisis point with just one patron.

It was a slow day, so when a local community college professor stopped by with a request for her class, Tracey and John saw it as an opportunity to help out and perhaps boost their library's image with the local college. In talking with the professor, they found out that classes that fall were focusing on twentieth-century American literature and authors such as Dos Passos, Upton Sinclair, and Edith Wharton. While the local college bookstore had the titles available for purchase, the professor hoped the library might be able to help, providing additional titles for the students on a closed reserve basis.

During this discussion with the professor, both John and Tracey looked at each other anxiously, knowing that due to the massive budget deficit, their materials budget had been significantly reduced. Somewhat hesitantly, they told the professor that while the library had a few copies of these popular works, there were not enough for the entire class, nor could they put their few copies on closed reserve.

Visibly agitated, the professor then asked about the possibility of using the library's online database subscriptions to access the books. Both John and Tracey again apologized, telling the professor that those resources had been discontinued. However, Tracey and John did mention interlibrary loan as a possibility, or perhaps other libraries in the city could help. It was too late though, and the professor stalked off, angrily shouting that if the library could not help her students, why did it even exist.

This was just one more problem added to many that John and Tracey had faced over the past few months as the library's hours and budgets were scaled back. Other patrons were upset when they had found out that many popular magazines and newspapers were discontinued. When it was explained that the money for these titles was not available, the patrons still grumbled and argued that the library had wasted the money.

The problems had even affected the library's genealogy department, a highly popular area that up until a few years ago had been used by many in the community. Previous staffing cutbacks and shorter hours had already reduced access to this part of the library to just a few days per week. Professional genealogists and family researchers had become discouraged, but the director had no choice, as the money was just not present in the budget for these services, nor would it likely be available in the near future.

The Problem

While the preceding scenario is fictional, for many of our communities and their libraries, it is all too close to the truth. Events in Michigan, Ohio, and many other states across America have highlighted the problems that popular community libraries continue to experience in light of a weakened economy, persistent unemployment, and uncertain future funding allocations. Under these circumstances, libraries are expected to do more on many fronts, from providing Internet access and related computer technologies to more new materials in the collection and increased volumes of day-to-day patron services.

Moreover, it's not just the public libraries that have experienced these problems, but other types of libraries as well. Libraries in higher education are also under attack, as campus administrators reduce staff, cut budgets, and still demand the same levels of service to the students and faculty. Business and other special libraries have not been spared either, as executives slash corporate libraries, considering them nonessential and a convenient way to reduce costs for shareholders and investors. In short, libraries of all types are experiencing these challenges now and surely will continue to in years to come.

Unfortunately, at the same time, continued internal structural problems are also affecting libraries, seen across the board in aging material collections, the ever-present flood of technological change, and unstable patron and/or community support. These are serious problems and in the next few years will become even bigger as libraries and their staff struggle to keep up. Let's look more closely at some of these internal problems.

Aging Collections

For many years, the heart of the library has been the collection. It has been the main focus of the budget and provided easy access to books and magazines in a wide variety of ways for all types of patrons' information needs. However, given the digital revolution in last 20 or so years, most everyone in the library world is finding out that these book and serials budgets are often in direct competition with the growing technology needs of the library. Computers, software, and integrated library systems are not cheap, and collection budgets, being the easiest target, have often been raided to keep up funding for continued technology hardware and software.

While in the near term, reductions in materials collections can be made to offset these and other needs within the library, the longer-term effects are detrimental in so many ways, from a lackluster and shallow collection to a raft of aging materials that no one wants to check out. For patrons who expect the library to have the physical materials on a diverse group of subjects and stories, this can be a huge disappointment. It goes without saying that this is a maddening conundrum for the library administration and staff as well!

Technology Access and Change

There's no doubt about it, technology in the library is the proverbial two-edged sword. It's expensive and very often a time trap for library staff. On the other hand, it's also helpful and expected to be present in today's library environment by both our patrons and staff. As noted in various publications from both the American Library Association (ALA) and the Online Computer Library Center (OCLC), library patrons have grown to expect technologies such as genealogy databases, technology training, public computer access, and even computer troubleshooting. This is the "new normal."[1] For bigger and better-funded libraries, this is not a terribly huge issue because they often have more funding options and adequate budgets; for smaller and mid-size libraries, this is a tremendous problem and one that is not going away any time soon.

Community Support

As noted in the articles cited in the preceding paragraph as well as our everyday experiences working in this environment, the library, specifically the public library, is continuing to, and has become quite often, the "default" focal point for many communities, in which residents and library users make heavy use of public meeting rooms and free computer-use stations as well as the more traditional storytime and summer reading programs.

However, in an ironic twist of circumstance, and because of failing levies, a faltering tax base, and other financial issues now existing in many communities, the library is often seen as an expendable place where cuts can be made. After all, as many would argue, would you rather have police and fire protection or the library open seven days a week? Unfortunately for many villages, towns, and larger cities, this is the decision that has to be made. When faced with these hard choices, communities often go without library access, which provides temporary relief, but in all actuality, harms their residents more than anyone realizes.

Our Changing Libraries and Patrons

While it may be easy to speak of the easily quantified and visible problems faced by libraries, are you, your patrons, or even the public at large aware of the quiet revolution from within? As we can see from the rise in popularity of digital materials and eBooks to the increased information expectations held by library patrons, this internal upheaval sometimes provokes more problems than almost any other issue.

For example, digital materials, in the form of eBooks and eReaders, while still a fairly new technology, are now assuming roles of primary importance within library institutions. Mentioned daily in the media, as well as being publicized and promoted by retailers such as

Amazon, Barnes & Noble, Kobo, and others, eBooks are changing the game for libraries in many ways. Vendors are advertising them, publishers are pushing them, and patrons are demanding them. If you don't think these technologies are important, consider that today, in many cases, it is understood that eBooks outsell paper books, especially as noted by retailers such as Amazon in their various press releases.[2]

If this surprises you, it shouldn't—and it's only the beginning. However you feel, the library, the one institution that most of us think would be in the forefront of these changes, is in many cases, just now coming to grips with this impending technological revolution. While some libraries and administrative staff are addressing these changes and planning ahead for the future digital library, quite a few are not, with some even refusing to consider eBooks at all.

The Rise of Electronic Content

As dramatic as it is, this revolution has not happened overnight. Thinking back to the early years of the Internet when Gopher and Mosaic were new, were we not all amazed at the amount of information that could be found even then? During the digital revolution and the rise of the Internet in the late 1990s, the concept of eBooks was one that while faint, was destined to grow, even if for some the thought of digital books taking over paper collections was almost laughable, a somewhat fanciful dream given the technology of the times.

However, technology and Moore's law both move fast and so did eBooks and easily accessed electronic information. More powerful computers, high-speed Internet, and the massive increase of software specifically designed for these new environments began to turn the tide from analog to digital. Through the first Internet bubble and beyond, the advances kept coming, and libraries—as well as library staff—were incorporating these changes as quickly as budgets would allow.

In today's world, we've gone far beyond those early pioneering Rocketbooks, PalmPilots, and others, and now have everyday familiarity with the new lightweight devices such as the Nook, Kindle, Kobo, the wildly popular iPad, and other types of tablets. The game is changing rapidly. It's not just hardware, however, as we've seen the standardization and acceptance of the eBook as a valid reading source, a turning point in how many people today view the entire reading experience. As noted by the Pew Internet & American Life Project in their report released in early 2012: " ... Altogether, 43% of Americans age 16 and older have read long-form writing in digital format as of December 2011—either e-books or newspaper or magazine material in digital form."[3]

While there's absolutely no doubt that paper-based books and other materials will be around for a long time to come, the prospect of digital reading on many types of devices is here to stay. Some in the popular press even argue that the whole perception of books, content, and materials are about to change, as noted in the discussions at **Unbound: Speculations on the Future of the Book**, a symposium held on May 3 and 4, 2012.[4] After looking through these resources and others, I need to ask you: Is your library ready?

Our Changing Patrons

As librarians and library staff, when we consider all of these transformations of materials and collections, it's easy to only look internally at how these changes affect the profession as well as the more general institution of the library as a whole. After all, we work every day at our library and have an interest in maintaining its place in the community or academic/business environment. Keep in mind, however, that no matter what type of library you work in, patrons in your city, county, school, or other location are a factor in your success. It's this demand point that keeps us all in business and functioning as part of the larger community.

In this light, and taking into account the displacements spoken about so far, you must also admit that your patrons are changing as well, both in what information they are looking for as well as how they acquire it. No longer are your patrons happy with old, stale information. No longer are your patrons bound to the reference desk, content to walk through the stacks, or patiently waiting in line until your library opens for the day. Fulfilling many of their information needs with search giants such as Google, Yahoo, and Bing, our patrons live in the age of instant answers, answers that are often electronic and communicated immediately. The primary channel of communications has become texting, instant messaging, and immediate response via social media giants such as Twitter, Facebook, and Pinterest. Anything less is looked on as slow, outmoded, and not as effective.

Let's look at this situation in somewhat more practical terms. The last time you were at a public event, how many people did you see using their phones while they were waiting? Not talking, but using them to acquire information in some format or another? Look at your own information usage. Look at your children. Note the almost explosive growth of the smart phone and the market saturation of iPhones, Android devices, Windows Phones, and iPads. As noted by the Pew Internet & American Life Project in their report released in early 2012, more than 46 percent of U.S. adults own or use a smart phone.[5] These digital choices are now fully mainstream.

Patrons—your patrons and mine—expect this same type of instant and informed response from their library as well. Patrons just don't want to wait. They want always available, always "on" access—24/7, 365 days a year. Commercial providers already do this—So why can't the library meet this need as well? This is the arena in which our profession and institutions have been placed, and we need to realize this.

However, have librarians accepted this? For the most part, one has to look no further than the many libraries and librarians on Facebook, Twitter, and other social media sites to see that many librarians realize that things are radically different and accepted methods must change. As professionals, librarians are attempting to go in new directions to find new methods of access and assisting patrons with their information needs as fast as possible.

However, there are libraries that have yet to accept this, not fully understanding how patrons truly use and expect information to be made available today. They don't seem to fully understand that pointing to a shelf of paper reference books or even a public catalog terminal is no longer adequate. These are the libraries that may have trouble in the future. These are the libraries that may be left wondering where their patrons have gone. What is your library doing about this? Digital resources, and access to them, will become more and more important to libraries seeking to have a place in their communities—and to remain relevant in these changing times.

Free Online Digital Book Sites and Collections: A Possible Solution?

Given then all of the challenges faced by libraries, what can we do as a profession? What can you do to change the situation within your local library? Is there even a solution? While so far there seems to be no "one-size-fits-all" magic answer, by looking at where technology has brought us so far, and with an eye to the future, one logical answer can be seen in the adoption of free online book sites into the library acquisitions and catalog collections process.

By utilizing the resources already available online, as well as taking advantage of new items coming online, our libraries can radically change for the better and meet these challenges head on. With these types of resources, the instant 24/7 access, and no additional costs, there's a lot to like. When patrons see the addition of millions of digital resources and easy access via the library's integrated library system (ILS) or website, they will see their library in a more favorable light.

This approach is not, however, as simple as just linking to available digital materials somewhere on the Internet. Advanced planning by both library staff and administration is needed, as is strategic planning and practical procedures to implement these additional resources. However the process goes, *all* libraries can benefit—from the small library with limited resources and staff to the larger, well-funded library. For too long, sites such as

Google Books and HathiTrust have been seen as supplemental to our regular collections, rather than core essentials that they should be.

Defining the Digital Book Collection

So just what is a digital book collection, and how does it work? Is it a proprietary vendor-driven product that each library purchases and then uploads digitized documentation and books to? Is it a purchased database that patrons can use to look for and download items from? Many people favor these types of approaches, and depending on your patron base and needs, this may certainly be a valid approach. However, I would argue that free online sites should be the main component of a digital book collection, considered part of the standard collection, and used alongside the standard print resources, fee-based subscription databases, and other materials. By centralizing the use of free online book sites such as HathiTrust and Google Books, any library can start small, perhaps with a pilot project, and then gradually grow and integrate these digital resources into the regular collection. Some might question the long-term viability and commitment of any "free" resources, but is this digital material ultimately any different than any other? Vendors and software are constantly changing as much as anything else, especially in today's economic climate.

The Process of Using Free Online Book Sites In Your Library

Given any library's choice to proceed with the integration of these sites into the everyday institutional workflow, the next decision is just exactly how this will get done. What's the plan? Some of the issues you need to think about in this process are staff training and education, technical issues, and building patron awareness. Let's look at each one of these in turn and see how they fit into our newly formed solution.

Staff Training and Education

It may not be the biggest issue faced by libraries when integrating these electronic resources into daily operations, but staff training and education on use of and integration with online book sites can be one of the bigger headaches faced by libraries and library administrators. As a result, this should be one of the first considerations addressed in the planning process. For example, who does the training? Who is responsible for working with staff to ensure that they understand the complexities (both good and bad) of this digital content?

Without a plan, without a trainer, without the necessary staff, the library is left to haphazardly implement these digital resources on a hit-or-miss basis, which in turn provides a lousy experience for the patrons, our customers. Consistency can be achieved only by adequate training and education to an agreed upon standard as well as dedicated staff to carry out the implementation.

For larger libraries and library systems, working within established computer support channels and information technology (IT) departments already present in the library is undoubtedly the first and best place to start. These professionals work with digital resources and computing information on a daily basis. Given the limits of the library's budget resources and time, this approach could work.

However, don't be overconfident, as sometimes the mixed nature of digital library materials makes it so they do not always fit the traditional IT and computing infrastructure that might already be in place. If the information technology staff is not library-trained or even aware of the unique technology approaches used, there are dangers. Careful planning and integration with library staff can help to alleviate these issues.

For special, academic, or smaller libraries, finding a solution for staff training and education can be considerably harder but at the same time not a totally impossible task. Certain tech-savvy staff can be appointed as the library's "go-to" resource for training and knowledge. Smaller libraries can also look to partnerships with library support organizations, usually found via their state library or existing nonprofit library membership organizations. Academic libraries, which most often have the support of on-campus information network colleagues, can work with faculty to provide group training options to address any other needs that might not already be supported. Special libraries can look to support organizations mentioned earlier in this chapter or look to internal groups within their organization or business unit that might offer options.

My experience in doing library training over the past few years has revealed that personnel-related issues, not necessarily the training process itself, can be hugely troublesome, especially when it comes to getting "buy-in" from staff in seeing the advantages that digital content can bring to the library and the patrons.

More than likely, you will find that certain staff members will absolutely love the new technology while others will not. Even when presented with all of the advantages these resources bring, some, more than likely, will still refuse to acknowledge or use these new digital resources. This lack of acceptance can be dangerous, however, as inconsistent usage and application is a precursor to inconsistent and uneven service—a big problem!

While there is no one simple answer when encountering staff resistance to all things digital, there are steps that can be taken to alleviate this. First, let your library staff have the time to become acquainted with the resources. Sometimes resistance to change can be addressed by giving staff time away from the desk or stacks and simply letting them explore what is out there and how easily it can be used. Negative thoughts can quickly turn to amazement when there is enough time to explore and fully understand what can be done without worrying about other job responsibilities.

Also, make sure that the technological tools needed to get the job done are available for use. In other words, if the public computing and staff workstations cannot properly read a PDF or ePub file, your staff will be less inclined to use these resources for learning about these resources or sharing them with patrons. As a final note, ensure that whoever is responsible for this actually follows up with staff after any training, helping to address any lingering questions or problems with the new materials and methods.

Technical Issues

Technology, especially new technology, can be fun. However, it does not come without costs, some of which are not always monetary in nature. Costs can be seen in implementation, everyday usage, and planning for future models of growth and integration. These themes can be troublesome for libraries that rush into things without planning ahead for possible roadblocks.

Take, for example, a library planning on incorporating items from Google Books into their website. Who is responsible for making the plan? Who will test the coding before going live—will it be the technology staff or the reference department staff? Who will make sure that the web browsers on the public workstations are up to standard and able to use the special technologies that are sometimes used by these sites?

From an everyday use perspective, what happens if something on the site breaks, or the web browsers or other software doesn't work as it should? Anyone who has been using technology for a while knows this is going to happen at some point. What sort of troubleshooting structures should the library have in place to address this?

Let's also consider future models of implementation. What happens if the vendor-based ILS refuses to cooperate with the Google Books application programming interface (API)? If your library hasn't adequately planned for potential technological issues, big problems await.

Patron Awareness

No matter how amazing and wonderful all of these online resources are or how excited your staff is, it doesn't mean a thing if your patrons are not aware of it. Patron awareness and use of the digital resources you are planning to add to your collection are paramount to successful implementation. Although there's really no one specific right way to do this, look to pre-established communication channels to funnel news and information about these resources to end users.

These methods can include signage, electronic communications such as email or the library website, and even working one-on-one with library staff and patrons as needed. For example, you could create special flyers or brochures to sit next to the public workstations, illustrating how to use Google Books or other sites. You might also encourage your reference and circulation staff to mention these resources explicitly when helping patrons looking for a title that may not be in your collection. By taking this direct route, you will ensure that your patrons are aware of these resources.

Academic libraries should make it a point to inform faculty so that they can tell students about these resources in class. They can also follow up with actual library visits and use these resources firsthand, explaining to students how they work as well as utilizing available library staff. Special libraries can also use these same avenues in providing these materials for employees and departments as needed. Publicity via in-house staff meetings or other pre-established communication methods are easy methods in which to get the message across.

The BIG Four!

Having defined a digital approach and discussed ways of training and incorporating these resources into the library, we now come to one of the biggest questions left to consider: Which sites or resources should be included in your library's digital strategy? What are some of the data points and information that library staff and administration should look for in choosing sites for adoption? It's not particularly easy, as almost every day it seems there is a new site being launched and a bevy of books and other resources that are just waiting to be downloaded and used. Given these realities, how can you ever hope to know which resources would be the most useful in your everyday library work?

While ultimately each library will have to make its own decision about which sites to use and integrate into the library's service offerings, at this point, there are four main sites, referred to here as **The BIG Four**, that offer libraries the most resources, the widest scope, and the most usefulness in terms of features. These sites also offer extensive search capabilities, additional software tools, and long-term availability. These four sites form the basis for this book and are discussed in depth in later chapters. These are:

- Google Books
- HathiTrust
- Internet Archive
- Open Library

Incorporating these four sites and their resources into your new digital strategy can benefit both your patrons and service offerings. Most importantly, your patrons will experience a bigger, better, more accessible, and more useful collection. The end result? No matter what type of library you have—be it public, academic, or special—everyone will benefit.

In case all or some of these sites are new to you, Table 1.1 provides more information about each. In it, you'll find the online locations of the sites as well as the more common book formats that can be found there. Figures 1.1 through 1.4 also show site logos for each.

Table 1.1   The BIG Four Online eBooks Sites: Location, Common Formats

Site	URL	Book Format	Downloads?
Google Books	http://books.google.com	Online viewer, PDF, ePub, text	Some
HathiTrust	http://www.hathitrust.org	Online viewer, PDF, text, images	Single pages
Internet Archive	http://www.archive.org	Online viewer, PDF, text, many formats	Yes
Open Library	http://www.openlibrary.org	Online viewer, PDF, text, many formats	Yes

Figure 1.1

Figure 1.2

Figure 1.3

Figure 1.4

Why Only These?

Now you might be asking yourself why only these four? What about the sites you've been using already or sites your patrons may have mentioned? After all, haven't some of these other projects been around for a much longer time and don't they have much more experience doing all of this? The reality is that yes, there are many other sites, projects, and initiatives, many of which have been around far longer than these four resources. However, as mentioned previously, when considered in terms of scope, material resources, and usefulness for everyday library workflow, these main four sites particularly stand out. Let's take a closer look.

Scope of the Sites

Libraries offer resources to patrons looking for information on any number of subjects. In the same sense, the Google Books project, HathiTrust, the Internet Archive, and the

Open Library do the exact same thing by virtue of their wide-ranging digital collections, which are not specific to a particular subject, time period, or even audience. In practical usage terms then, these four sites immediately become valuable resources to libraries looking to either supplement or expand their collections with additional titles, or to address patrons' information needs that go beyond the typical request.

Let's say you have a patron looking for information on early aviation in the United States. While it's more than likely you will have some information about this topic in your local collection, the online sites we're focusing on contain digitized product manuals, aviation magazines, military flight resources, and much more. These are materials that in many cases can be downloaded by your patron and used at her leisure, when she needs the resources.

When you offer these resources, presented in an effective manner, your patrons see the library as a more valuable resource, one that they are more likely to continue to use or even advocate that others use. With this approach, the library becomes much more than a physical warehouse of dusty books and more of a place where answers can actually be found. In short, a valued and up-to-date community, academic, or business resource.

Material Resources

Knowing that the depth and breadth of content offered by these online sites can be invaluable to you and your patrons, also consider the *types* of material resources found there. While it's easy to find fictional classics such as *Treasure Island* and *Tom Sawyer*, you can also find popular magazines such as *American Woodworker*, *Prevention*, and even *Popular Science*. More importantly, you can also find government documents, family genealogies, scientific pamphlets, public domain works, and a whole lot more.

Consider how these resources could bridge the physical collection sitting on your library's shelves and the screens of your patron's computers, mobile devices, and tablets. This supplemental value makes these digital resources even more important. While other sites offer some of the same content, you would be hard-pressed to find as many titles in the smaller ones as are contained in any one of these four. Just looking at some of the following relative numbers can help to quickly illustrate this:

- The Google Books Project, 30 million titles[6]
- HathiTrust, more than 10 million titles[7]
- Internet Archive, more than 3 million titles[8]

Usefulness and Ease of Use in Everyday Work

Another hallmark of the big four is their demonstrated usefulness and ease of use in everyday library work. These sites, once you and your patrons have worked with them, become easy to understand and search, and they offer many benefits. For example, let's say your patron is looking for some historical information about Carnegie libraries in New York City. While you may have some resources on your shelves and possibly even more in vendor-supplied databases, could you find hundreds of books, magazines, and other historical articles? Just doing a sample search for the phrase "Carnegie Library" in HathiTrust reveals over 445 individual resources to choose from! This is just one search on one of the sites we've mentioned! If you combine this with the other resources, your patron will have a virtual cornucopia of information on Carnegie libraries.

Beyond just searching, however, these sites also offer downloads and other methods of using the source material. They get your patrons the information they need when they need it. Smaller sites and subscription database resources may offer some of this but probably not the depth you will find on any one of these four.

On the Other Hand

Even with the features and advantages the big four offer, I would be remiss not to mention the many other smaller sites that exist and can also be useful. Although not the main focus of this book, some of these will be discussed in later chapters, including Project Gutenberg, DailyLit, and ManyBooks, all of which could be integrated into your library to serve your patrons' information needs or integrated with these four primary sources.

Important Points to Remember

No one would argue that the Internet has not changed our world in many ways. Whether you consider music, books, movies, or any other facet of contemporary life, you must agree that we live in a far different world than in the early 1990s—and the next few years will see equal amounts of change. Our libraries, although today bound with economic troubles and material transformations, are poised to make changes as well, becoming much different institutions than they are now. Taking advantage of these digital resource sites now can help you and your library to make that leap.

Let's review some of the points mentioned in this chapter. Use these as memory joggers, talking points for your own planning, or even in conversations with your staff or your library's board. These points can also get your staff thinking about where they fit into this change. Finally, think about the following in relation to budgets, ongoing projects, and even possible grants.

The Problem

- Funding the library
- More service, less local support
- Aging collections versus technology
- The burden of training for technology changes

Our Changing Libraries and Patrons

- Digitization becoming the primary service?
- Changes in patrons and information seeking
- Libraries becoming aware of these changes
- Libraries living up to patron expectations

Free Online Digital Book Sites and Collections

- Solutions to ongoing problems
- Defining the digital collection
- Integration of the digital collection—no longer separate!
- Staff training and awareness of the paradigm change

The Big Four

- Google Books, HathiTrust, Internet Archive, Open Library
- Scope of resources, everyday ease of use
- Other sites' disadvantages (small, not as comprehensive)

Notes

1. American Library Association (ALA), "State of America's Libraries Report 2012," 2012, http://www.ala.org/news/mediapresscenter/americaslibraries/soal2012; Online Computer Library Center (OCLC), "Perceptions of Libraries, 2010: Context and Community," http://www.oclc.org/reports/2010perceptions.html.

2. Amazon.com, http://phx.corporate-ir.net/phoenix.zhtml?c=176060&p=RssLanding&cat=news&id=1449176.

3. Pew Research Center, "The Rise of E-Reading," 2012, http://pewresearch.org/pubs/2236/ebook-reading-print-books-tablets-ereaders.

4. "Unbound: Speculations on the Future of the Book," http://futurebook.mit.edu/.

5. Pew Research Center, "46% of American Adults Are Smartphone Owners," http://pewinternet.org/Reports/2012/Smartphone-Update-2012/Findings.aspx.

6. The New York Review of Books, "The National Digital Public Library Is Launched!," http://www.nybooks.com/articles/archives/2013/apr/25/national-digital-public-library-launched/.

7. HathiTrust, http://www.hathitrust.org.

8. Internet Archive, http://www.archive.org/texts, May 2012.

Resources

Digitization Trends in Everyday Life: Libraries and Patrons

Like it or not, digitization is fast becoming the norm, both in libraries and in the daily lives of our patrons and the rest of society. The following links give some background on these trends, which can be especially useful when formulating your own library's policies and/or strategic planning for the years to come.

LibConf.com, "CIL Opening Keynote Panel,"
http://www.libconf.com/2011/03/21/cil-opening-keynote-panel/

Pew Research Center, "E-Reader Ownership Doubles in six Months,"
http://pewinternet.org/Reports/2011/E-readers-and-tablets.aspx

Pew Research Center, "46% of American Adults Are Smartphone Owners,"
http://pewinternet.org/Reports/2012/Smartphone-Update-2012.aspx

Pew Research Center, "Younger Americans' Reading and Library Habits,"
http://libraries.pewinternet.org/2012/10/23/younger-americans-reading-and-library-habits/

TechCrunch, "That Was Fast: Amazon's Kindle Ebook Sales Surpass Print (It Only Took Four Years),"
http://techcrunch.com/2011/05/19/that-was-fast-amazons-kindle-ebook-sales-surpass-print-it-only-took-four-years/

Library Crisis—Library Changes

We all know our libraries are changing and being hit with funding issues as the economy struggles to regain its footing. The following sites address some of the issues faced by fellow librarians and their libraries.

American Libraries, "England's Libraries and the Funding Crisis," http://americanlibrariesmagazine.org/news/09072011/england-s-libraries-and-funding -crisis

Education-Portal.com, "Libraries in Crisis: What Budget Cuts Mean for CA Libraries," http://education-portal.com/articles/Libraries_in_Crisis_What_Budget_Cuts_Mean_for _CA_Libraries.html

LibraryJournal.com, "Coping With The Terrible Twins: Periodicals Price Survey 2012," http://lj.libraryjournal.com/2012/04/funding/coping-with-the-terrible-twins-periodicals -price-survey-2012/

Changing Libraries, Changing Approaches

As mentioned in this chapter, our approach to change should be ongoing; we should always be willing to shift to new technologies and methods of getting necessary information to our patrons. Thus the following resources outline some of the current issues we all face.

ALA TechSource, "Coming to Terms with Mobile," http://www.alatechsource.org/blog/2010/04/coming-to-terms-with-mobile.html

The Digital Shift, "Q&A: Dan Cohen on His Role as the Founding Executive Director of DPLA," http://www.thedigitalshift.com/2013/03/digital-libraries/qa-dan-cohen-on-his-role-as -the-founding-executive-director-of-dpla/

LibraryJournal.com, "The Voices of Librarians and the DPLA," http://www.libraryjournal.com/lj/home/889797-264/the_voices_of_librarians_and.html .csp

LibraryJournal.com, "What is the DPLA?" http://lj.libraryjournal.com/2013/04/ future-of-libraries/whats-is-the-dpla/

Poudre River Public Library District, "eBooks and eReaders in Public and Academic Libraries," http://www.poudrelibraries.org/about/pdf/ereader-report-2011extended.pdf (Via TeleRead and InfoDocket)

ReadWrite, "Will Your Local Library Lend E-Books (Or Can They?)," http://www.readwrite.com/archives/will_your_local_library_lend_e-books_or_can _they.php

The Big Four: Organization and Application

My main argument, and focus of this book, is that the big four sites can fulfill many of your library's information needs and bring millions of resources to your library. In this following section, find out more background information on these sites.

Ars Technica, "Exercises in Democracy: Building a Digital Public Library,"
http://arstechnica.com/information-technology/2012/05/exercises-in-democracy-building-a-digital-public-library/

Google, "Google Books History,"
http://www.google.com/googlebooks/about/history.html

Internet Archive, "About the Internet Archive,"
http://archive.org/about/about.php

New York Times, "An Elephant Backs Up Google's Library,"
http://bits.blogs.nytimes.com/2008/10/13/an-elephant-backs-up-googles-library/?ref=technology

ReadWrite, "7-Year Battle to Stop Google from Digitizing Libraries Is Ending with a Whimper,"
http://readwrite.com/2012/10/12/google-closes-two-chapters-in-ongoing-books-fight

Wesleyan University, "Google Books and Hathi Trust,"
http://ptully.blogs.wesleyan.edu/2011/03/25/google-books-what-is-the-fuss-about/

Other Digital Resource Sites

While the emphasis in this chapter has been on the bigger digital resource sites such as the Google Books project and HathiTrust, many other valuable sites exist as well. These will be mentioned in a later chapter, but the following links describe some of the sites as far as origins, collections, and other information.

LibraryJournal.com, "Colorado Library Consortium Adds Project Gutenberg eBooks to Library Catalogs,"
http://www.libraryjournal.com/lj/home/888596-264/colorado_library_consortium_adds_project.html.csp

University of Texas Libraries, "Electronic Books,"
http://www.lib.utexas.edu/books/etext.html

Appendix

Table 1A-1 The BIG FOUR Online eBook Sites: General Information

	Google Books	HathiTrust	Internet Archive	Open Library
Estimated Counts (February 2013)	30,000,000 scanned*	10,643,103 total volumes^	3,883,214 available titles^	1,000,000+ eBooks^
Multiple Formats Available?	Yes (ePub, PDF, Plain-Text)	Yes (Images, PDF, Plain-Text)	Yes (Multi)	Yes (Multi)
Can Create Online Collections?	Yes	Yes	Yes	Yes
Has Developer Resources or API's?	Yes, some restrictions	Yes, some restrictions	Yes	Yes
Bibliographic Record Access?	No	Limited	Yes	Yes
Advantages or Disadvantages?	Widespread collections, good for academic and general reading; ties into online eBook store	Good for academic research, but item downloads somewhat limited; excellent online catalog with multiple search options	Good across the board resources, good for both academic and general reading; obscure titles available, including government documents, tax rolls and court proceedings	Can directly upload and edit individual records; ties into the resources available on the Internet Archive

^Counts as noted on each individual website as of February 2013.
*Estimated as of early 2013. Sourced from The New York Review of Books, "The National Digital Public Library Is Launched!," http://www.nybooks.com/articles/archives/2013/apr/25/national-digital-public-library-launched/.

Table 1A-2 Other Online eBook Sites: General Information

	Project Gutenberg	DailyLit	ManyBooks	ibiblio	Baen Free Library
Multiple Formats Available?	Yes (ePub, PDF, plain text)	Yes (images, PDF, plain text)	Yes (images, PDF, plain text, other)	Yes (multiple)	Yes (ePub, Kindle, plain text, other)
Can Create Online Collections?	Yes	Yes	N/A	Limited*	Yes
Has Developer Resources or API's?	Yes, some restrictions	N/A	N/A	Limited*	Yes
Bibliographic Record Access?	Yes	Limited^	N/A	N/A	N/A
Advantages or Disadvantages?	Multiple formats, Dropbox integration, historical and some current titles, diverse subjects; thought of as one of the original eBook sites	Unique delivery methods (email, RSS), popular and classic fiction resources	Multiformat, extensive genre selections; includes popular and classic fiction; around 29,000 titles	Best for collection searches and topics; individual eBooks found within collections	Smaller selection, current fiction titles and popular authors; part of the larger commercial Baen Books

^RSS feeds.
*Not in the traditional sense, but by becoming a contributor, you or your library can create online access and collections along with other resources.

Table 1A-3 Common Availability of Various Material-Type Formats^

Resource:	DailyLit	ibiblio	ManyBooks	Google Books	HathiTrust	Internet Archive	Project Gutenberg	Open Library
Audio			◆			◆	◆	
ePub			◆			◆	◆	◆
DAISY				◆		◆		◆
HTML	◆	◆	◆				◆	
Kindle			◆			◆	◆	◆
MOBI			◆				◆	◆
On-Screen		◆	◆	◆	◆	◆	◆	◆
Other	◆	◆	◆		◆	◆	◆	◆
PDF		◆	◆	◆	◆	◆	◆	◆
Plain Text	◆			◆	◆	◆	◆	◆

^Availability and material types as noted from each individual resource as of February 2013. Details and updated information on specific other file types is available on each specified resource website.

Chapter 2

Getting Started with the Google Books Project

Figure 2.1

One of the first and most easily recognizable of all the online book sites, the Google Books project is well known by many in the library world. Easy to use for both patrons and staff, this site and its millions of resources offer more than just books and magazines for your patrons' use. In fact, this site can serve both as the cornerstone for your library's digital strategy and as a worthy addition to your physical collection. From classic serials such as *LIFE* and *Popular Mechanics* to obscure eighteenth- and nineteenth-century resources on literature, history, and more, the Google Books project is truly amazing.

In this chapter, you'll start from the beginning, with background on the origins of the project, and then move on to practical information about how to use it in your library, assisting your patrons with their information needs. You'll also explore other ways to integrate the Google Books project into your integrated library system (ILS), public website, and more. Finally, we'll also sneak a peek at some of the other neat applications and options offered by the project.

Discover buried treasure.

It pays to dig deep, because quite often the passages you need – the information that can make your research sparkle – are hidden in unexpected places.

With Google Book Search, you can quickly search the full text of a book, from the first word on the first page to the last word in the final chapter. That's why, when it comes to finding that perfect books for your purposes, you can't beat Google Book Search and your local library.

books.google.com

Find the book you want in three easy steps:

Go gle

Figure 2.2

Origins and Issues

Officially launched in 2004, according to the project's history,[1] unofficial beginnings of the project can be traced back to 2002, as noted in Steven Levy's work *In the Plex*. In his book, Levy writes about Larry Page, Sergey Brin, and other Google officials discussing different options about a proposed book-scanning project.[2] From the acquisition of sources to the actual mechanics of the scanning process itself, Levy tells of many obstacles that Google initially had to overcome to begin a project of such size and technological scale. Once underway however, Levy goes on to say that Google determined to "get every book ever written in its search engine."[3]

From these beginnings, the project has grown exponentially, adding millions of titles as well as library and publishing partners. Along the way, Google has changed both public perceptions of book digitization and the data that these millions of titles contain, as noted in Figure 2.2. However, this process has not been without controversy, as can be seen by the continuing lawsuits over the project, both from authors and those in the publishing and literary fields. Even in early 2013, disagreement about Google Books continued as legal decisions remain up in the air, still waiting to be completely finalized, as evidenced in various legal opinions and news citations.

No matter the final outcome, through the Google Books project, both the public and libraries now have access—24/7, 365 days a year—to many titles that have not been accessible for years, locked away in dusty archives. These are not just a few titles either. In fact, as of early 2013,[4] it is estimated that over 30 million titles had been scanned and added to the project, with no end in sight.

Where Do the Books Come From?

Given these massive numbers, one of the first questions that might come to your mind is just where does Google find all of these titles? Although bookshops and estate sales might be great places for you and I to pick up books, a project of this size demands a unique approach. In fact, Google has gone a different route, choosing to partner both with book publishers and libraries. Within these relationships, Google and the Google Books project has obtained a breathtaking array of materials that provide a unique depth and breadth of information. Let's look more closely at how these partnerships work to provide unique contributions to the project.

Book Publishers

Working with many established businesses in the book publishing industry such as Arcadia, Osprey, and others, the Google Books project gives consumers and library patrons the ability to preview and read many popular and current titles and genres. One can access Lee Child, Terry Brooks, and other authors of popular fiction. But we can also find books such as the *Second Treatise of Government* from John Locke and technical/historical nonfiction such as the highly specialized *Condensed Analysis of the Ninth Air Force in the European Theater of Operations: An Analytical Study of the Operating Procedures and Functional Organization of Tactical Air Power as Developed by the Ninth Air Force in the War of Western Europe.* This wide array of titles is simply amazing and can open up new avenues of discovery for your patrons!

Libraries

While there's no doubt that publishers—with their new and backlisted titles—are important to the project, it's libraries and their massive collections that help to provide the depth and breadth found in the online selection of books contained by the project. In actively seeking materials from all types of libraries, both public and academic, Google has established ongoing partnerships with a wide array of institutions, ranging from the New York Public Library to the University of California library system, the University of Wisconsin–Madison, and others.

Google also has worked with international libraries, including the Austrian National Library and the Oxford University Library. A complete list of Google Books project partners can be found at the Google Books Library Project,[5] but Table 2.1 gives a good picture of the partnerships currently in place.

Library partnerships within the Google Books project continue even today as new resources are added to the site, providing special access to collections that would otherwise be unavailable for study or use. In 2010 and 2011 alone on the Google Books project blog

Table 2.1   Examples of Google Books Library Partners

Library	Type
Columbia University	Academic
Cornell University	Academic
Princeton University	Academic
New York Public Library	Public
Keio University	Academic
University of California	Academic
Committee on Institutional Cooperation, (CIC)	Nonprofit

Inside Google Books[6] (currently archived but still available for reading online), Google announced special collaborations with the Bavarian State Library, the National Library of the Netherlands, the British Library, and others.

The Material Collection

Given the many millions of titles in the Google Books, let's also take a moment to consider the types of materials that can be found there. Having used Google Books for several years, I know it has a broad mix of sources—from books and magazines to government documents, genealogies, and even current selections in fiction and nonfiction via the Google Play online eBook store. This alone brings both a value and depth of information to anyone using the project for their information needs.

No Physical Limitations

Unlike the local library, where physical space and patron demand often drive the focus and intent of the collections, Google Books has no such limitation. Digitally scanned books are easily compressed to a few megabytes and can be stored among Google's vast online storage network of data centers. As a practical demonstration, consider the area of American literature and specific title, Upton Sinclair's *The Jungle*, as seen in Figure 2.3. A classic of American literature, both for its transformative effects on American culture as well as its portrayal of a unique time in our nation's history, this particular title can easily be found in the Google Books project in many different editions and from many different publishers.

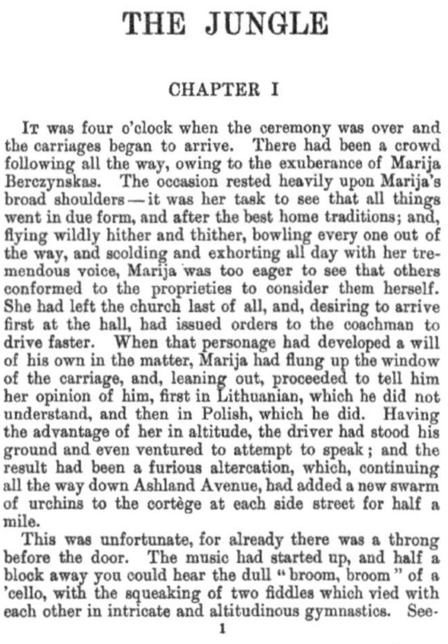

Other classic works are available as well. Have you ever had patrons ask for the Civil War classic *The Red Badge of Courage* only to find that your only physical copy is checked out? No longer is this a worry, as simply steering your patrons to the Google Books project gives them many different editions to consider. (See Figure 2.4 for an example)

A staple of most public and academic libraries, due to its continued use in student classes, *The Red Badge of Courage* and many other titles like it are just part of a rich vein of materials that are available for your patrons to access in a wide variety of ways, either on a library-based PC, the patron's home computer, or even a mobile devices such as the Nook, Kobo, and iPad.

THE JUNGLE

CHAPTER I

IT was four o'clock when the ceremony was over and the carriages began to arrive. There had been a crowd following all the way, owing to the exuberance of Marija Berczynskas. The occasion rested heavily upon Marija's broad shoulders—it was her task to see that all things went in due form, and after the best home traditions; and, flying wildly hither and thither, bowling every one out of the way, and scolding and exhorting all day with her tremendous voice, Marija was too eager to see that others conformed to the proprieties to consider them herself. She had left the church last of all, and, desiring to arrive first at the hall, had issued orders to the coachman to drive faster. When that personage had developed a will of his own in the matter, Marija had flung up the window of the carriage, and, leaning out, proceeded to tell him her opinion of him, first in Lithuanian, which he did not understand, and then in Polish, which he did. Having the advantage of her in altitude, the driver had stood his ground and even ventured to attempt to speak; and the result had been a furious altercation, which, continuing all the way down Ashland Avenue, had added a new swarm of urchins to the cortège at each side street for half a mile.

This was unfortunate, for already there was a throng before the door. The music had started up, and half a block away you could hear the dull "broom, broom" of a 'cello, with the squeaking of two fiddles which vied with each other in intricate and altitudinous gymnastics. See-

1

Figure 2.3

Serials

While books are what primarily come to mind when we think of libraries, magazines and other types of serial materials are available on the project as well. This wide selection of current and historical magazine titles spans the spectrum of subjects, from *Ancestry* and *Baseball Digest* to *Popular Mechanics*, *LIFE*, and *Women's Health*. You can also find long out of print and historical nineteenth-century periodicals that are not often easily located and used today, including titles such as *Scribner's Magazine* and the early editions of *Popular Science* and *Popular Mechanics*. See Figure 2.5 for an example of *Scribner's Magazine*.

What Isn't There

Knowing the amount of materials contributed by publishers as well as the many titles scanned from partner libraries, you might think that almost any paper-based materials would be available on Google Books. But there are actually many resources that you will not find, either due to legal issues over copyright or the format of the material itself.

Let's look first at copyright and legal issues, a thorny set of questions for many, not just libraries and librarians. While copyright law is fairly unambiguous about titles published before 1923 in the United States, the situation gets a little murky for titles published later. Google Books has scanned a whole class of titles that are technically under copyright protection but whose copyright has not been renewed or whose author cannot be found. Because of their unknown (also known as "orphan") status, many of these cannot be viewed on Google Books. Most often for these titles, you will see either a catalog record or perhaps a small snippet of information about the work.

Figure 2.4

Figure 2.5

This can be challenging for your library, especially if you make the Google Books project a major focus of your ongoing digital strategy. Unfortunately, with this particular issue, there seems to be no resolution in sight. Even in the early part of 2013 there remained a wide area of disagreement between Google, book authors, and even a few publishers, with cases still winding their way through the courts. No truly firm decision has been made.

Second, beyond just the legal and ownership rights, you will also not find documents such as maps, pamphlets, and other types of ephemera. While these are valid resources, and quite often highly popular in our own libraries, these types of materials seem not to be a primary focus of the project at this time, although things may change in the future. This is not a deal-breaker by any means, but if these types of materials are important to your library or your patrons often seek them out, this could be an issue.

Impact on Your Library

So what does Google Books mean to you as a librarian? What does it mean to your library's mission and your patrons' needs? Any decision about using the Google Books project for your library's information mission depends on a variety of factors, ranging from the types of information your patrons are seeking to the kinds of materials that are already contained in your physical collections. If you are a library director or are involved in actively managing the library in some way, it's important to consider this both in current and any future strategic plans. Any or all of these can significantly impact your decision about utilizing the Google Books project.

With this in mind however, and whether you are a public, academic, or business library, some of the ways that Google Books can be implemented into your institution can be seen in the following list:

- Collection backup
- Primary resource for research
- Digital branch collection

Let's take a closer look at each of these along with some specific examples.

Collection Backup

For most libraries, the budget determines the size and scope of the collection. This is an unfortunate but real aspect that we must deal with. However, utilizing and integrating Google Books into your collections as a backup or supplement to your paper resources can substantially enhance your library's collection offerings, enlarging both subject coverage and depth while at the same time incurring no additional costs. With the ability to import these listings into your integrated library system (ILS) via the Google Books application programming interface (API) as well as various book cover and book embedding options, this opens up a world of access to resources that your patrons would otherwise be without.

Let's look at this in a practical sense. Take for example, the topic of medieval armor. While most libraries contain more than a few resources on this subject, it's hard to compete with Google Books as a backup resource.

Sample searches, as seen in Figure 2.6, on medieval armor showed more than 10,000 available titles on this subject as of early 2013. If one branches out into subtopics, which is something our patrons so often do, the list of available titles grows exponentially.

Figure 2.6

This is just one example, of course, but your patrons could find similar resources related to any number of topics. The end result? Local libraries can acquire and maintain only a finite number of physical copies, but with almost infinite space and certainly no collection restrictions, the digital volumes maintained by the Google Books project can incredibly boost your library's quality.

Primary Resource for Research

In today's library environment, databases and access to the Internet in general have become more widespread than ever, but many patrons still have the need to use primary resources, especially for some of the more esoteric subjects in genres such as history, literature, scientific research, and genealogy. While for larger libraries this is not so much of an issue, for smaller institutions, this can be troubling to say the least. In these cases, quite often the patron does not find what he or she needs or is stuck waiting for photocopies or an even slower interlibrary loan process, which can take weeks for any resolution.

This too can be resolved by implementing the use of Google Books at the library. By providing this free access to lower-use items that are otherwise too expensive for the library to acquire, your library—regardless of size or location—can become a research powerhouse. This can be a huge budget-saving measure, allowing even small libraries to concentrate on more popular subjects and not have to rely on meeting their patrons' research needs via paper-based copies or slow interlibrary loan delivery.

Digital Branch Collection

In today's harried world, with private and work lives a swirl of interconnected jobs, duties, and activities, time for patrons to visit their local library is often at a premium. In addition, many libraries have had to curtail hours due to budget cuts and staffing issues. The end result? Your patrons lack access, and communities see libraries as not important to their current information needs.

Figure 2.7

However, by integrating the Google Books project into your library via the online catalog as well as local programming events, this barrier can be effectively broken. With this approach, the "digital branch" of your library is always available for patrons no matter their location and the time. In today's world, 24/7 access can help us quickly connect with patrons who might not otherwise think of the library due to the more traditional hours our libraries now are open. While this approach obviously does not replace a full-scale library, it can serve many of your patrons' information needs, especially if it can be combined with access to other digital resources and databases that the library already has access to.

Searching Google Books

From high-level implementation to more practical uses, let's now go directly into searching Google Books. I will share tips and tricks, as well as help explain some of the amazing capabilities built into the site that can help you and your patrons find the necessary bits of information. In this section, you'll learn how to form specific search queries, both basic and advanced, as well as become better acquainted with specialized operators. You'll also learn about practical issues ranging from techniques for actively implementing Google Books at your library to utilizing found resources in your interaction with patrons and their information needs.

Methods of Searching

When using the site for the first time, it's natural for you and your patrons to have many questions. From just getting started to figuring out what type of search works best, knowing the answers to certain questions will help you and your patrons better understand and use the Google Books project.

To understand how a search works in Google Books, it's important to note that three main types of search are available. These include:

- Basic searching
- Advanced searching
- Searching within results

Let's consider each one in turn.

Basic Searching

One of the givens of any Google product is ease of use. The basic search option in Google Books reflects this and is as simple as going to the project site and typing in what you are looking for, be it an author, title, keyword, or even phrase.

One of the first things you will notice as you begin your search is the integration of the same autocomplete method that is used on the traditional Google search page. For most us, this is a welcome feature, as it provides keywords and phrases that might steer us to what we are looking for.

Figure 2.8

However, for your patrons who may have never been exposed to this feature before, it might be distracting or even cause confusion, leaving them to wonder if they should stop typing or continue on. Knowing this, remember to take a few moments with your patrons and ensure that they understand this particular feature.

For now, give it a try. To get started, simply navigate your computer's web browser to the home page for the Google Books project, which can be found at http://books.google .com/books. Once there, let's start by performing a sample search for information about Carnegie libraries. First, type **Carnegie libraries**. What are your results? (See Figure 2.8 for an example.)

As of early 2013, this quick search returned over 1.3 million hits! This is a staggering number of results, and of course as you may already know, many of them are neither accurate nor close to the topic at hand, including one particular title that I ran across called *Catalog of the Wheeler Gift of Books*. If you scan the results of your own search, you will no doubt see other misses as well.

Why did you and I get so many unrelated results? The answer lies within the design and construction of the Google Books project. Unlike traditional library catalogs or other database resources, where for the most part records are searched only via indexed terms such as keyword, author, title, subject headings, or other entries commonly found in the machine-readable cataloging (MARC) records, every word of every title in the Google Books project is searchable!

This full-text search is a positive step in many respects, providing additional resources (possibly) related to what you might be looking for. It can also be a point of frustration, with the results containing many false hits, or titles that may contain the words or phrases that were being searched for but that are not directly related to the query at hand.

Your patrons, especially those who are less experienced with the project or who lack knowledge about how libraries and library catalogs are structured, might not be as aware of this particular approach to searching and may give up when faced with a seemingly insurmountable number of resources to sift through. Is there a method you can use to reduce the clutter *and* give you accurate results? Yes, you do have options to solve this particular dilemma.

Because Google Books is based on the same Google technologies and searching mechanisms that are used for all areas of the search giant's many sites, it's accurate to say that you have voluminous search methods from which to choose. However, for quick basic searches, especially when faced with inaccurate initial results or many thousands of false hits, both phrase searching and the use of special modifiers can be effective timesavers. Let's take a closer look at these methods and give some examples.

Phrase searching via the quotation limiter instructs Google search to find only results where these words are grouped together and is usually the best initial method to narrow results. In this case, let's redo our previous search for Carnegie libraries, only this time use the quotation limiter like this: **"Carnegie libraries."**

What sort of results do you get? Earlier, just searching for the two words, over a million results were returned. Now you'll see that by using phrase searching, a more manageable 30,000-plus entries are returned. Granted this is still a huge number of titles and too many to look through, but it's possible to see how phrase searching can help winnow things down considerably. From here, at least for this example, you might experiment with a more complex phrase or even a series of phrases to get even fewer and more specific results. Take a few minutes now and redo your search using your own phrase. See what works best for you.

The use of *special modifiers* involves adding special symbols to the query that instruct the Google Books search process to ignore certain terms, add others, or group items in a special way. You may be familiar with this approach, and you may even use it in your own online catalog or other types of library databases. Some of the more common modifiers supported in the Google Books project include:

The "–" modifier

The "OR" operator

The "*" modifier

Let's look at these in depth and show you specific methods in which they can be used.

The "–" modifier tells the Google search engine to exclude certain words. Take, for example, a patron who is looking for information on Theodore Roosevelt, but not Franklin Roosevelt. In this case, using the special modifiers in the preceding list, a possible solution would be **Theodore –Franklin Roosevelt**. This would return a list of titles with the singular use of the search term **Roosevelt**, but any direct references to **Franklin Roosevelt** only would be excluded.

The "OR" operator is powerful and tells Google to search for two or more terms at once. Let's say your patron is looking for books on the history of the Olympics from either 1932 or 1936. In this case, the search phrase could be constructed as **Olympics 1932 OR 1936**. Returned results would include any titles related to either of those two years.

You can also team up the OR operator with the quotation marks used previously, which is especially handy if you are looking for certain phrases.

The asterisk, while not used as much as the other operators, can stand for any number of letters or words, which is helpful if you are looking for phrases or you are unsure how to spell a specific word. Let's say for example, your patron is looking for resources on historic bombers of the U.S. Air Force. In this case, a search term could be constructed as **"bomber B-*"** By utilizing quotation marks to symbolize a phrase search, your results would include any number of aircraft models or nomenclature that include the B-designation.

For now, redo your initial search on Carnegie libraries and use the special operators discussed in this section. Use any combination of the operators and see what your results look like. Depending on what operators you choose as well as how your search is constructed, various numbers of titles will be returned, but overall, your results should include many fewer resources to search through. You might see something similar to this particular title: *A Book of Carnegie Libraries: Free to All; Carnegie Libraries and American Culture*, and probably others. The point is that while they are often overlooked in today's world, specialized search operators can be quick and effective.

In addition to the specific special operators mentioned already, there are other operators and combinations of searching techniques available for use on Google Books. These include the **"$"** as well as the **"&" operators**. If you haven't used special operators or search techniques much in your daily work, it's worth familiarizing yourself with them, as well as with the type of results that they can help return. For additional information on each of these and other types of information on this topic, consider taking advantage of the many search help pages that Google has made available for use online.[7]

Now that you know about the special operators and performing some sample searching, it's important to remember to show your patrons the same operators. Using special operators in a basic Google Books search can be extremely helpful, but to persons unfamiliar with this approach, it may be confusing. Be aware of this as you work with your patrons, and demonstrate a few sample searches to ensure that they understand both the operators as well as the searching process. If, after a while, you are still not getting anywhere with results and/or sample searches, consider using the advanced search options outlined in the following section.

Advanced Searching

Depending on the topic, sometimes a basic search of the Google Books project is just not effective or returns results that are not related to the information your patron is looking for. Rather than waste time repeating searches or even giving up, consider using the advanced searching capabilities found within the project. With a multitude of operators

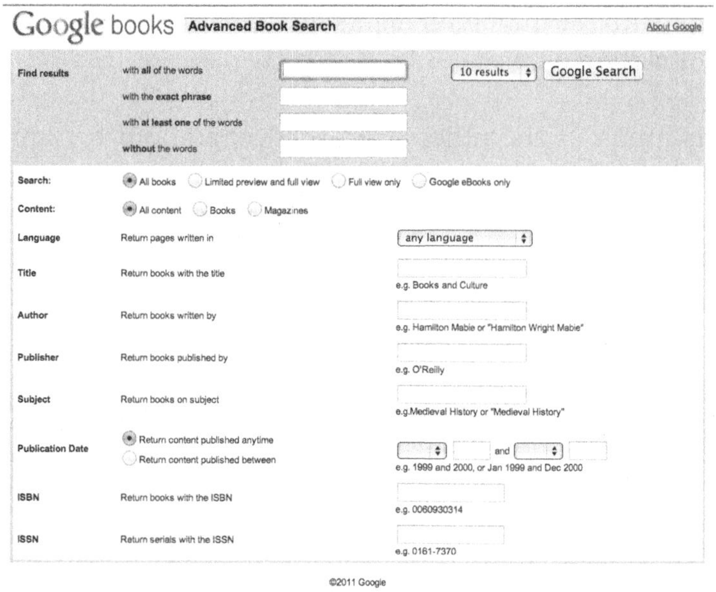

©2011 Google

Figure 2.9

and many ways to search for very specific types of data, this approach can save time, energy, and (in some cases) extreme frustration.

While it's possible to get to the advanced search options from within the project itself, the easiest way to do so is to use this link: http://books.google.com/advanced_book_search. See Figure 2.9 for a detailed view of what is available on the page or simply try the link in your web browser.

If you take a few moments to either look at the preceding screenshot or the actual advanced search page in your browser, a few things should be readily apparent. Notice that no special operators, esoteric letters, or punctuation marks need be entered into this page. In fact, it's as simple as filling in the blanks! This is a time-saving approach that can help cut down on possible confusion or the need to remember the specific roles the specialized operators perform. You will also notice a few new search options to consider, including limiting by content and publication date, and some new terms that include **Limited preview**, **Full view**, and **Google eBooks**. And don't overlook the availability of the more traditional limiters such as author, subject, publisher, ISBN, and ISSN.

Conducting your search with this method is more efficient and enables you to obtain specific results quickly. Note that it's also possible (and easy) to "stack" searching options on this page, filling in multiple fields for complex queries. For most patrons and searches, the advanced search box is probably the best default method, if only because of the many options. I've also found that the advanced search is also the best method of looking for magazine articles within the Google Books project, especially if you have only part of the titles or are unsure of the exact spelling.

For now, however, let's go back to our previous search for information on Carnegie libraries. Do you remember from our last search that it was time-consuming to narrow our search results to a manageable number, and you and I both had to employ various special modifiers to achieve any form of success? Now, using the advanced search page, let's perform the same searches again. Use some or all of the advanced options and see how this affects your results. What works better? What doesn't? What happens when you stack search quantifiers? Does this get too specific, or is it effective? Practice this for a while until you feel comfortable with each option.

Table 2.2 Examples of Search Options Available Within Google Books

Date Options	Google Options	Book Options
Nineteenth century	Everything	Any type of book
Twentieth century	Images	Previews enabled
Twenty-first century	Videos	Google eBooks
Custom range	Multi	Free Google eBooks

Searching within Results

One final search method that you should know well is searching from *within* specific results. After performing either a basic or advanced search within Google Books, you will have an initial list of titles to examine. Located at the top of your returned search results, you'll find additional tools that you can use to quickly refine and limit these results dynamically, winnowing down an unmanageable list to something fairly concise and accurate. Table 2.2 summarizes some of these options:

When you are faced with an overwhelming number of search results, this additional feature can save you from having to redo the initial search and is much more efficient!

For now, let's go back to our previous search for information on Carnegie libraries and see how these additional tools can help. Let's say you are specifically looking for books or magazines published about Carnegie libraries in the post–World War I years of 1919 and 1920. Do either a basic or advanced search and examine your initial results. How hard or easy was it to get these results?

Now try the same search, only this time just search (basic or advanced) for the term **Carnegie libraries**. Now with your results in hand, try some of the tools listed in the top panel to dynamically change your results. You will likely find that using the tools is a great method for quickly improving your accuracy without having to completely redo the search.

As you do this, don't forget the many calendar options available, as shown in Figure 2.10. Notice that by selecting the date options, you can set both the start date and stop date via a quick pop-up calendar. From here, it's a simple matter of filling in the required years and redoing your original search. The end result? Accurate results!

Plan on spending some time with each of these options, examining both how they work and how they do not. Becoming familiar with these will make

Figure 2.10

them much easier to explain to your patrons when you are assisting them with their own searches. Remember, many patrons have never used nor have they been aware of these very specific tools, and it will be up to you to transfer your knowledge to them in an effective manner.

Caution!

Over the past few years, the Google Books project, much like Google itself, has continued to change, integrating the project with other Google services such as search and shopping. This reflects ongoing changes in the online environment as well as competition from other companies in the market such as Facebook and Microsoft.

You will also notice more aggressively displayed links to the online Google bookstore, **Google Play**, as well as the new social/sharing network known as **Google +**. For most of us who use Google on a daily basis, this is no big deal. But your patrons who don't might be confused. If you sense a patron is getting confused, make sure to clarify the different aspects of the various products. Try to steer your patrons strictly to Google Books, but do make them aware of the other offerings. Take the time to explain the similarities and differences between Google Books and Google Play if at all possible.

Metadata and Indexing: A Cautionary Note!

Up to this point, we have focused on the basic and advanced searching skills needed to successfully use the resources on the Google Books project. However, let's go even further and talk about cataloging, indexing, and the book metadata found within the project. While an in-depth discussion of these issues is beyond the scope of this book, they're worth mentioning briefly here to address some potential problems.

Library cataloging standards are often somewhat mysterious to library patrons, yet how we catalog—and how accurate our records are—can really impact how well patrons are able find the information that is sitting on our library's shelves. Similarly, the Google Books project has been criticized for its irregular and non-library methods of indexing metadata for the millions of titles in the project. While most libraries use classification schema such as the Dewey Decimal System, the Library of Congress Classification, or even the Superintendent of Documents Classification Scheme (SuDoc), Google uses a variety of indexing terms and methods, including the Book Industry Standards and Communications (BISAC) subject headings,[8] which are found more often in bookstores than in libraries.

This discrepancy was specifically noted in the *Chronicle of Higher Education* on August 31, 2009, in a post entitled "Google's Book Search: A Disaster for Scholars."

It was also mentioned in a later article (also in the *Chronicle*, published in May 2010) entitled "The Humanities Go Google." In particular, many variances in book metadata were noted among the resources scanned into the project. Researchers found inaccurate publication dates, as well as errors in how the titles are classified. People have continued to note errors as well, which are highlighted online at *Inside Higher Ed* in an article by Matthew Reisz entitled "Catalog of Errors?"[9]

Google has responded to these criticisms in the past, but a particularly good example is noted through the blog Language Log (dated August 29, 2009,[10] under a post titled "Google Books: A Metadata Train Wreck"). In the article, Google admitted there were errors, but given the number of books in the project and the many sources of provided titles, asserted that mistakes were inevitable. While there is no doubt that this is certainly true—we all know from working in our own collections that there are many errors and corrections that continually need to be made, what does this mean to librarians who want to use the project? What does this mean to our patrons? How about our libraries?

In the end, as you use the Google Books project in your library, keep in mind the size of the database and that searching the project is different from searching the library's online catalog. What works well with your library system might not necessarily work well for the Google Books project. You more than likely will end up experimenting a bit, if only to get a sense of how searching for subjects and specific items in the Google Books project actually works. As an additional note, and for more backstory details on this ongoing controversy, check out the *Library Journal*'s article, "Google, The Last Library; and Millions of Metadata Mistakes," published online September 3, 2009.[11]

Viewing and Using Your Results

Being able to successfully search Google Books is a significant achievement, but being able to interpret those results and then either use them for yourself or help your patrons find what they are looking for is also important. In this section, you'll examine how to view results, use them, and refine them as necessary.

Search Results

A popular perception is that using all things Google is easy and that no explanations are needed to understand how things operate on the Google Books project site. Nothing could be further from the truth. Having a user-friendly interface is great, but both you and your patrons must also be able to use the results that you find. This part isn't always so simple, especially with complex queries or when the returned results are off target or too numerous to count. So let's consider some specific areas to concentrate on, including viewing results and their listings as well as looking at how each is constructed.

We will also explore smaller items to pay attention to, such as tag clouds, reviews, and even the use of citation managers and QR codes.

Viewing Results/Listings

After conducting your search query, your results are returned in standard list format and include information about each resource. These most often include title, author, publication date, and cover image. Also provided as part of these base results is information about how much of the book is available online for viewing. This ranges from no view (i.e., no part of the text is available for online viewing) to previews or even full views (i.e., some or all of the work is available for viewing). This is directly related to the publisher's requests and/or the item's copyright status. Regardless of status, clicking on any of the titles in the list will take you immediately to the work's full record.

Individual Listings Components

Let's move from looking at lists of returned results and take a few moments to see how individual titles are presented in the Google Books project. As you do this, think about this process. What do you see on the screen? What components allow you to view and easily use the titles that you have found? Being comfortable with how these components work will enable you to have the necessary skills to assist your patrons as they access the Google Books project in your library. To help get you started, let's look back to our previous search on Carnegie libraries and examine at one of the returned titles: *A Book of Carnegie Libraries*.

As you can see from Figure 2.11, individual title results are similar to the page of returned search results you received before, but there are several distinct elements, you should pay attention to. These include:

Figure 2.11

- Main viewing area
- Information pane
- Viewing controls

Main Viewing Area

The **main viewing area** is just that, the area of the screen where you can see the individual resource. No matter how you choose to view a title, it will always show up here, without any pop-up windows or other browser tabs to distract you. Within this viewing area, you will have options to read the title in either single page or double page, depending on your monitor and reading needs. You also have the option, in many cases, of thumbnail views, which can help you quickly scan a many-paged resource.

Information Pane

To the left of the main viewing area lies what I have labeled the **information pane**, which provides additional information about the title you have chosen. The top part contains bibliographic and related details about the work, and will often contain reviews written by other Google Books users. While they are certainly not held to the same professional standards as a more formal review that you might find in the *New York Times Review of Books* or *Library Journal*, they can be helpful in determining if a resource is worth further investigation.

As noted in Figure 2.12, in this same area of the information pane, you will also find integration of the Google Books project with the new **Google +** social networking service. Similar in some respects to Facebook and other social media sites, this new offering has been integrated across most of Google's other software and services options. For what it's worth, by using these **Google +** options within the project, you will find it easy to share title and resource information with your patrons or even the public in general. Most commonly, this is expressed within Google Books by the **+1** option, similar in many respects to the now nearly universal Facebook like.

However, it's important to be aware that any use of the service will appear on your or your library's Google profile[12] and might also appear in the regular Google search results. From a library's perspective,

Figure 2.12

this can be an effective marketing and visibility tool, especially if your library makes use of Google-based products and services. From broadcasting new digital items in your collection or even books that have been added in the standard method, it's a fast and unique method of getting your message out!

In the same area of the screen as the **+1** option, you'll find a star rating system. This is similar to many of Google's other ratings systems is especially useful if you are hurriedly considering multiple resources and do not have time for an in-depth investigation of each one. However, do note that these ratings are held to no particular standard and that they can vary wildly.

The **search bar** section, located directly below the star rating option, can help you search for specific words or phrases within the resource. Remember, *all* of the books in the Google Books project have been digitized, and every word in the text is searchable. Once you have a specific resource, use this type of search to quickly zero in on the information you are looking for. Note that results of this type of search are indicated across the top row of the current title you are examining.

The second part of the information pane, **About This Book**, can provide a wealth of related and additional information, including:

- Details on finding the item in a local library

- Adding the item via the **My Library** option

- Purchasing the item through a commercial vendor

- Finding items related to this resource and your search in general

- Purchasing a Google eBook version, if available

Let's take a few moments and look over these additional components.

If you find a resource that you have been searching for, **Find in a Library** is a great option to consider. Clicking on this link takes you to the Online Computer Library Center (OCLC) and their associated WorldCat catalog, where you'll find a list of libraries that own the resource in question. From here, you can try to borrow the physical item from one of these libraries. Note that while it's fairly easy for librarians and library staff to distinguish between the Google Books project and the WorldCat catalog, some of your patrons might not be as knowledgeable. If you notice your patrons consistently choosing WorldCat, you might consider signage or on-the-spot assistance as needed, to help distinguish between the two different services.[13]

The **My Library** option, as noted in Figure 2.13, enables you to add a specific resource to a custom online Google Books bookshelf. If your library has a Google Books account, this is a great way to keep highly requested items easily accessible! You can either hide or show bookshelves, as you choose. Note that both bookshelf options—in the regular Google Books and in My Library in Google Play—refer to the same set of resources. Take time to familiarize yourself with these options. They can be confusing, especially if you have never used the Google Books project before.

Figure 2.13

Google Books also lists commercial providers such as Amazon, AbeBooks, and Barnes & Noble that may sell the title in question. Clicking on these links transfers your search to the sellers' websites. If the item is in their catalog of available titles, you will be taken to a listing. If not, you'll see a list of related titles. You can also find additional bibliographic information such as pricing or user ratings.

The **related books** option is a great way to find titles similar to the one already retrieved. For patrons who need additional citations or just want to broaden their research, this is a great alternative to performing search after search. For magazines, results include identification numbers such as LCCN and ISBN. You can either click on individual related titles or on the link for all related titles.

In many cases, you will also be given the option to buy digital versions of the resources via Google Play. Although you won't be able to obtain every resource this way, many are available for purchase. Google Play is discussed later in the chapter, but it's worth noting here that this option can be confusing, especially if all you want to do is read the resource you've found. It's essential to understand that Google Play is the online bookstore and is not strictly part of the Google Books project.

Don't overlook the many additional possibilities available for your selected title as well. These include QR codes, additional bibliographic information, tag clouds, and even the various citation export options for BibTex, EndNote, and Reference Manager. Citation exporting is a great shortcut for your patrons who may be working on a professional publication or even just homework. Already used extensively in the library community and elsewhere, QR code generation is an effective way to mesh online titles with your physical collection or set up special displays in the library.

Viewing Controls

Once you've found a specific resource on the project, you will find great flexibility in using and viewing the information from that particular title. I've called these **viewing controls**, and it is easy to become familiar with them. Take a look at Figure 2.14.

Figure 2.14

Note that the search bar for the project is still available at the top of the page. This enables you to do additional searching without having to go back to the original search page in the browser (as do some of the other online eBooks sites we've covered so far.).

Notice the individual title-level **viewing controls** for the particular resource you have found. Use them to enlarge or shrink the display, change from single to double to thumbnail views of the item in question, and even jump to hotlinks in the text enabled through the table of contents. Other controls include full-screen viewing, clipping text options for public domain and free titles, and sharing link options (if you want to share what has been found with others). Because these controls are embedded in the page, you can stay within a single browser window, rather than having to use multiple tabs or windows to read the material you're searching. The thumbnail option is not appropriate for reading, but it can be helpful in tracking down specific photos or other art. Note that you can click on any of the thumbnails and immediately be taken to that particular page for a closer look.

Figure 2.15

From the left control menu, we now move to the right side of the page and the second set of book viewing controls. As noted earlier in this chapter, for most titles, this includes a linked table of contents and the index. Choosing any one of these listings will immediately takes you to the page in the work. See Figure 2.15 for a detailed look at these options.

These embedded viewing controls make it easy to manipulate the page images to fit your viewing needs and particularly the reading device you are currently using to examine the title. When explaining these options to your patrons, don't forget that with some titles, mainly for those considered to be in the public domain, you can directly clip plain-text quotes or entire sections. Because you can switch between page images and plain text, you can directly import portions of the text into other documents. See Figure 2.16 and 2.17 for details on these options.

If you are working with a patron on a particular title, plan on spending a few moments talking about these controls. Although they are not hard to understand, there may be

Figure 2.16

Figure 2.17

confusion, particularly with the various clipping options. This might also occur if your patron wants to download the resource to his or her own device. Also, you might want to explain that the ability to download to specific devices may or may not be available, depending upon your library's rules and policies.

Just for Libraries and Librarians: Going beyond the Basics

Now that you've explored Google Books and have learned how the site works to search for and view results, it's time to learn about some of the more advanced capabilities of the project. These options can be used in libraries to make the Google Books project even more valuable to your patrons and staff. In particular, we will consider integration with your current library system, different mobility options, and other specific Google Books extras that you should be aware of. Table 2.3 offers a brief summary of some of these.

ILS Integration

One of the biggest parts of many libraries' technological efforts is their integrated library system (ILS). Consisting of back-office functions such as circulation, cataloging,

Table 2.3 Examples of Google Books Advanced Options for Libraries

Name	Function
Online bookshelves	Collection development
ILS integration	Catalog expansion/development
RSS feeds	Patron awareness
Book embeds	Extending library value
Google Books API	App development and server-side integration

and acquisitions, as well as the front-facing online public catalog, the ILS has become an essential part of the library. The Google Books project can both add and supplement this local system, complementing the collection, and adding to the depth and breadth of information the library can offer its patrons. How is this done?

In these days of tight budgets and rising expenses, adding to the collection of physical materials often involves tradeoffs between what is needed and what can be afforded. Google Books offers a way to bridge this gap. Utilizing technologies such as the Google-provided application programming interfaces (APIs), libraries can access and integrate many of Google's eBooks directly into their catalog, offering patrons access to millions of titles that would otherwise not be accessible.

It's more than just a catalog supplement, however. Developers can use the Google Books API to directly pull information from the Google Books database and use it on the local library website or wherever the library is online—at zero cost! As noted in Figure 2.18, there is extensive information on getting started.

Here's a practical example. Let's say your library wants to expand the local genealogy collection and integrate these selections into the online catalog. However, the budget just isn't there to digitize the source materials or acquire additional database sub-scriptions. What do you do? The solution is simple. Using a free account from Google and the Google Books API, your staff can directly pull public domain genealogy resources from the project and integrate them directly into your catalog as needed. The only thing your library needs to contribute is a small amount of staff time to get the project underway!

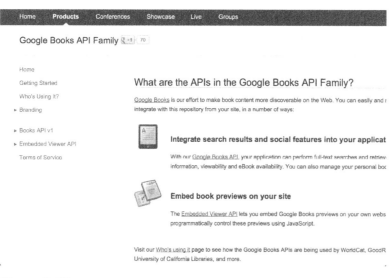

Beyond the technical part of this integration, the project also allows your library to include embedded books, book covers, and even ports of texts available from the project. All of these features provide and extend the services your library can offer the patrons and the community at large. For smaller libraries, this is extremely beneficial and a zero cost option that can really be effective.

Figure 2.18

Going Mobile

Today's library patrons are mobile, and their use of cell phones, tablets, and other portable electronic devices is not going to diminish anytime soon. Can your patrons use the Google Books project with these types of devices? Yes and no. As originally stated on the Google Books blog in 2009,[14] a mobile reading platform of over 1 million public domain titles was initially made available for use by mobile devices. You can find the platform here: http://books.google.com/m.

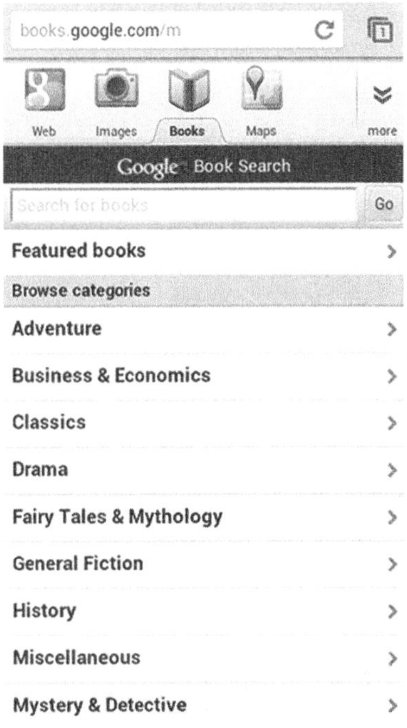

As seen in Figure 2.19, using this small subset of the total Google Books project, which is devoid of extraneous information and graphics, your patrons can have access no matter what type of device they are using.

However, technology advances swiftly, and with the advent of a redesigned Google Books site as well as the integration of Google Play with the project for the purchase of online books, it is now possible to view Google Books resources on almost any mobile platform, without any need for special sites or programming. Access does depend on the types of devices being used as well as the source materials, but for the most part, Google Books can be accessed via the main site.

Figure 2.19

The Google Online Bookshelf (My Library)

As shown in Figure 2.20, the Google Books **Online Bookshelf** (integrated with the **My Library** option) is easy to implement and makes your patrons and community aware of special library resources and projects. It also helps satisfy patron demands for popular items in an effective manner. The way it works is really simple.

Start by using a Google account to log into the Google Books project. This can be a library, staff, or personal account. Once you are logged in, click on **My Library** on the left side of the page. Then you'll see a set of default bookshelves. From there, click on **New Shelf**. You have just created a new online bookshelf! As noted in Figure 2.21,

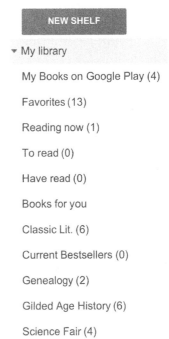

Figure 2.20

Figure 2.21

you can now rename the bookshelf, tell a bit about the materials it will contain, and decide whether to make it public or private.

At this point, your new bookshelf is empty. How do you add titles? Simply use Google Books to find titles that you want the bookshelf to contain and add them to it. Viewing the individual items and using the viewing controls, you can quickly fill your bookshelf with materials. Other advanced considerations at this point include the ability to do custom title ordering, changing how the items appear on the bookshelf, and even import and export options, including the ability to add titles by ISBN and ISSN.

Practical Usages

So what are the practical implications of these online bookshelves? Is this option really helpful for your library? Let's examine this question by using the topic of science fairs, which are popular in libraries across the country. If you work in a public library and your local schools hold science fairs, you know that keeping hard copies of titles related to science and science fairs available for all your patrons is almost impossible, if only because of the numerous students that need resources for their projects.

However, by adding digital resources via the bookshelves options in the Google Books project, you can create specific science fair bookshelves by grade, science topic, and even resource type. You can then use these resources to actively supplement your paper-based collection. Patrons can also view the shelves via a link from your library catalog or the library's website. From a service perspective, if it is after regular library hours, patrons can use your online bookshelves to do their own research, viewing titles online, finding links to another library, or purchasing titles outright on Google Play or another bookseller. The end result is a boost to your library's effectiveness within the community, schools, and even individual patrons.

Special Google Digital Projects

One of the highlights of the Google Books project is that the technology is extensible, with this ability to be used in other Google digital projects that scan not just ordinary books, but special resources that otherwise would have never been viewable unless by researchers on site at the resource.

As noted on the Inside Google Books Blog,[15] these special projects include partnerships with European libraries such as the Oxford University Library and the Municipal Library of Lyon. Using this technology, now more than 550,000 titles from the sixteenth, seventeenth, and eighteenth centuries are available for anyone to use! This same technology is also applied via the Digital Dead Sea Scrolls Project.[16] Recently updated, this amazing digital project is bringing the Dead Sea Scrolls to the Internet and to our patrons in ways never seen before. While the Dead Sea Scrolls are not directly related to Google Books, their new accessibility is a natural outgrowth of the project and yet another valuable resource for your library to consider.

Google Play!

In response to rapid development of iTunes, as well as Amazon's and Barnes & Noble's on-line portals for selling software, eBooks, movies, and more, Google has developed a similar portal called **Google Play**. Found online at https://play.google.com/store/books, this site offers current books, both nonfiction and fiction, as well as applications, movies, and music. While similar to the other offerings, Google Play is also incorporated directly into the Google Books project, which enables patrons and libraries to purchase some titles found there.

However, there is great potential here for confusion among your patrons about the mixing of these two services. Should they search Google Books or Google Play? What if they click on a title that is only available via Google Play? Many eBook links start out in the Google Books project but end up pointing users to the Google Play bookstore. Given this, patron education becomes especially important. Stress this to your staff, and give them a chance to become completely familiar with how the integration works. As patrons use Google Books, your staff will then be able to answer these types of questions.

Besides potential confusion over the mixing together of the Google Books project and the online bookstore of Google Play, 2013 has also seen the expansion of the mobile application, Google Play Books. Available on the majority of mobile devices now carried by our patrons, this even further blurs the lines between the two separate projects. If we combine this with the recent Google option to upload eBooks to one's individual Google Books library in May of 2013 (see https://support.google.com/googleplay/answer/3107421 for details), it's important to carefully plan how to use these as well as Google Books in your library.

Important Points to Remember about Google Books

In conclusion, what follows are some of the important points mentioned in this chapter. You can use these when training your staff on the Google Books project or to help yourself remember the high points from each section. These items are also excellent starting points for signage or presentations related to patron training.

Origins and Issues

- Partnerships with libraries and publishers
- Publishers can determine how much of each of their titles are seen online
- Libraries can choose their level of commitment
- Copyright and legal issues remain a major issue

Site Structure and the Materials Collection

- The project contains both basic and advanced search capabilities
- Many serials and other magazines are available for use
- Project emphasis on books and traditional sources, not ephemera
- Don't confuse Google Play with the regular Google Books project

Searching Google Books

- Many methods of search, from basic to advanced, are available.
- Searching options abound both within the catalog *and* the individual titles.
- Stackable searching is possible with modifiers.

Viewing and Using Your Results

- Sources can be viewed online or downloaded
- PDF and ePub formats dominate, and plain text is an option
- Outbound links to WorldCat and other online booksellers

Just for Libraries and Librarians: Going beyond the Basics

- Share your collection via online public bookshelves
- ILS integration and book covers
- Some mobility options for other devices
- Other digital projects as outgrowth of Google Books

Introducing the Future: Google Play

- Includes bestsellers and public domain items
- Specialized applications for many devices
- Read within the web browser options

Questions for You to Try

The Google Books project is an amazing resource, one that can help your library expand its collection and help your staff answer the many patron questions that come up almost daily. Use the following practice questions to learn more about the site and get your searching skills up to date and ready for the reference desk!

Answers to these questions are at the back of this book, so if you get stuck, take a sneak a peak to see how they can be solved. Also note that there are many ways to get answers to the following questions, and you might have an alternative method of getting the same results.

Google Books Site and Structure

1. You're working the reference desk and a teacher from the local high school pulls you aside for some special assistance. She is teaching British literature this semester and is concerned about having enough copies of the books available for students to use. How can Google Books help, and what's the best method to help this teacher find what she needs?

2. Your director is planning a major eBook push for your library in the upcoming strategic plan to be presented at the next board meeting. What are some ways Google Books can be incorporated into the plan? Specifically, how can Google Books get eBooks to your patrons easily, quickly, and for free?

3. The children's librarian is going to be giving a talk to a local high school class next week about using Google Books to find articles for a persuasive essay. Considering the site and its structure, what's the best method for the students to browse for different subjects?

Searching Google Books

1. Your local genealogical society has expressed interest in learning more about various genealogical resources that might be available via the Google Books project.

In particular, they are looking for family histories. What sort of search strategy would you recommend for them and why?

2. It's science fair time at your library again, and as usual, all of your science books are checked out. How can the Google Book project help? How would you go about searching for supporting materials, and what sort of results might you find?

3. You work at a small college library, and your director is looking to implement a digital book strategy for downloadable public domain titles. Using Google Books, find four or five resources that can be downloaded. Which do you find more of—PDF or ePub format?

Viewing Results

1. You've been helping a patron find more information on *Billboard* magazine from the 1950s. However, she is not quite sure what viewing options would work best. Knowing the multiplicity of views that are possible, which one would you recommend and why?

2. Look for public domain resources that are downloadable. How would you copy the text to a Word document? Which method is best?

Notes

1. Google, http://books.google.com/intl/en/googlebooks/history.html.

2. Steven Levy. *In the plex: How Google thinks, works, and shapes our lives.* New York: Simon and Schuster, 2011, 355–75.

3. Ibid., 350.

4. The New York Review of Books, http://www.nybooks.com/articles/archives/2013/apr/25/national-digital-public-library-launched/.

5. Google Books project, http://books.google.com/googlebooks/library.html.

6. Google Books Search, http://booksearch.blogspot.com/.

7. Google Inside Search, http://support.google.com/websearch/bin/answer.py?hl=en&answer=136861.

8. BISG, http://www.bisg.org/what-we-do-0-136-bisac-subject-headings-list-major-subjects.php.

9. Inside Higher Ed, http://www.insidehighered.com/news/2011/12/08/scholar-continues-find-flawed-metadata-google-books.

10. Language Log, http://languagelog.ldc.upenn.edu/nll/?p=1701.

11. Oder, Norman, "Millions of Metadata Mistakes," *Library Journal*, published online September 3, 2009 and found online at http://www.libraryjournal.com/article/CA6687562.html.

12. Google, http://www.google.com/+1/button/.

13. OCLC, http://www.worldcat.org/whatis/default.jsp.

14. Google Books Search, http://booksearch.blogspot.com/2009/02/15-million-books-in-your-pocket.html.

15. Google Books Search, http://booksearch.blogspot.com/2011/05/books-from-16th-and-17th-centuries-now.html.

16. Digital Dead Sea Scrolls, http://dss.collections.imj.org.il/.

Resources

Project Background and Information

Bodleian Libraries University of Oxford, "Oxford's Google Books Project Reaches Milestone," http://www.bodleian.ox.ac.uk/news/oxfords-google-books-project-reaches-milestone20121009.

CNET, "Google, Authors Wrangle in Court Again Over Digital Books," http://news.cnet.com/8301-1023_3-57583461-93/google-authors-wrangle-in-court-again-over-digital-books/.

Darnton, Robert, "The National Digital Public Library Is Launched!," The New York Review of Books, April 25, 2013, http://www.nybooks.com/articles/archives/2013/apr/25/national-digital-public-library-launched/.

Google, "1.5 Million Books in Your Pocket," http://booksearch.blogspot.com/2009/02/15-million-books-in-your-pocket.html.

Google, "About the Google Books Project," http://books.google.com/googlebooks/about.html.

Google, "The Point of Google Print," http://googleblog.blogspot.com/2005/10/point-of-google-print.html.

Howard, Jennifer, "Google Begins to Scale Back Its Scanning of Books from University Libraries," *Chronicle of Higher Education* 58, no. 28 (March 16, 2012): A27. MasterFILE Premier, EBSCOhost (accessed August 12, 2012).

National Public Radio, "The Secret of Google's Book Scanning Machine Revealed," http://www.npr.org/blogs/library/2009/04/the_granting_of_patent_7508978.html.

Kelly, Kevin, "Scan This Book," *New York Times Magazine*, May 14, 2006, http://www.nytimes.com/2006/05/14/magazine/14publishing.html.

Pike, George H., "Divide and Conquer: Update on the Google Books Lawsuit," *Information Today* 29, no. 2 (February 2012): 1. MasterFILE Premier, EBSCOhost (accessed August 12, 2012).

Searching Google Books

Google, "Basic Search Help," http://www.google.com/support/websearch/bin/answer.py?hl=en&answer=134479.

Google, "Find Out What's in a Word, or Five, with the Google Books Ngram Viewer," http://booksearch.blogspot.com/2010/12/find-out-whats-in-word-or-five-with.html.

Language Log, "Google Books: A Metadata Train Wreck," http://languagelog.ldc .upenn.edu/nll/?p=1701.

James, Ryan, and Andrew Weiss, "An Assessment of Google Books' Metadata," *Journal of Library Metadata* 12, no. 1 (2012): 15–22.

Google Play

CNET, "How to Upload Documents, eBooks to Google Play Books," http://howto .cnet.com/8301-11310_39-57585097-285/how-to-upload-documents-e-books-to-google -play-books/.

Google, "Discover More Than 3 Million Google eBooks from Your Choice of Book-sellers and Devices," http://googleblog.blogspot.com/2010/12/discover-more-than-3 -million-google.html.

Google, "Google Play Help," http://support.google.com/googleplay.

Mobileread, "Google Books Offers ePub Downloads of Free Books," http://www .mobileread.com/forums/showthread.php?t=55071.

The Google Books Project and Your Library

Google, "Google Books Family API," http://developers.google.com/books/docs/ getting-started.

Google, "LIFE Magazine Now Available on Google Books," http://booksearch .blogspot.com/2009/09/life-magazine-now-available-on-google.html.

Open, "British Library Encloses the Public Domain," http://opendotdotdot.blogspot .com/2011/06/british-library-encloses-public-domain.html.

Swiss Army Librarian, "Linking from the Catalog to Google Books," http://www .swissarmylibrarian.net/2011/05/24/linking-from-the-catalog-to-google-books/.

Chapter 3

HathiTrust

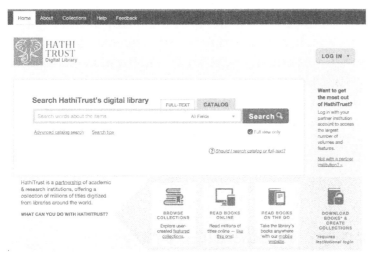

Figure 3.1

Now that you've had a chance to examine and use Google Books, let's move on to another online eBook project called HathiTrust. While similar in many ways to the other sites discussed in this book, Hathi-Trust differs substantially in design and implementation as well as in goals and usage, often taking a more academic approach with individual library memberships and sharing of digitized resources.

In this chapter, you'll examine the project from its beginnings up to the present and even into the future. Along the way, you'll learn how to effectively use this resource and integrate it into your library workflow as an everyday reference for your staff and an information source for your patrons. To understand the project's approach, consider the following scenario. It's about Josh, the director of a small academic library in Ohio.

Budget Problems!

It was 10 p.m. and Josh was still in his office, working and reworking the library budget numbers. Frustrated, he deleted the spreadsheet he had been working on for some time and started again with a fresh copy. No matter how he tried, the updated budget just didn't work out with any sort of sustainable numbers.

As director of a small academic library in Ohio, Josh had just learned that his budget had been cut again for the upcoming academic year. Now at an impasse, he somehow had to provide library resources without the budget to do so. His only alternative at this point seemed to be to cut his serials collection or his staff. The serials budget was already looking thin, and as far as staffing went, the only remaining option was to replace highly competent reference librarians and catalogers with student help. As great as he knew the students could be, there was no way he could replace highly trained and knowledgeable librarians.

As he started punching numbers into the spreadsheet, Josh looked around for his budget and saw the pamphlet on the desk. He'd picked it up at a recent academic library conference. Leafing through it, he saw it was about a digital book resource site called HathiTrust. It seemed too good to be true, offering both free access to millions of titles and membership options for academic libraries. He remembered that many of the other librarians at the conference had raved about it, but he wasn't too sure. eBooks seemed to be growing as a sustainable resource—but not having titles on the shelf and available at the library still seemed a little too risky. Dropping the pamphlet back on his desk, he thought maybe tomorrow he would investigate HathiTrust a bit more. Maybe it would help him address the declining budget numbers staring back at him from the computer screen.

Origins, Partnerships, and the Academic Library

Although the preceding story isn't real, academic libraries today are facing many of the same problems. As you likely know all too well, increasing expenditures for both electronic resources and the materials-based collection along with rising staff costs have created multiple headaches for library administrators. Coupling this with reduced allowances and lack of funding has only compounded these issues.

At the same time, both faculty and students are asking, and sometimes even demanding, more services and books in the collection. Under these circumstances, challenges can often seem insurmountable for both library staff and administration. If you are a librarian or on staff at an academic library, then more than likely this is a familiar story.

However, these problems are not just limited to academic libraries. In fact, libraries of all types, from public to academic, special and educational, are all experiencing these same increased financial and service pressures. Quite often, there's really no easy answer.

A Way Out?

Given all of these issues, the HathiTrust project just might be a way forward for academic and other types of libraries. While primarily originating from and used in the academic library environment, HathiTrust is freely available for use by everyone and is easily accessible via its public website (www.hathitrust.org). Offering over 10 million digitized volumes and growing, HathiTrust has become a thriving membership option for libraries and an excellent information resource that we can offer our patrons and the public in general. To get a better understanding of the project, let's look more closely at how it all began.

Origins

According to the HathiTrust website, the project began in 2008 via an agreement between academic libraries from institutions such as the University of California, the University of Virginia, and academic consortiums such as the Committee on Institutional Cooperation (CIC). Taking its name from the Hindi word for elephant, the goals and objectives for HathiTrust are quite comprehensive.

Project Goals

HathiTrust's goals separate this particular project from the many other digital books sites we will discuss, reflecting its sharp focus as well as the needs of the member libraries. As noted on the HathiTrust website, these objectives include:[1]

- Creation of a digital archive of materials owned by member libraries

- Access to contributed materials by both member libraries and the public

- Preservation of the knowledge obtained from the physical volumes by various digitization strategies

- Long-term reduction of the costs of physical storage by member libraries and their contributed collections

- Creation of technical tools that meet member libraries' needs and address individual concerns about their collections

If we consider these goals on an individual basis and compare them to the other projects covered in this book, it becomes readily apparent that HathiTrust is unique.

The project assists academic institutions and libraries achieve their own goals while at the same time providing a larger amount of digital information to all of us—a contribution that can be used by your library as well as your patrons and even your community!

Table 3.1 Examples of HathiTrust Library Members

United States Library of Congress	New York Public Library
Stanford University	Texas A&M University
The Ohio State University	University of Florida
University of Michigan	University of Minnesota
John Hopkins University	California Digital Library
Dartmouth College	Duke University
Massachusetts Institute of Technology	Purdue University

Who Can Join?

As noted in Table 3.1, HathiTrust is open to libraries of all types, although most members at this point are from academia. In addition to the names mentioned previously, other notable members include the University of North Carolina at Chapel Hill, Yale University, The Ohio State University, and the Triangle Research Libraries Network. Not static by any means, membership and interest in the project continue to grow as its successes and volume of digitized materials continue. The following link can provide more information about current materials contributions from member libraries (as of April 2013): http://www.hathitrust.org/updates_april2013.

Current Operations and the Future

While we now know of the project's overall goals and ensuing growth, of particular interest is continued investment of project resources and time into various subprojects, all of which benefit the membership as a whole. Some of these smaller works are meant for internal use only, helping to maintain administrative focus or a coherent digitization strategy. Other parts are for external use, providing patrons, staff, and the public with better access to the information that is already available.

The complete list can be found online,[2] but some of HathiTrust's more notable features include:

- Digitization and use of orphan works
- Growth of library members and external partnerships

- Easy mobile access

- Full title downloads

Let's now take a closer look at these.

Digitization and Use of Orphan Works

A fairly controversial topic for many in the library, publishing, and academic worlds, orphan works are invariably brought up when considering online eBook sites such as HathiTrust. Given all of the notoriety and news stories, it's easy to get confused about the whole topic. In fact, let's take a look at just what the definition of an orphan work is and how these titles play a role in online eBook sites such as HathiTrust.

According to most popular and current understandings, orphan works are titles whose author or publisher cannot be found, yet remain covered by copyright law. Under this system, even though these titles are not claimed by anyone, they cannot be scanned, digitized, or otherwise made available for use because those actions would not have the owner's authorization, whether that author is an individual or publishing company. The end result? Many millions of titles are effectively in a form of stasis, not able to be used by anyone. Even if HathiTrust or some other online book site has previously digitized these titles, their availability online is almost nonexistent due to ongoing legal and copyright concerns.

HathiTrust, in partnership with the University of Michigan,[3] is addressing this issue with the aim of making orphan works available within the project. A pilot project began the process of finding copyright owners, and from 2008 through 2011, the project made great strides in identifying orphan works and making many of them available via the site.[4]

However, since then, this work has been legally challenged in court, and controversy about digitizing and using the titles has become widespread.[5] In fact, in late 2011, HathiTrust halted its current work with these orphan works because of a lawsuit filed by the Authors Guild. This suit charged that HathiTrust had not correctly identified the true copyright owners and therefore did not have the right to copy or distribute the titles that had been grouped into the orphan works category. While in October 2012 the courts ruled in favor of HathiTrust's efforts to identify these digital orphans,[6] no permanent decisions have been made.[7]

Growth of Library Members and External Partnerships

HathiTrust continues to add libraries as knowledge of the project grows. Notable new members include Boston College, Notre Dame, and the University of Florida. At the same time, HathiTrust's model of membership has evolved. While all member organizations are equal in standing, there are two different options for joining the project. As noted on the

HathiTrust website,[8] libraries can choose to contribute materials to the project via digitization and other methods, or they can simply become members without contributing physical content.

Even without contributing materials for digitization, these secondary members help the project both monetarily and nonmonetarily via committee participation and helping to set long-term strategies. Some of the committees currently in effect at the project include project end-user support as well as communications and usability design. This library involvement has helped the project address many changes in a thoughtful and ongoing way. For complete information and news about these new members as well as committee and meeting information, see the following link: http://www.hathitrust.org/news_publications.

Prototype Catalog

Figure 3.2

Beyond partner libraries, HathiTrust has reached out to the nonprofit and commercial world to help further the project, as can be seen with the ongoing discussions between both the Online Computer Library Center (OCLC) and Elton Bryson Stephens Company (EBSCO) Publishing. Well known in the library world, OCLC is currently working with HathiTrust to offer a combined digital catalog consisting of traditional OCLC resources and the materials available via HathiTrust.[9] As noted in Figure 3.2 and available online at http://hathitrust.worldcat.org, this tool can help patrons and librarians/staff increase their searching efficiency and locate materials in a wide variety of physical locations and online at the same time.

HathiTrust has also employed a strategy to offer digital resources through the EBSCO Discovery Service.[10] With this approach, in addition to subscription databases offered by EBSCO, library end-users can also access the many millions of resources offered by HathiTrust. At last count, according to various resources, this included more than 8 million individual titles![11]

Easy Mobile Access

With the continued growth of the use of mobile applications and hardware along with near universal Internet access via the same mechanism, HathiTrust has forged ahead to provide a mobile catalog for the project. As seen in Figure 3.3 and available at http://m.hathitrust .org, the slimmed-down interface has great functionality and is easy to use by both library staff

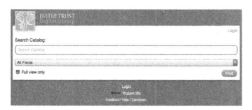

Figure 3.3

and patrons. Although by no means complete, the mobile catalog offers options to read items in full view on your mobile device of choice as well as to examine detailed catalog records. Search is also supported and includes the common fields: title, author, subject, ISBN, publisher, series, and year of publication. Testing on a variety of devices, I was able to use the site and gain access to materials without a problem. You'll learn more about these features later in the chapter.

Full Title Downloads

One of the biggest questions you are likely to encounter about the HathiTrust project, and one that is potentially frustrating to staff and patrons alike, concerns the inability to download the full source material. While **some** full title downloads are publicly allowed for selected works, most notably those in the public domain or with allowable licenses to do so, for the majority of the collection this is not the case. While guest accounts are permitted and give you the opportunity to build online collections, you cannot download the full source material—at least not yet. However frustrating, the reason behind this policy is sound, especially if we consider the tangled web of copyright restrictions and the presence of works whose copyright status is unknown. For more details and information on this approach, try the following link: http://www.hathitrust.org/help_digital_library.

However, for patrons whose libraries are HathiTrust project members, title download policies are a bit more lenient, including many more public domain titles and resources.[12] The key point here is additional license and copyright clearance.[13] This may limit the use of the project for some nonmember libraries or the general public, but overall, given the easy access to many millions of titles, for those with specific information requests, it should not limit the effectiveness too much.

Technological Change

The HathiTrust project is in itself a technological wonder, especially if you consider its ever-growing content. But the future seems even brighter as new methods of access and retrieval become available. With the continued growth and implementation of the WorldCat search engine as well as additional agreements with OCLC, HathiTrust is destined to become a method people use to access and search resources previously unavailable to many libraries.

You can see shades of these changes in the current partnership between the project and Serial Solutions' Summon product. As noted on the HathiTrust website,[14] linking library serial and other holdings with information from HathiTrust will give patrons much greater access. The practical implications? Your patrons can be more efficient and effective as they search in a single place for copies on your library shelf as well as HathiTrust.

So What Does This Do for Your Library?

Given the growth of the project and the incredible number of available resources, you should consider the practical everyday benefits of using HathiTrust in your library. Offering

Collection Name

English Short Title
Catalog

Collection Description

Published between 1473
and 1800 mainly, but not
exclusively, in English in
the British Isles and North
America

Figure 3.4

content such as genealogy information, history, science, magazines, and many other resources that are no longer available for purchase or interlibrary loan due to age or condition, HathiTrust can greatly enhance your library's collection and scope. At the same time, these benefits are provided at no additional cost to you, your staff, or your patrons. Note, for example, Figure 3.4 as a small sample of the types of materials offered.

Let's also look at a practical example. Consider a patron who comes into your library looking for information on Pittsburgh's formative role in the Sesqui-Centennial International Exposition of 1926. It might seem that information on this particular event would be limited to general reference materials on your shelf or would involve directing your patron to the Internet and their favorite search engine. However, through HathiTrust, it's possible to quickly pull up many titles that deal directly with this particular subject.

The end result? You've helped your patron find answers, and your library is seen as an essential information resource. Using HathiTrust as part of your library's digital strategy just makes sense as you extend your library's information offerings to the community and become a more valuable resource to your patrons.

Of course, some would argue that making resources such as HathiTrust part of your information strategy puts your library at risk and makes it too dependent on outside services. However, couldn't this be said for many of the vendors and services that libraries already depend on for collection development and information technology? While there is no denying that depending on HathiTrust entails some risk, I believe the benefits outweigh the dangers.

Another argument in favor of HathiTrust comes down to simple economics. Being part of the group lowers library costs, improves access (through millions of additional titles), and brings the library a wealth of knowledge. From a membership standpoint, the library can help give direction to the project by participating in decisions and committee membership. For non-member libraries, the advantages are apparent as well. Even with access to only a small portion of the total collection, patrons can still use millions of resources that cost the library absolutely nothing other than staff training and perhaps integration with the local online catalog.

Site Structure and Materials Collection

Having looked at both origins and goals, let's look more closely at the HathiTrust project, in particular the design of the online catalog as well as the types of materials that can be found there. Familiarity with these aspects of the project will facilitate making it an everyday tool for yourself, your library, and your patrons. As with your on-site collections, having the skills and knowledge to successfully navigate HathiTrust means that your library can benefit that much more.

Framework And Structure

Although comparable in many ways to the Google Books project, the Internet Archive, and the other sites profiled in this book, the structure of the HathiTrust catalog and website does differ. As you search the various indexes, use the full text item search and explore the collections, the differences HathiTrust brings will quickly become apparent. Let's examine in depth some of these differences via the following categories:

- Methods of search

- Examining results

- Public collections

Methods of Search

Getting started with your search is as simple as navigating to the HathiTrust homepage at http://www.hathitrust .org and deciding which search method you would like to start with. As seen in Figure 3.5, options include catalog searching, advanced catalog searching, full text searching, and advanced full text searching. Each of these approaches has strengths and weaknesses, depending on the types and amounts of information you are searching for.

Figure 3.5

Catalog searches give the most options when you are searching for a specific piece of information and include full text and advanced options. **Advanced catalog searches** enable you to begin "stacking" results from your query, starting with a particular field and adding on additional qualifiers and limiters to cut down on the results you have to examine to find a good resource. Including fields such as title, author, subject, and ISBN, advanced catalog searching is the most flexible and usable for intricate data queries. **Full-text searches** differ from catalog searches in that they bring back occurrences of your term (or terms) wherever they

Table 3.2 Search Methods Available on HathiTrust

Type of Search	Best For
Basic, Advanced Catalog Searching	Specific titles, authors, etc.
Full-Text	Word or phrase within full view items
Advanced Full-Text	Word or phrase PLUS specific titles, authors, etc.

appear in the full text of items that are available. **Advanced full-text searches** offer the best of both worlds, giving you the ability to search across the full text of items in HathiTrust as well as the traditional fields of title, author, subject, ISBN, and others. The following table summarizes the approaches available on the site.

Examining Results

Although searching is easy in HathiTrust, ultimately what you are looking for are answers related to specific information needs. Given this, you must be familiar with how results are formulated in HathiTrust and how they differ from other digital book sites. In HathiTrust, your results are returned in list format and can in many cases be sorted by relevance, date, and title, depending on whether you are searching the regular catalog or by the **Full View** option. Even more interesting is the breakdown of the returned results on the sidebar, where it's easy to refine your search, adding new details to query for or narrowing down your initial thoughts, particu-

Figure 3.6

larly as noted in Figure 3.6. Note also on the sidebar that you can quickly jump to related authors and subjects, saving some research time and weeding out entries that are not pertinent.

Once you search the project, there are multiple ways to view your results. HathiTrust allows titles that are considered to be in the public domain, for which the copyright has not been renewed, or to which the publisher has granted access, to be fully viewed online—that is, you can read the entire text. For titles that are still under copyright, to which the publisher has *not* granted access, or those with an uncertain copyright status, the full contents are not shown. Instead, for these titles, the most you will see is the catalog record, as shown in

Figure 3.7. Upon initial viewing, this can be confusing and is a potential trouble spot for your patrons. Plan to make your staff well aware of these distinctions and educate them about orphan works issues that determine whether materials can be shown in the project. The following link offers some background information that may help you understand the difference: http://www.hathitrust.org/help _copyright#RestrictedAccess.

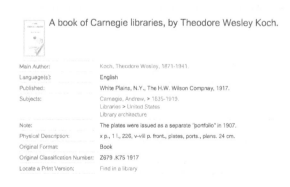

Figure 3.7

Note that there are also special viewing options for patrons with physical disabilities or who otherwise cannot view the titles online. These options include the use of the keyboard to turn pages when viewing titles as well as special versions of public domain titles (currently undergoing testing at the University of Michigan, according to HathiTrust). For more details and information on these updates and other access options for your patrons, try the following link: http://www.hathitrust.org/accessibility.

Public Collections

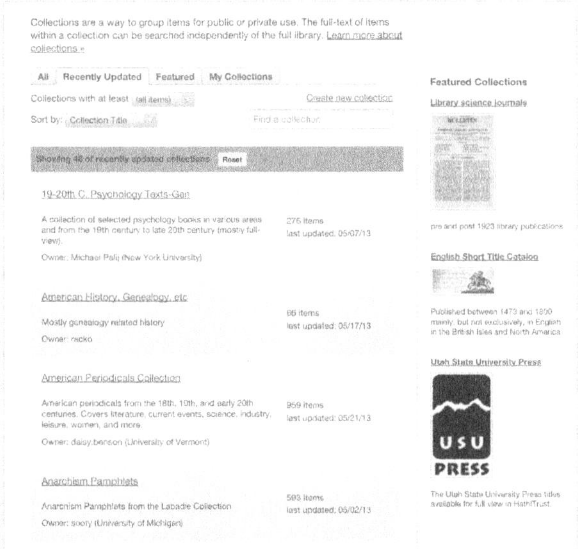

One of the most flexible and appealing features of HathiTrust is the ability to view, use, and create personal collections of materials. Similar in scope to the bookshelves found in the Google Books project, these are lists of digital resources that can be used within the site. Some examples of collections found currently on the site are:

- Titles about Japan in the nineteenth century
- Cookbooks
- Resources on silent films
- Adventure novels

Figure 3.8

From a patron's viewpoint, as noted in Figure 3.8, access to these collections offers a great way to speed up searching, and it's an entry point to highly used materials. Imagine your local library's genealogical collection combined with any of the available family research collections available on HathiTrust, and you can begin to see the possibilities.

Materials

The heart of the HathiTrust project is its digital collection. The collection is large and continues to grow as existing members contribute new digital materials and new members join with their own collections. As of this writing, the current HathiTrust statistics provided by the project include:[15]

Table 3.3 HathiTrust Digital Collection Statistics

Category	Count
Total Volumes (as of 2013)	10 Million Plus
Serials	270,000 Plus
Public Domain volumes	3 Million Plus

Materials Aspects

But raw numbers do not adequately describe the many types of digital materials that can be found in the HathiTrust project.

For example, consider serials. While you are likely aware of the general consumer magazines and academic journals currently in your library, how about having access to dozens of historical serials such as the following that can be found on the project:

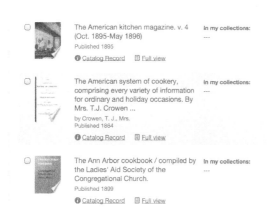

The American kitchen magazine. v. 4 (Oct. 1895-May 1896)
Published 1895
In my collections: ---
ⓘ Catalog Record · Full view

The American system of cookery, comprising every variety of information for ordinary and holiday occasions. By Mrs. T.J. Crowen ...
by Crowen, T. J., Mrs.
Published 1864
In my collections: ---
ⓘ Catalog Record · Full view

The Ann Arbor cookbook / compiled by the Ladies' Aid Society of the Congregational Church.
Published 1899
In my collections: ---
ⓘ Catalog Record · Full view

Figure 3.9

- *Brill*
- *Magazine of American Genealogy*
- *Texaco Star*
- *The Century*

As seen in the above list and Figure 3.9, these are just the tip of the proverbial iceberg. A wide range of other serials are also available, ranging from foreign language magazines such as *Mesures* and *Bulletin de la Section de Geographie* to governmental serials like *Register of Officers and Cadets* and even the relatively obscure *United States Customs Court Reports.* Other types of titles include encyclopedia sets, maps, atlases, cookbooks, and even city directories.

Becoming familiar with the many types of materials accessible via HathiTrust allows your library to use it to supplement your local collections or enhance your resources for particular types of patron requests. For example, if your library has continued demand for genealogical resources, HathiTrust can be a natural add-on, with massive numbers of titles available for use such as *Genealogy of the Cutts Family in America; Parkersburg, 1907;* and *A Souvenir of the City of Parkersburg.* Access to these types of materials can help you respond to patron queries at a lower staff cost, which reduces delay and saves time.

Searching HathiTrust

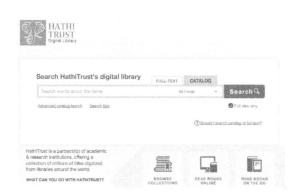

Figure 3.10

Now let's shift the focus to searching for materials in the project. In this section, you'll learn about the four main search methods on the site, as well as specific examples and explanations of each. At the same time, you will find out how these different search techniques and methodologies can influence your library's use of the project. Finally, you'll discover a radical new searching mechanism for HathiTrust, which while still in development, promises an exciting new way to search for digital materials in the near future.

As you read about each tool, technique, or example in this section, follow along with your own computer if you have one available. Comparing your results to the examples shown in the book will help reinforce what you learn and will help you think of additional questions. Also, check out the practice questions at the end of the chapter. Use them to review what you've learned.

Multiple Search Methods: An Overview

Unlike other digital online book sites, HathiTrust offers a broad spectrum of search tools. In addition to the well-known basic and advanced catalog searches, you have access to the full text search, collection browsing, and search-specific techniques that involve wildcard operators, Boolean operations, and more. Let's look at each of these via the following four categories:

- Searching the main catalog
- Searching the full-text of digital items
- Searching with Boolean operators and special modifiers
- Searching, browsing, and using the collections
- Searching within individual source materials

Searching the Main Catalog

Navigating to the HathiTrust home page at www.hathitrust.org, you will find the project offers two initial searching options: Catalog searching with indexed keywords and traditional query terms such as author, title, and so on, and a **Full-Text** option, which gives you the ability to search across the entire text of the resources available in the project. What do you do? What works best? How will your patrons react to these choices? Unfortunately, there's really never an absolute answer, either for yourself or your patrons. For the most part, in my experience, the choice of searching options depends on the type of information that you're looking for.

Consider this. Traditional **Catalog** searching will retrieve information about the items in the catalog, whereas the **Full-Text** option retrieves information from within the individual items in the catalog. For broad subject searching or for specific authors and titles, regular catalog searching can be both fast and efficient. For broader themed searches, specific keywords that may or may not be indexed (or even time periods, obscure names, and other specific bits of trivia), the **Full-Text** option can be powerful. For this section, let's consider the regular **Catalog** search options and how it works within HathiTrust.

To get started searching, select the **Catalog** tab from the main search box, as seen in Figure 3.11, type in what you are looking for, and click the **Search** button. This type of quick search utilizes all

Figure 3.11

available fields in the catalog records. If you are looking for a specific author, title, or subject, you will want to use a qualifier from the drop-down options listed. The following table lists all of the options available via this method:

Table 3.4 Selected Fields in HathiTrust Catalog search

Author
ISBN/ISSN
Publisher
Series Title
Subject
Title

Figure 3.12

Now, let's do a quick query across the regular HathiTrust catalog, looking for information on Carnegie libraries. As noted in Figure 3.12, select the **Catalog** tab once again from the main search box and enter the following terms: **Carnegie libraries**. What results do you get? Was this more or less than you expected?

With no limitations and searching every field, my initial search for information on this topic returned more than 400 different resources. However, for most information queries, this can still be a lot of titles to examine and sift through. Let's try narrowing our search just a bit. While there are many ways to do this, try looking for only the term "Carnegie libraries" within items that are labeled **Full view only** in the site.

At the same time, also remember that in the catalog search, you are not actually searching the full text; rather, you are searching only fields such as author, title, and subject. Performing this search, you can see that your results include more than 260 items that have the search term **Carnegie libraries** and are available in full text in the HathiTrust project.

Searching the Full Text of Digital Items

One of the highlights of the HathiTrust project is the ability to search across the full text of materials that are available in the catalog. Instead of relying on just the common headings such as author, title, and subject, the project's search engine scans the digitized *contents* of the items in the catalog, which has the potential to return many more titles than you would receive using the more traditional catalog search. This is an extremely powerful method of searching and when combined with the sheer number of volumes available in the project has the potential to help you find what you're searching for.

However, this technique does not come without some inherent drawbacks. Simply put, because there is

Figure 3.13

so much more information being searched, the potential for too many results and false hits becomes an issue. It's possible, especially when searching for common terms or phrases, to get thousands of results that are not really relevant to what you are actually searching for. The **key to solving these issues** is careful construction of search queries. This is when we—as librarians and library staff—conduct a thorough reference interview with our patrons. Knowing what types of information they are looking for can determine the best approach.

Okay, now it's your turn to give it a try. Remember our earlier search for information on Carnegie libraries? Try the same topic, only this time perform a full-text search across the catalog. From the home page of HathiTrust, select the **Full-Text** tab and enter this query: **Carnegie libraries**. What results to you get?. As noted in Figure 3.14, in early 2013, my search returned more than half a million items and over 150,000 online viewable titles! While it's

Figure 3.14

always good to get results when searching, in all reality, these results are really not helpful in any way. There are just too many results to sift through. Understand that without proper guidance and knowledge about how to properly search HathiTrust, many of your patrons **will do just this**, spending too much time paging through the vast listings and getting frustrated in the process. Is there anything you can do to bring down the numbers so that your patrons will have an acceptable list of results in cases such as this?

Initially, you can go back and rephrase the search, looking for alternative ways to construct it to reduce the number of results. However, this can be tricky, especially if you do not know much about the topic. One good method is redoing the search to look for only items that are available full text. This might reduce the number of hits somewhat, but there will still be far too many resources to wade through. In the full-text search, you can also use the same Boolean operations and special operators that were used in previous examples. In fact, phrase search by this method is powerful. To see an example of this at work, try doing a full text search again for Carnegie libraries, only this time use quotation marks to indicate a phrase. You will note an immediate decrease in hits and perhaps a results list that is a bit more accurate.

The next option to try is searching the topic again, only this time utilizing the advanced full text search options available within the project. Similar to the traditional catalog searching that you performed earlier, this type of search enables you to search the full text of titles in HathiTrust as well as the regular fields such as author, title, and subject. This method can reduce the returned results to a more realistic number.

Let's try this type of search now using our previous query topic of Carnegie libraries. This time, use the **Advanced full-text search** option. In the search box, type **Carnegie libraries** and

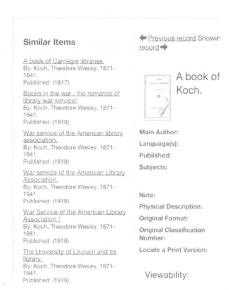

Similar Items

A book of Carnegie libraries.
By: Koch, Theodore Wesley, 1871-1941.
Published: (1917)

Books in the war : the romance of library war service/
By: Koch, Theodore Wesley, 1871-1941.
Published: (1919)

War service of the American library association.
By: Koch, Theodore Wesley, 1871-1941.
Published: (1918)

War service of the American Library Association.
By: Koch, Theodore Wesley, 1871-1941.
Published: (1918)

War Service of the American Library Association /
By: Koch, Theodore Wesley, 1871-1941.
Published: (1918)

The University of Louvain and its library.
By: Koch, Theodore Wesley, 1871-1941.
Published: (1919)

← Previous record Showin record →

A book of Koch.

Main Author:
Language(s):
Published:
Subjects:

Note:
Physical Description:
Original Format:
Original Classification Number:
Locate a Print Version:

Viewability:

Figure 3.15

Refine Results

Subject

Library science (207)

Libraries (202)

Library science Periodicals. (186)

United States (92)

Bibliography (91)

more...

Author

Carnegie Library of Pittsburgh (107)

Carnegie Library of Pittsburgh. (91)

American Library Association. (49)

Library Association. (33)

H.W. Wilson Company. (32)

more...

Language

English (1,803)

Unknown (22)

French (13)

Undetermined (7)

Portuguese (5)

more...

Figure 3.16

choose the limiting options of **this exact phrase**. Next, limit the years of search to between 1890 and 1917. Perform the search. What sort of results to you see? Are the returned titles more on topic? Performing this search in early 2013, I received approximately 2,261 results for all items, with over 1,800 of them online and viewable. That's still a lot, but the list is vastly more manageable than what we received on our initial search. Remember this alternative method of searching when you work with patrons. The only caution is to ensure that your patron is comfortable with the many available opportunities. If possible, spend a few moments with them, ensuring they understand the various selection options.

There is yet another possibility you should consider and one that might work as well for your patrons. By examining the **Catalog Record** option for any individual title on the project, you can retrieve other resources via the **Similar Items** menu choice. Let's give this a try. Redo the initial search as you did before, using the **Advanced full-text** search. Examine your results. Next, briefly look at a title that is close to our example topic of Carnegie libraries. Choose the Catalog Record option and examine the list of **Similar Items**. What do you find? You might see titles such as *The Carnegie Branch Libraries in Brooklyn* and *Cornerstone Laying of Steensland Library*. Examine Figure 3.15 for examples.

As you do this, don't overlook the many sidebar options available for you to use (see Figures 3.16 and 3.17).

The sidebar options—choosing a particular subject, format, or date of publication—can also reduce incredible numbers of results to something more manageable. When examining these, note that they also give the number of resources available for each option. While your trial search for Carnegie libraries was intentionally generic, if you were actually looking for a specific patron's topic, it would be easy to use language, author, format, and perhaps even year to limit the results.

While we've really only examined a few matters in this section, searching the project is something that you and your staff need to be proficient in. By knowing these techniques, you can help your patrons search the project both quickly and easily, thereby relieving the potential for frustration that can happen when searching a project as large as Hathi-Trust. As an additional aid, you might also consider signage in the library or even mini-training sessions for your patrons, time permitting.

Searching with Boolean Operators and Special Modifiers

Although not as popular as simple searching, wildcard and Boolean phrase searching remain powerful options for both librarians and patrons when used properly. Wildcard searching enables you to search for both full and partial words by allowing common symbols to stand in for letters or numbers. According to HathiTrust's help documentation,[16] the asterisk (*) can be substituted for several letters, while the question mark (?) substitutes for a single letter. Consider, for example, **TEA***. In this instance, returned results (depending on other fields you may have searched) could include tea, teabag, tea-bags, teachers, and teasing. This sort of wildcard searching can come in handy, especially if you are unsure of the exact subject or even the spelling of the subject in question.

Boolean phrase searching is also available for use within the project. Let's take an example phrase: **Teachers AND Students**. Notice in this instance that you are search-ing for items that contain information on *both* teachers and students. Here's the same search reproduced graphically, as noted in Figure 3.18.

Place of Publication
United States (1,492)
United Kingdom (185)
England (179)
No place, unknown, or undetermined (84)
Canada (23)
more...

Date of Publication
1900-1909 (721)
1890-1899 (609)
1910-1919 (519)
1907 (166)
1897 (116)
more...

Original Format
Serial (1,133)
Journal (994)
Book (697)
Biography (76)
Conference (26)
more...

Original Location
University of Michigan (557)
University of California (409)
New York Public Library (279)
Princeton University (198)
University of Wisconsin (70)
more...

Figure 3.17

The arrow points to the group of returned results that contain the requested term. Now redo your search, only this time, add the wildcard operator "*". Your example search should look like this: **Teachers AND Student***. In this instance, you've used Boolean logic as well as an additional wildcard operator to tell the search engine to look for instances of the term **teacher** as well as variations of **student**, which would work to pick up both **student** and **students** as potential matches.

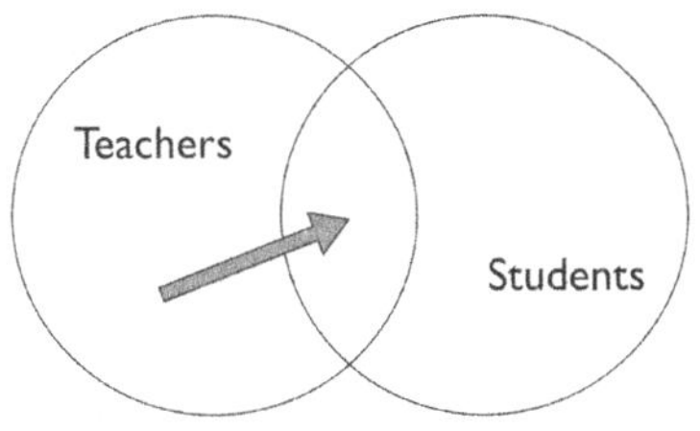

Figure 3.18

As you can see, even with the sample search being fairly clear and understandable, Boolean logic and wildcard oper-ators, while powerful, are not easy to understand and use, especially in these days of simple one-box searching that most of us are used to. This is especially important to

Figure 3.19

remember when helping your patrons. If possible, try to spend extra time with them, ensuring that they understand the various searching mechanisms and are receiving results pertinent to their information needs. For more background on wildcard operators as well as accepted Boolean configurations in the project, follow this link: http://www.hathitrust.org/help_digital_library.

Within HathiTrust, you're not limited to the basic item metadata fields such as author, title, and subject. HathiTrust offers advanced options for catalog searching as well. If your first search does not come back with relevant results or if your search query is more specific, choose the **advanced catalog search**. As you can see in Figure 3.19, it's possible to include multiple search quantifiers as well as years of publication, language, and even format. Also note that you can stack multiple search terms for detailed and very specific materials searches. Note in Figure 3.20 some of the language types that are available.

Figure 3.20

Examine Figure 3.21 to see the option to limit your search to specific types of materials. Although it is a common tool in library catalogs, this type of search is not as common among online eBook sites. If you are looking for an electronic resource or something that is not in traditional book format, consider using this option. Examples of this would include newspapers, photographs, and computer files, just to name a few. Many patrons often overlook this option, but if used properly, it can return an avalanche of needed information.

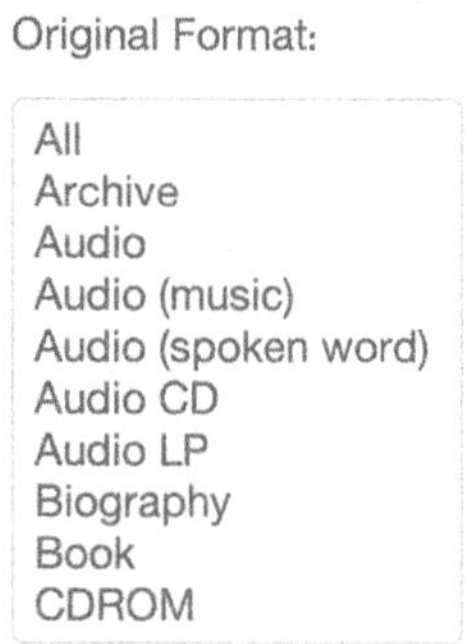

Original Format:

All
Archive
Audio
Audio (music)
Audio (spoken word)
Audio CD
Audio LP
Biography
Book
CDROM

Figure 3.21

Searching, Browsing, and Using the Collections

One of the additional search methods offered by HathiTrust usually isn't considered searching at all. This involves the **Collections** option available on the site. Similar in scope and approach to the previously discussed Google Books project bookshelves option, this feature enables you to search for a collection of materials on a topic as well as search the items within the collection itself. Getting started is easy. Let's first navigate to the **Collections** start page.[17] You can use the specific address of http://babel.hathitrust.org/cgi/mb?colltype=all or just go to the HathiTrust homepage and choose the **Browse Collections** link. Once done, you will see a list of the collections currently available in the HathiTrust project (see Figure 3.22).

From this point, you can search, browse, and use the various collections as needed. Notice along the top the various tabs that include **All**, **Recently Updated**, **Featured**, and **My Collections**. Each on of these can serve as the basis for your further use. For now, though, let's try an example search across all of the collections.

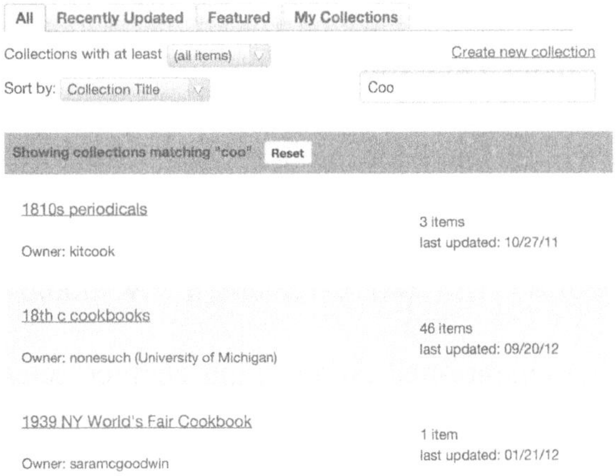

Let's say you are helping a patron look for titles on HathiTrust about historical cookbooks or cooking. To begin, type the following: **Cookbooks**. Notice that as you begin typing, the list of returned collections begins to change—results appear as you type. An example of this is seen in Figure 3.24.

Figure 3.22

Figure 3.23

Once you've typed in your query on cookbooks, you will find multiple returned collections within the list. From this point, you can choose to examine any or all of the lists that appear interesting. For this search example, I've chosen **19th Century Cookbooks**. When you click on the link, you'll see a list similar to the one in Figure 3.25.

From here, you could go into any title in the list or simply scan the complete range, searching for titles that are close to the subject you are looking for. However, do not overlook the option at the top of the page to **Search in this collection**. If you are looking at a vast number of titles in a particular collection or if you want to quickly find your information, this

Figure 3.24

Figure 3.25

secondary search option is a great method to use. Once you've selected and searched within the collection, you'll find your results in the window below, which gives you the opportunity to examine them on an individual basis. Note here that in searching these collections, you can use the same methods as when performing a **Full-Text** search across the entire project.

Let's give this a try with the collection we found previously about nineteenth-century cookbooks. Using the search box, see what you can find out about creating salads. What sort of results did you get? A few titles returned in early 2013 that I found while searching included *Salad and Salad Making*, *What To Eat*, and *How to Serve It*. Remember that as you begin to look through your own returned results, there might not be an indication that the keyword you searched for was present within the title. However, once you select an individual work, it is possible to find more information.

Searching within Individual Source Materials

From querying collections, let's now shift our focus to methods of searching individual items. In this instance, let's

Figure 3.26

assume that you have narrowed the search down to a few specific resources, and you want to search them for more information on your topic. What sorts of searching possibilities exist, and how do you implement them? Many strategies can be considered at this stage, so to get started, let's go back to our original search for information on Carnegie libraries. In this case, I've redone our previous search and have selected the following title as an example: *A Book of Carnegie Libraries* (see Figure 3.26 for details). You can either search for the same or similar title or do your own search and follow along.

As mentioned earlier in this chapter, selecting any title from your list of returned results, there are a couple of different methods to investigate. The first option might be to fully examine the cataloging record for the item in question. Note the example in Figure 3.27.

Looking at the catalog record for an individual item, there really isn't a search function as such, but you do have options displayed on the left for finding similar titles. Or you could click on the subject links within the record itself. Either of these

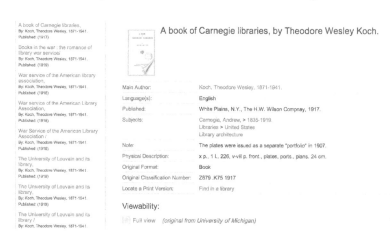

Figure 3.27

routes enable you to further your search, though you will not be able to enter new search terms via these options. If you do not find any helpful or additional information in this manner, move on and view the full text record to explore additional searching options (as noted in Figure 3.28).

At this point, you can also search within the item itself. For example, using

Figure 3.28

the same record as noted previously, let's do a quick search within the title for our familiar phrase of **Carnegie libraries**. What are the results?

As seen in Figure 3.29, our returned results actually reveal quite a bit of information. Notice that our search terms are highlighted in contrasting colors, which are important cues when you are phrase searching, helping you quickly notice and identify potential areas of interest. Also note that separate instances of each word in our search phrase are identified. Upon examination, what does this show you? In this particular case, what you see is similar to our other search results earlier in the chapter, that is, the search engine will query the database for each instance of the word you choose to search with. While correct in doing this, it's not very helpful to you when looking for a particular area of interest or phrase.

In this case, redoing your search to include the phrase within quotes would reveal more accurate results related to what you are looking for, as noted in Figure 3.30.

At this point, you can view the individual pages listed in your results list or go back and redo the search, adding or subtracting terms until you find a closer match. Remember that you can also perform Boolean search strategies within the content, much as you did with the earlier site searching when Boolean and wildcard searches were explained.

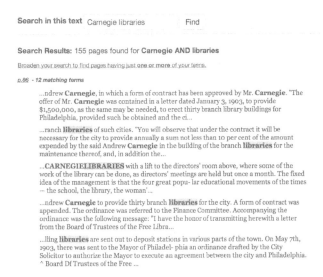

Figure 3.29

The Best Search Method?

Now that you have had a chance to get acquainted with the many ways you can search the digital resources available through the HathiTrust project, is it safe to say that one method is best? Does one method consistently return the most accurate results time after time? Is there one technique that you should emphasize in your library? Ultimately, there's no single best way to search. It all depends on what you are looking for. In my estimation, your best options are to completely familiarize yourself with **all** of the selections, rather than focusing on the easiest or simplest. Be sure to stress this approach with your patrons as well.

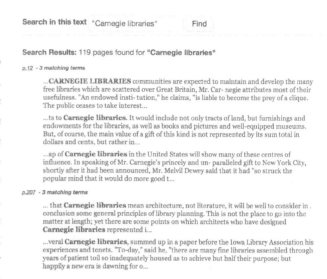

Figure 3.30

To illustrate this a bit further, let's say you are working at the reference desk one day and a patron shows up looking for information on post–World War II economics in the United Sates, in particular auto company operations in postwar Detroit. Directing your patron to the HathiTrust project to get started, you might think it most beneficial to go immediately to the full-text search, thinking this would give the quickest and longest list of results. However, knowing now how the project is designed and how the search engine works, we know that more than likely, this is not the most efficient search method to employ, mostly because of the likelihood of too many false hits and resources to sort through.

A far more effective method would be to steer the patron toward an initial catalog search using key subjects, words, or possibly even titles that came to mind. By doing so, you would weed out resources that by virtue of the keywords might be listed but are not really related to the topic. Once this is done and a sublist of possible titles is in hand, you could then search specific resources or use them as a starting point for closer investigation.

On the other hand, let's say a patron is looking for titles on the Works Progress Administration (WPA) that were published in the 1930s. A full-text search might work better. A single topic search for a broad subject area such as this is often more successful than a detailed singular search such as with our first example. Ultimately, it all comes down to the classic reference interview and being able to fully define (as much as possible) what your patron is looking for. Even in this digital age, the interaction between you and the patron remains an almost certain key to success.

Viewing and Using Your Results

Being able to successfully search the digital collections held by HathiTrust is only the first step in taking full advantage of the project. The next step is being able to take your results and use them to either answer a question or revise the search for better outcomes. In this section, you will learn to do just that. You will examine how search results are returned and explore the individual components that make up those results. Along the way, you'll rediscover some practical applications you can use in your everyday library work and learn how this affects your patrons' information searching.

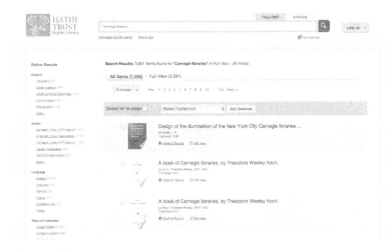

Figure 3.31

Viewing Results

No matter what your topic is or which method you've chosen for your search, in HathiTrust, your results are always returned in an ordered list. And you always have the opportunity to review and revise your initial search (as is mentioned previously in the chapter.) Let's look again at this process in the following screenshot (Figure 3.31).

On the left is the sidebar, within which are clickable links that allow you to revise your search or search for related topics. In the middle of the window are your results, ordered and with more information about each digital title. The top of the window contains a quick-search box that you can use to revise your query without returning to the main search page and starting over.

Viewing Individual Records

Let's assume you have found a particular record that you feel will best answer your information request. What's the best method of viewing and using this record? Can you view multiple pages? Can you download the entire book? How about printing? These are questions that you may already be asking about the project—and you know

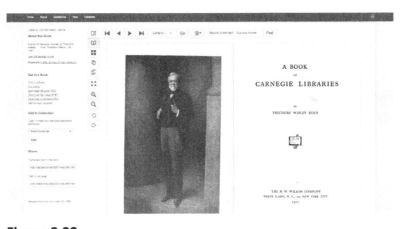

Figure 3.32

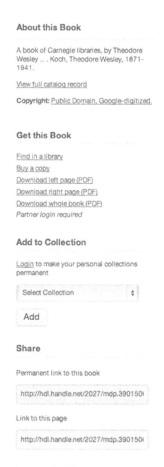

Figure 3.33

that your patrons will be asking these as well. To answer in the affirmative, there are many methods of access that makes using these found records easy for your patrons. Let's take a look at (Figure 3.32) and explore what options are available.

As you can see with this particular title, viewing individual titles results in a layout that is similar to the initial results page, with the main reading area in the center and additional options to the left and top. However, there are new controls for viewing and reading your selected digital item.

Looking at the left side of the page when viewing our title (as shown in Figure 3.33), you will see a succession of information that includes the catalog record, copyright status, and other locations in which to find copies of the work, both digitally and in paper format. Note that you can also add the title to a collection or share it with others you might be working with. This last feature—the ability to quickly and easily share items from the project—offers a great way for you to help patrons in remote situations, such as over the phone, email, instant messaging, or even short message service (SMS).

Notice as well the permanent link offered by HathiTrust. Because the links are unchanging, it is easy to include this resource in your library's online catalog, website, or wherever it is needed. The result? A quick and easy method to enhance your local collection and offer additional resources to your patrons. This also works around any sort of access issues your library may be experiencing, especially for patron' after-hours access to resources when your physical locations are closed.

Viewing Items on the Screen

How about viewing the item or items in question on screen? What special controls and options exist for doing this? Actually, there are quite a few, and some of the recent updates by HathiTrust make this experience even easier than before. Let's take a look at Figure 3.34 and explore what is offered.

As shown, there are five primary views to any title. This includes **Scroll**, **Flip**, **Thumbnail**, **Page by Page**, and **Plain Text**.

Figure 3.34

Under **Scroll** view, you are presented with a single page at a time. With this method—and depending on what type of hardware, operating system, and web browser you are using—you can save individual images, view them in other web browser windows, or even copy them to a standard word processing document. Also in this view, it's like reading a standard paper book, with a single page presented at a time.

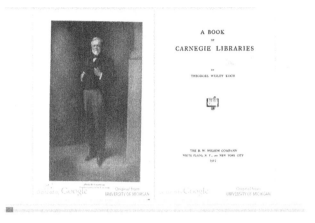

Figure 3.35

As seen in Figure 3.35, the **Flip** option, similar to what is offered by other eBook projects such as the Internet Archive, gives titles viewed on HathiTrust a more book-like reading experience, including animated page turns as you view the item. This same viewing option can be used on many hardware platforms, including laptop, desktop, and tablets such as the iPad. When combined with standard controls, this view works well and might be an experience your patrons find the easiest to use.

Figure 3.36

If you have decided to explore a particular item further but still need to investigate whether the content is relevant, the **Thumbnail** option is a great way to view all of the content at once. Let's take a look at this through Figure 3.36.

As seen in the screenshot, it's possible to scale the title source pages. Although not readable or legible, one of the biggest advantages to thumbnail viewing of source pages includes the option to quickly scan for particular images. Rather than having to go through the source page by page, the thumbnail option can drastically enhance efficiency and enable you to quickly locate needed information.

Let's consider a practical use for the thumbnail view. Let's say, for example, a patron comes to your reference desk one day and is looking for original illustrations related to trunks and hats from the now-classic Sears Roebuck series of catalogs. This is a very specific topic. Using the HathiTrust project, this type of information can quickly be found. First, retrieve the title from the project. Second, once the title is on screen, switch to the thumbnail view. At this point, it becomes easy to scan the pages until the necessary illustrations are found.

It's important to note that some custom preferences are available with this option, including the number of pages that will show up on the screen at one time. There can be drawbacks in using this, especially if bandwidth is a concern, because it does take time to download even the smaller images for each page. This is worth mentioning if your patron is not in the library or is experiencing slow Internet access.

The **Page by Page** option is similar in some respects to the **Scroll** option (outlined earlier in this chapter); however, the biggest difference lies in how different pages are selected and viewed. Unlike the smoothing page-by-page approach to the **Scroll** option, this display requires you to use the page controls as presented.

The **Plain Text** option does not contain book formatting, layout, or any sort of special typographical treatments/fonts. It is simply the digitized plain text of the document. You can copy the text or use the on-screen controls to read through the item. Unlike the other presentation styles that are in an image format, this style lends itself well to patrons who might actively be using the project for research and is a great method of using portions of text without having to retype citations or passages from the individual title.

Other Controls

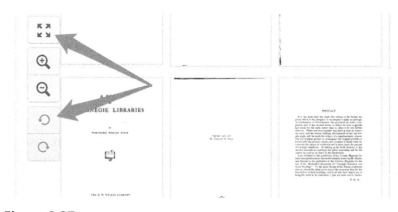

Figure 3.37

Finally, consider the additional controls built into the interface that enable you to move around inside the digital materials or change your viewpoint once within a work. While these features are somewhat ubiquitous to online digital book sites, HathiTrust's implementation is particularly easy to use. Note Figure 3.37 and Figure 3.38 for more details.

The options include the ability to move page-by-page through the source, jump to specific pages within the source, zoom in and out, and alter the orientation of the source materials. Especially in the case of maps, illustrations, or oddly shaped titles, having the ability to change orientation adds a nice touch and brings added flexibility to the interface. If your patron has

Figure 3.38

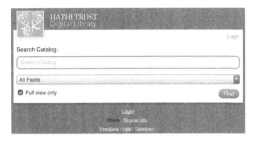

Figure 3.39

never viewed resources in this manner, spend some time with him or her, pointing out the controls and options contained within them. Intuitive as they may be to you, your patrons may have never used them before.

Going Mobile

Do you have a smart phone? How about an iPad or another tablet? To access information these days, you don't need to be locked down to a desktop or laptop. Mobile information access is growing and is important in today's fast-paced world. In light of these developments, there's a fairly new implementation of the Hathi-Trust project that provides users with mobile access to the site. In particular, consider this new feature in relation to searching and viewing results.

Searching

Without the luxury of the full HathiTrust cata-log interface, the mobile version is naturally some-what lacking in options, though certainly not in searching power. After typing in your search query, you can select fields for the search, including author, title, subject, ISBN, and ISSN, as shown in Figure 3.40. From here, it's also possible to search for just the catalog record of the items in question or for the full-view versions that are available.

Figure 3.40

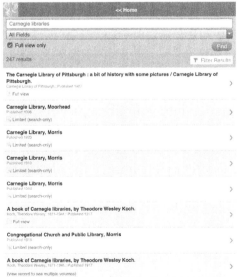

Figure 3.41

Viewing Results

The results of your search are viewed on an easy-to-use interface that gives basic information about each title, including record information and a link to the full text if it is available (see Figure 3.41). Note that you can also filter your results—by subject, author, language, and other features.

If you choose to view individual results from your search, you'll find a new interface that is different than the one in the main site but also effective and easy to use (see Figure 3.42). Note that you can view the catalog record as seen here or jump directly to the full text item on the screen as shown in Figure 3.43.

Viewing documents and other titles while on the go makes this approach highly effective and a great tool for your patrons who might not be able to make it into your library to use the full site. (As a side note, I've tested this interface on a variety of devices, including my Android phone, my iPad, and even my Nook tablet, and I've found it easy to use and read on all of them.)

A book of Carnegie libraries, by Theodore Wesley Koch.

Author: Koch, Theodore Wesley, 1871-1941.

Published: White Plains, N.Y., The H.W. Wilson Compnay, 1917.

Language: English

Subjects:

Carnegie, Andrew. > 1835-1919.

Libraries > United States

Library architecture

Note: The plates were issued as a separate "portfolio" in 1907.

Physical Description: x p., 1 l., 226, v-viii p. front., plates, ports., plans. 24 cm.

Original Format: **Book**

Original Classification Number: Z679 .K75 1917

Locate a Print Version: Find in a library

Figure 3.42

Just for Libraries: Going beyond the Basics

You've now had a chance to examine HathiTrust and its many features and functions, from searching and viewing results to using them. Now take a look at some of the methods for integrating the resources from the project into your library ILS and website. Let's start first with the HathiTrust application programming interface (API) and move on to various forms of webpage widgets that you can put on your ILS or your library's website.

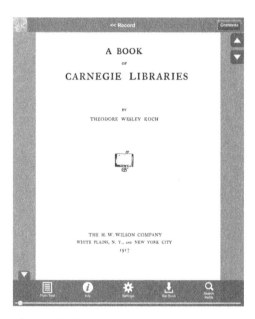

Figure 3.43

Application Programming Interface (API)

Using the web browser is the most obvious way to search and use the resources available on the project, but there are other methods of accessing HathiTrust resources. Two of the methods mentioned on the project site are the **Bib API** and the **Data API**.[18] With these two mechanisms, it's possible to build website and other applications that automatically query HathiTrust and return resources such as records, titles, and even individual pages. You can integrate these data into your library ILS or just paste the returned information into your library's website.

While the preceding methods enable your library to access individual bits of information about titles available in HathiTrust, the project also offers your library the ability to download and use entire data records that are publicly available. Not just bits or pieces of records, these are sets of entire texts that can be downloaded and used in your local library. There are some related restrictions, so it's best to become well acquainted with the regulations on use of the data. You can examine detailed information at this link: http://www .hathitrust.org/datasets.

While it's likely that the offered HathiTrust APIs and downloadable data sets will provide resources or information access methods that you will need in your daily interactions with patrons and other library staff, these technical hooks into the HathiTrust project can help your library better use the information that is available. This includes directly offered data links via your ILS catalog, library website, and even social media sites such as Facebook, Twitter, and others.

Widgets

We already commonly use small pieces of HTML code known as widgets to provide links to our libraries' social media sites such as Facebook and Twitter, and this same opportunity is available for HathiTrust resources as well. With these small pieces of code, you can offer the HathiTrust project's resources to your patrons in a wide variety of ways, including catalog searching and full text searching.

As seen in Figure 3.44, using these options is as easy as copying the provided code and pasting it into your library's ILS public access pages or website. No coding experience is needed, and you can implement these without too much effort. Try this direct link for additional details: http://www.hathitrust.org/widgets.

What the Future Holds!

HathiTrust continues to grow in both membership and resources, and the future is bright, with tremendous new options for change and expansion. Is there

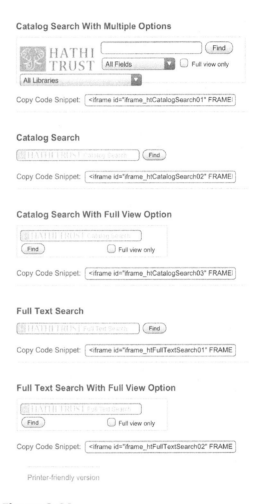

Figure 3.44

any way of getting a glimpse of some of the changes in store for the project? Of course, I have no crystal ball, but by looking at the site, news articles and announcements, and current activities and committee information, I've identified a few possibilities that are being explored. I've loosely grouped these into types of changes under the following headings: membership and materials, project technology, and orphan works. Let's examine these speculations.

Membership and Materials

As the HathiTrust continues to grow, membership has expanded in many directions. Libraries, particularly academic libraries, see the project as an opportunity to allow continued access to materials without the costs associated with storage and retrieval of paper-based resources. This factor alone will drive HathiTrust forward, particularly as more library budgets suffer cutbacks and other restrictions. In addition, the growth of the project's holdings and its wide range of resources will allow member libraries access to more materials than could be obtained on site for their faculty, staff, and patrons. Digital access to a wide variety of materials is a driving force in the library world and one that once experienced will not soon go away.

Project Technology

One of the highlights of HathiTrust since the beginning has been the expansion of the project from a technological standpoint. As of early 2013, this continues to be the case. As noted on the project website, February, March, and April 2013 alone saw the redesign of the main online website and catalog, full text searching updates, **PageTurner** updates (one of the interfaces used when viewing individual titles on the project), and changes to how full text search operates within the project. For more complete details on the various technology updates that have been performed or are still in process, check out the following link: http://www.hathitrust.org/news_publications.

Orphan Works

Orphan works issues were mentioned earlier in the chapter, and HathiTrust has so far taken the lead on these issues and continues to play a role in their discovery and use. While as of this writing progress has stalled and previously identified orphan works have been removed from public view, this this isn't the end to this issue. In the future, I feel that it is likely that part of or all of these titles will be available again, once all concerned parties come to a suitable agreement. It's a delicate situation that libraries and archives face in this digital age, and it is one that will be settled in one way or another. Once this is accomplished, the flood of materials available for your patrons will be impressive. For now, however, it's a waiting game, as noted by HathiTrust in response to the latest ruling in the ongoing controversy (http://www .hathitrust.org/authors_guild_lawsuit_ruling). Because the project previously took the lead on this issue, I can foresee the project once again tackling this issue as soon as possible.

Important Points to Remember about HathiTrust

What a remarkable thing HathiTrust can be for our libraries! Easy to access and with millions of resources, this site can be used both as a collection enhancement tool and an online backup to your collection. HathiTrust can be a resource for reference departments, and it can offer specific information that isn't available via the more popular Internet search engines.

To help you remember specifics about the project, review the following highlights and specific points about the project. You can use these for self-review or as you present the site to your staff or patrons. Mix these talking points in with your own points.

Origins and Background Information

- Partnership of libraries
- Maintain access and continued growth for the long-term
- Signed partnerships with OCLC and Serials Solutions to enhance basic digital access services

Site Structure and Materials

- Many types of materials available for use
- Includes series and multivolume sets
- Millions of digital titles available for use

Searching HathiTrust

- Four methods of searching: catalog, full text, collections, individual items
- Full text availability for many titles
- Collections searching both at subject and individual level

Viewing Results

- Results one page at a time
- Variety of formats that include text, image, and PDF
- Collections and accounts enable long-term storage of found titles

Beyond the Basics and Library Tools

- WorldCat Search partnership with OCLC
- API access to database as well as dataset downloads
- Widgets available for your library's website
- Mobile access across a range of devices

The Future

- Continued membership growth
- Increased access to millions of materials via library additions
- Improved access to orphan works a possibility

Questions for You to Try

What follows are some sample questions for you and other library staff to answer by searching HathiTrust. Each set revolves around a specific part of the site and reflects what you've hopefully learned so far. Remember, there is no absolute wrong or right in how you answer these questions. The important thing is to answer them as best you can. Use these for self-review or in a staff training session. Remember, practical everyday use of the site will help you feel comfortable using it yourself and implementing it as you answer your patrons' questions!

HathiTrust Site and Structure

1. Given the many methods of searching, which method would you start with if you were asked to put together a library pathfinder of sources for the history of the Federal Reserve? What specific searching methods could you use to save time when creating this bibliography?

2. Name three types of materials (in addition to regular book volumes) that can be found on the site. Write down a few specific titles. What sorts of materials are **not** common to HathiTrust?

Searching HathiTrust

1. You're working at the reference desk, and a patron comes to you looking for historical information on the World War II writer Ernie Pyle, specifically a quote from one of his books about England during the war. The quote is: "Heroes are all the people . . . " Given this information, how would you instruct the patron to begin her search? Can you find what title this quote is from?

2. Do a regular catalog search on HathiTrust, focusing on titles about the American Civil War. How many results do you find that are available for full text use on the site? How many results are only catalog records? Now limit your search to the immediate postwar years of 1870–1890. How does this affect your results?

3. Browsing the public collections can be illuminating, both from a materials standpoint and for just learning more about the project. Using two public collections found on the site, find five resources related to topics that appeal to you. Once you've found them, write down titles and authors.

Collection #1 _____

Title One: _____

Author: _____

Title Two: _____

Author: _____

Title Three: _____

Author: _____

Title Four: _____

Author: _____

Title Five: _____

Author: _____

Collection #2 _____

Title One: _____

Author: _____

Title Two: _____

Author: _____

Title Three: _____

Author: _____

Title Four: _____

Author: _____

Title Five: _____

Author: _____

Viewing Results

1. Imagine you're working at the reference desk and a patron comes up looking for information on Charles Lindbergh. In particular, he's looking for some digital results that he can view on his Nook. How would you find materials for the patron? Name some titles that might fit his need and explain how you would go about making these titles viewable on his reading device.

2. HathiTrust makes source materials available in three primary formats. Name these formats and give examples of when each would be appropriate.

3. Imagine you're working at the reference desk one afternoon and an older couple comes to you looking for a fast method for finding and using genealogy resources. Using the collections function in HathiTrust, what can you find on genealogy, and what options in the collection can help them quickly sort the titles?

Notes

1. HathiTrust, http://www.hathitrust.org/mission_goals.

2. HathiTrust, http://www.hathitrust.org/news_publications.

3. University of Michigan Library, http://www.lib.umich.edu/imls-national-leadership-grant-crms.

4. University of Michigan Library, http://www.lib.umich.edu/orphan-works.

5. Chronicle of Higher Education, "Wired Campus," http://chronicle.com/blogs/wiredcampus/quickwire-major-libraries-join-controversial-project-to-publish-orphan-books-online/32974?sid=wc.

6. HathiTrust, http://www.hathitrust.org/authors_guild_lawsuit_ruling.

7. ReadWrite, http://readwrite.com/2012/10/12/google-closes-two-chapters-in-ongoing-books-fight.

8. HathiTrust, http://www.hathitrust.org/partnership.

9. OCLC, http://www.oclc.org/us/en/news/releases/2011/20114.htm.

10. EBSCO, http://www2.ebsco.com/EN-US/NEWSCENTER/Pages/ViewArticle.aspx?QSID=492.

11. No Shelf Required, http://www.libraries.wright.edu/noshelfrequired/2011/09/08/hathitrust-full-text-soon-searchable-in-ebsco-discovery-service-and-oclcs-worldcat/.

12. HathiTrust, http://www.hathitrust.org/help_digital_library#Download.

13. Creative Commons, http://creativecommons.org/.

14. http://www.hathitrust.org/blogs/perspectives-from-hathitrust/hathitrust-and-discovery.

15. HathiTrust, http://www.hathitrust.org/statistics_info.

16. HathiTrust, http://www.hathitrust.org/help_digital_library.

17. HathiTrust, http://babel.hathitrust.org/cgi/mb?a=listcs;colltype=pub.

18. HathiTrust, http://www.hathitrust.org/data.

Resources

Being able to use and understand the HathiTrust project takes time. From the various ongoing digital collection projects to future goals and the role of the project in the library community, there's a lot to learn. From a librarian's standpoint (administrator, librarian, or staff), integrating and using HathiTrust in your everyday library work can be challenging and complex. However, there are many available resources, web links, and additional information about the project. Use these to learn more about the HathiTrust project, share with other library staff, and perhaps even let your patrons know about them as well.

Origins

HathiTrust, "Our Partnership," http://www.hathitrust.org/partnership.

HathiTrust, "Statistics and Visualizations," http://www.hathitrust.org/statistics _visualizations.

Controversies

Cohen, Dan, The Atlantic, "The Fight Over the Future of Digital Books," The Atlantic, September 23, 2011, http://www.theatlantic.com/technology/archive/2011/09/the -fight-over-the-future-of-digital-books/245577/.

Kolowich, Steve, "Abuse of Trust?" *Inside Higher Ed*, September 19, 2011, http://www .insidehighered.com/news/2011/09/19/michigan_admits_flaws_in_hathitrust_system_for _identifying_orphan_works.

Role in the Library Community

Booth, Char. "Unlocking HathiTrust: Inside the Librarians' Digital Library," *Library Journal*, June 9, 2011, http://www.libraryjournal.com/lj/newslettersnewsletterbucket academicnewswire/890917-440/unlocking_hathitrust_inside_the_librarians.html.csp.

Wieder, Ben, "HathiTrust Makes Text of Its Digital Library Searchable Through Summon Service," *Chronicle of Higher Education*, March 28, 2011, http://chronicle.com/blogs/ wiredcampus/hathitrust-makes-text-of-its-digital-library-searchable-through-a-new -partnership/30593.

Young, Jeffrey R., "QuickWire: Major Libraries Join Controversial Project to Publish 'Orphan' Books Online," *Chronicle of Higher Education*, August 24, 2011, http://chronicle .com/blogs/wiredcampus/quickwire-major-libraries-join-controversial-project-to-publish -orphan-books-online/32974?sid=wc.

Resources & Materials

About.com, "HathiTrust Digital Library – A Researcher's Guide," http://genealogy .about.com/od/history_research/a/hathitrust.htm.

Helft, Miguel, "An Elephant Backs Up Google's Library," *New York Times*, October 13, 2008, http://bits.blogs.nytimes.com/2008/10/13/an-elephant-backs-up-googles -library/.

Technology

HathiTrust, "Papers and Presentations," http://www.hathitrust.org/papers_and _presentations.

HathiTrust, "Technological Profile," http://www.hathitrust.org/technology.

Chapter 4

The Internet Archive

Figure 4.1

More Than Just Web Pages: Origins of the Internet Archive

While you are probably well aware of the Internet Archive for the massive amounts of historical web pages contained in the now-famous **Wayback Machine** (http://archive.org/web/web.php), you might not be as aware of the tremendous digital book resources available on the site as well. With a huge online presence, the Internet Archive is a virtual treasure trove for librarians looking to use and integrate digital materials into their libraries. With over 4 million digitized items,[1] specialized BookReader software, and many other digital resource initiatives, this is one site you should definitely know about.

In this chapter, you'll examine the Internet Archive to discover what is available. You'll learn methods of searching, evaluating, and using the materials that are on the site as well as tips on integrating this project into your everyday library workflow. Let's start first, however, with a story, one that might be familiar.

An Elusive Family Member

Stacy put the last of the family genealogy books on the book cart and felt a wave of relief wash over her. It had been a long day, and she'd spent most of the afternoon doing original cataloging on a set of family genealogies contributed by the Friends of the Library group. It was a unique resource and would go a long way toward helping to address the many books and other information that had been lost in the library fire last year. That disaster had been terrible, and resulted in the loss of most of the contributed family histories and other local history resources that had been added to the collection over the years. Even though the staff and firefighters had saved a few titles before the building went up in flames, the loss was incredible. Given the library's active genealogy department and close partnership with the local genealogical society, it was a tremendous blow to all involved.

Since then, the staff had been working diligently to restore the genealogy collection to its former state, but because of the age of many of the titles, progress was slow. Recently however, another librarian working with Stacy had mentioned an online resource that she said might contain a large number of the books that had been destroyed. Not really believing this at first, Stacy checked and was surprised to find so many titles that were indeed available online. Since then, she had been devising a plan with the other librarians to directly integrate these resources into their newly formed digital genealogy library. What was the site she had found? To her surprise, it was the Internet Archive.

Origins and Goals

Established in 1996 by Brewster Kahle,[2] well known for his work in the eBook and library arenas, the Internet Archive can be found online at http://www.archive.org and physically located at their main offices in San Francisco, California. The Internet Archive is a nonprofit organization with the goals (according to their website) of creating a "digital library" that everyone can have access to and use for free,[3] and enabling "universal access to all knowledge."[4] Today, this has resulted in a wide spectrum of digital materials being available at the site, ranging from web pages to software, music, movies, and even digital eBooks!

Given such wide-ranging goals and a huge task involved in bringing this together, the Internet Archive has not worked alone. It has cultivated partnerships with a wide range of literary, library, and other types of groups. From membership in the American Library Association to projects with organizations such as the National Aeronautics and Space Administration (NASA) and the Open Content Alliance, the Internet Archive continues to be a model for information access, standing in stark contrast to the old models of inaccessible or discarded information.

How Is It So?

Given your introduction to the Internet Archive so far, you might be asking yourself, "How does this all work?" That's a very good question. How does a single organization implement something of this scale? How did they start with essentially nothing and then just a few short years later provide access to over 4 million digital titles and other electronic resources? While we've seen a variety of methods employed with the other sites profiled so far in this book, from the commercial model of Google Books to the ongoing library membership model of HathiTrust, the Internet Archive has achieved this success via many different extents, including acquisitions and ongoing projects.

As librarians and library staff, acquisitions are a central focus of our organization both as we work to add items to the physical collection as well as when we evaluate and weed the current titles we already own. The Internet Archive is not too different in its approach. The project is continually adding materials to the collection via scanning centers in many different countries[5] and at the same time encourages outside organizations and individuals to donate items to the project. These outside organizations include libraries as well as the Open Content Alliance.

Found online at http://www.opencontentalliance.org, the Open Content Alliance works with major partners such as Lyrasis and the Consortium of Academic and Research Libraries in Illinois (CARLI) to share digital texts, bibliographic information, and even multimedia. The Open Content Alliance, working in conjunction with the Internet Archive, continuously uploads and makes available to end users these digital resources from the servers at the Internet Archive.

While acquisitions involves actively adding items to the Internet Archive, it's the organization's ongoing projects that has also lead to its current measure of success. Two good examples of this include the BookServer project and the Open Library project.

The BookServer project concentrates on improving the computing structure needed for sharing eBooks and other digital resources, regardless of where they are located and on what devices or computer they are needed, removing roadblocks to resource sharing commonly found online today. By doing this, as noted recently by the Internet Archive,[6] this computing framework enables readers to access content found across a number of systems, not just a single catalog or website.

The Open Library project has been a tremendous success as well, adding both cataloging information and a unique searching interface for digital materials of all types (see Figures 4.2 and 4.3).

Figure 4.2

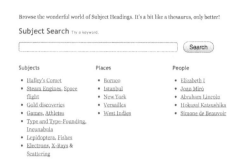

Figure 4.3

More than just a searching mechanism and provider of downloadable digital content, the Open Library project offers a comprehensive way to access, edit, and download digital content of all types. With their project mantra of "one web page for every book published," the Open Library offers a fascinating new way to connect readers and content of all types.

Site Structure, Materials, and Components

The core of any library is the collection, be it analog, locally stored digital data, or online resources. A product of many years of adding, weeding, and keeping existing resources up to date, it's absolutely vital to the success of the library as an organization. In this same way, we can examine the wide-ranging digital collections made available through the Internet Archive and understand the reasons for its continued popularity. A vast array of materials in many formats can be searched and used—books, videos, software, music, and more. The scope of the contained content is amazing as well, with a depth and breadth that's hard to match—it's not just limited to public domain or government documents. Let's look at some specifics!

Site Structure

We'll start first by examining how the Internet Archive's website is constructed and how you should navigate, search, and use the resources that you've found. A successful website design should be transparent, not taking anything away from the end user who may be just browsing or from someone who is looking for something specific. Does the Internet Archive website accomplish this? I would argue that it does. Consider the following screenshots of the site and layout in Figure 4.4.

In the preceding image, you will notice that the design is consistent across the site, regardless of the types of

Figure 4.4

resources that are being examined. For example, look at the top navigation and search area and then the bottom half of the page, which is reserved for the different categories of materials available on the project. For comparison, now click on the **Texts** portion of the site.

When you look at Figure 4.5, you will again notice some of these consistencies.

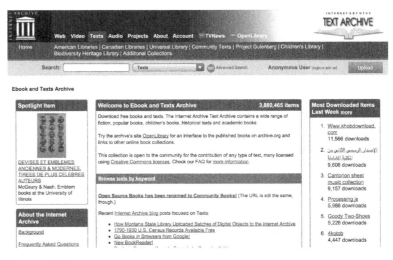

Figure 4.5

The top component, the header bar, stays the same, helping you navigate to other areas of the site without having to go back to the beginning page. As shown in Figure 4.6, notice the availability of the search bar, which enables you to search for all types of materials within the project, regardless of where you are on the site.

Below the header and search bars, you'll find the main content area, which provides more information about each specific section that the user is looking at.

Figure 4.6

To the left and right are the update sections consisting of additional information on downloaded items, staff favorites, and more. If you are looking at individual titles, this main content area will have specific details such as copyright information, date, and other identifiers. In addition, when viewing individual titles, to the left you will find links to different versions of the text for different digital platforms such as Kindle, ePub, and HTML.

The biggest difference you'll find on the site will be when you actively search for something. After your initial search, the results listing will completely change the interface and navigation. For example, let's search for our favorite subject, **Carnegie libraries**. After entering the query in the search box, here's the screenshot of our initial results as seen in Figure 4.7.

Figure 4.7

As you can see, the list of results has replaced the framed main page, with search quantifiers to the right. From here, it's easy to select individual items to explore more deeply or to refine the search with new terms or quantifiers such as those listed on the right (see Figures 4.8 and 4.9). Refining your search can help you to shortcut the search process and find related titles more quickly.

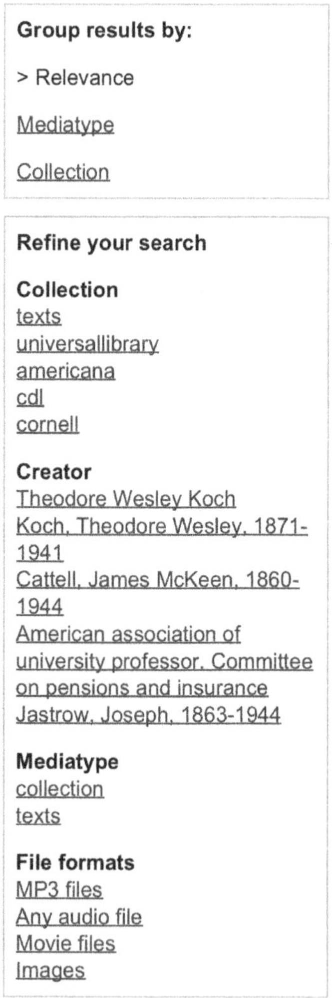

Group results by:

> Relevance

Mediatype

Collection

Refine your search

Collection
texts
universallibrary
americana
cdl
cornell

Creator
Theodore Wesley Koch
Koch, Theodore Wesley, 1871-1941
Cattell, James McKeen, 1860-1944
American association of university professor. Committee on pensions and insurance
Jastrow, Joseph, 1863-1944

Mediatype
collection
texts

File formats
MP3 files
Any audio file
Movie files
Images

Related collections

americana

biodiversity

cdl

blc

umass_amherst_libraries

Related creators

Carnegie Institution of Washington. Dept. of Marine Biology

Carnegie Institution of Washington. Tortugas Laboratory

Carnegie Library of Pittsburgh

Carnegie Museum

Kislak Reference Collection (Library of Congress) DLC

Related mediatypes

texts

collection

Figure 4.8

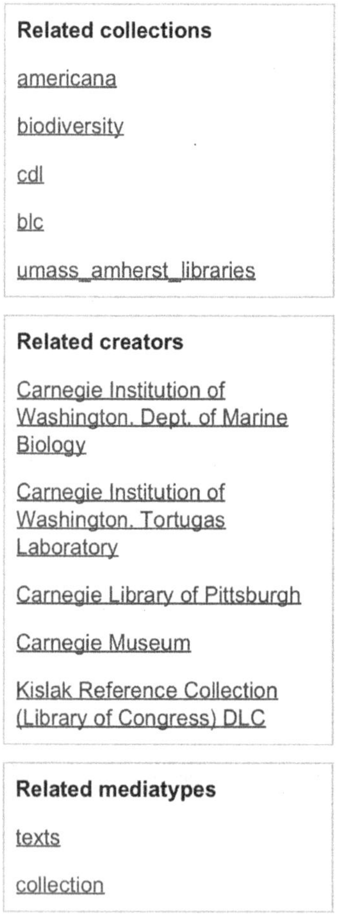

Figure 4.9

Composition and Collections

While we have mainly been searching digital eBook content, remember that the project maintains extensive collections of material in other media formats as well, including many different types of audio, video, and software. You can use these collections along with the eBook content you find, or you can use them as standalone resources. Each of these formats is accessible on the Internet Archive and has its own unique uniform resource locator (URL) (See Table 4.1.)

Knowing this brings additional depth and breadth when you provide answers to your patrons or just give them leads to additional informational resources. Let's take a quick look at some of the other collections you will encounter on the site.

Table 4.1 Internet Archive Content Types and URL's

Material Type	URL
Books	http://www.archive.org/details/texts
Movies/TV	http://www.archive.org/details/movies
Software	http://www.archive.org/details/software
Audio	http://www.archive.org/details/audio
Projects	http://www.archive.org/projects/

Video (Including Movies and Television)

The Internet Archive's video collection is vast. Feel like watching a movie? Spend some time viewing Alfred Hitchcock's *The 39 Steps*[7]. Visit the Prelinger Archive[8] and watch some NASA (as noted in Figure 4.12) or classic TV commercials from Folgers, Tupperware, and others. As noted in Figure 4.10 and Figure 4.11, don't overlook the many home movies and other videos that have been uploaded also, all of which you can use to supplement the more traditional digital eBook resources found on the site.

Software

The Internet Archive also contains a diverse collection of software that can be freely used and downloaded to your computer—from open source software to shareware and more, as noted in Figure 4.13. If you or your patrons are looking for classic games or productivity software, or are just browsing around, make sure to click on the following link to get started: http://www.archive.org/details/software.

Audio

From old-time radio to current podcasts, news, music, and more, the audio resources at the Internet Archive are extensive and easy to use. Use the regular Internet Archive search engine to search for materials. Once found, the embedded audio player on the site makes it easy to preview different shows, as noted in Figure 4.14. If you want to take audio for offline use, check out the various download options, which range from Ogg Vorbis to MP3 formats. It would also be easy to weave these resources into your library's audio collection, either via links in your library

Sub-Collections	
Animation & Cartoons Whether you want to watch classic cartoons from a bygone era, Brick Films made with your favorite building toys, Machinima patched together from video games, or the artful computer animations...	1,715 items
Arts & Music This library of arts and music videos features This or That (a burlesque game show), the Coffee House TV arts program, punk bands from Punkcast and live performances from Groove TV. Many of these...	916 items
Community Video Open Source Video has been renamed to Community Video! (The URL is still the same, though.) You are invited to view or upload your videos to the Community collection. These thousands of videos were...	227,358 items
Computers & Technology Featuring two television programs popular in the 1980's and 1990's: Computer Chronicles and Net Café, this library showcases videos about computing and technology. Collection topics include BBS, the...	10,910 items
Cultural & Academic Films This library of academic and cultural films features collections from the Academic Film Archive and the Media Burn Independent Film Archive, as well as a selection of documentaries created by Dorothy...	3,826 items
Ephemeral Films Ephemeral films are non-fiction films usually made for educational, industrial, or promotional purposes. The two classic ephemeral film collections found on the Archive are the Prelinger Archives and...	1,109 items

Figure 4.10

Welcome to Drive-In Movie Ads	158 items

Super short advertisements used during intermission at drive-in movie theaters during the 1950's and early 1960's to get people to consume junk food from the concession stand, may be viewed here.

Warning: watching these ads may make you hungry!

Browse Collection
Browse by Subject / Keywords

All items (most recently added first) - RSS

Figure 4.11

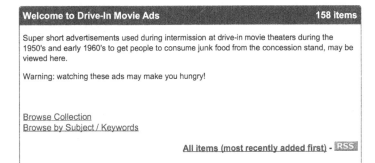

Figure 4.12

Figure 4.13

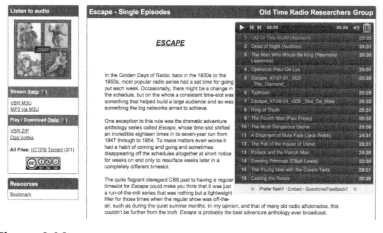

Figure 4.14

Figure 4.15

catalog or by placing bookmarks, posters, and handouts within easy reach of your patrons to emphasize what is available on-line at the site. For more details on types of audio content and format, the following link can quickly get you up to speed: http://www.archive.org/details/audio.

Digital eBook Collections

Now that you've taken a look at some of the other collections maintained by the Internet Archive, let's look at the main reason for including the project in this book: the digital eBook collections! Accessing the main page at the project (http://www.archive.org/details/texts), you will immediately see the quantity of resources to choose from, including lists of popular downloads, different types of digital eBook resources, and overall collection information as noted in Figure 4.15, 4.16 and 4.17.

While all of these resources in one spot may be somewhat intimidating to grasp, becoming more familiar with them can easily be accomplished by viewing the subcollections, which aggregate various types of eBook content into categories such as **American Libraries**, **Project Gutenberg**, and the **Universal Library**. While it's possible to search all of the available digital eBook resources through the main search box at the top of the page, these additional links can help you quickly zero in on a particular topic. Table 4.2 provides a quick way to find them.

Choose one of these subcollections to explore, and you'll find a more detailed page on each, with options to search by popular topic, title, contributor, and more. Note that each page also contains forum options, RSS feeds, and other contact details, as seen in the following screenshot.

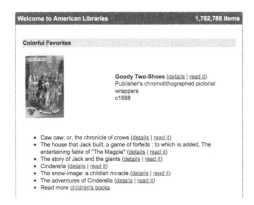

Figure 4.16

Notice as you explore that the search bar automatically changes to the collection you are in, in case you want to search directly for specific resources instead of just browsing. This is a great feature and one that can help you and your library's patrons to narrow your search results.

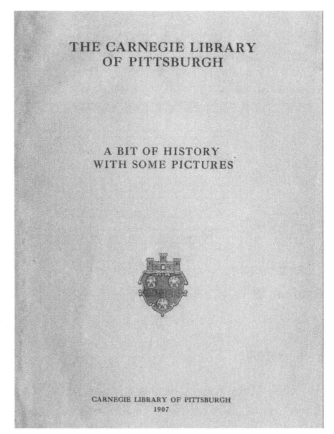

Figure 4.17

Table 4.2 Internet Archive Text Sub-Collections

Name	URL
American Libraries	http://www.archive.org/details/americana
Canadian Libraries	http://www.archive.org/details/toronto
Universal Library	http://www.archive.org/details/universallibrary
Community Texts	http://www.archive.org/details/opensource
Project Gutenberg	http://www.archive.org/details/gutenberg
Children's Library	http://www.archive.org/details/iacl
Biodiversity Heritage Library	http://www.archive.org/details/biodiversity
Additional Collections	http://www.archive.org/details/additional_collections

Collections and Your Library

Having a single page for each subcollection (as seen in Figure 4.18) is a great way to learn more about what types of digital resources are available at the Internet Archive. In doing my own research for this chapter, I spent time exploring the **American Libraries** and the **Canadian**

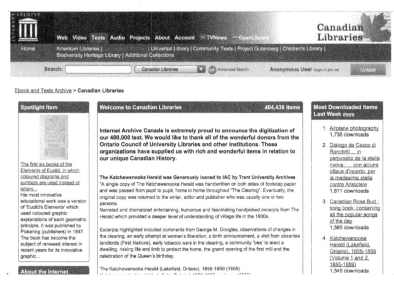

Figure 4.18

Libraries sections, and I came across fascinating historical titles such as *The North Carolina Booklet* and *Songs of a Sourdough*. I also dug up the U.S. Census, which can be found on the Internet Archive for 1790 through 1930. While titles like these may have limited practical value on our everyday bookshelves, they often contain important genealogical and historical resource information. Don't overlook these subcollections as a great research starting point!

Format

One of the biggest issues with digital reading is format. There are so many different eReading devices and formats that it can be confusing, both to the library and the patron. With this in mind, it's a relief to note that on the Internet Archive, many different formats are available for using online through the web browser or downloading for later use in other programs and applications. Some of the more popular ones are shown in Table 4.3.

Table 4.3 Internet Archive Common File Formats

File Format
PDF
Plain text
DAISY
ePub
MOBI

While you're undoubtedly familiar with PDF, plain text, and HTML, many other formats are also available for resources found on the project, including ePub (an up-and-coming standard supported by a large variety of eReading devices), Mobi (the older Mobi Pocket–based eBook format), and DAISY (which enables readers who have reading difficulties to have access to digital resources). However, what you won't find much of in the Internet Archive are titles limited by digital rights management (DRM). Although it is enabled for some titles,[9] most of the resources on the Internet Archive have no such restrictions, so you can use and share them freely with your patrons without having time limits or needing to download special software.

Figure 4.19

Searching the Internet Archive

No matter how impressive the collection, whether it's digital or analog, if you can't search it, you can't find it! As a librarian or library staff member, you are already keenly aware of this. Therefore, it is absolutely critical that you, your staff, and your patrons become experts on how to search the Internet Archive. Without this base knowledge, it's possible that you will end up both frustrated and empty-handed. In this section, you will learn both basic and advanced searching skills necessary to effectively use the site, giving you what you need to successfully help your patrons fully utilize the many resources.

Words of Warning!

While you are undoubtedly familiar with the easy one-box searching of Google and other online databases and search engines, querying for topics and resources currently available through the Internet Archive can be a different experience. Choices abound, from fast basic searching to detailed queries. As you go through this section, take the time to familiarize yourself with all of the options. Following along with your own web browser is a great way to learn, as you can refer to the site in real time. Beyond just your own learning, think about your patrons, those who may not be familiar with anything more detailed than a basic Google or Bing search. Use your skills and your experience with interviewing patrons to help them be successful when using the Internet Archive.

Basic Searching

For simple data queries, getting started with basic searching at the Internet Archive is done by navigating to http://www.archive

Figure 4.20

.org/details/texts and filling in the search bar with your keyword, author, or topic and then scanning for results. This basic quick search strategy can often be effective and returns results quickly.

To help illustrate this, let's do a quick and simple search for digital resources on Chicago history. Using our search bar as noted previously, type in ***Chicago history***. What do your results look like? Some of the returned titles are fairly impressive, with resources such as *History of Chicago and Chicago, A History and Forecast*. For this basic query, we received excellently focused results for our search. There was no distinction between words or phrases, and we were able to find what we were looking for.

However, this is not always the case. Let's go back to our search bar and look for information on Carnegie libraries (as seen in previous chapters). Type **Carnegie libraries** and select the **Texts** option (see Figure 4.21).

Figure 4.21

Search Results

Results: 1 through 50 of **653** (0.012 secs)
You searched for: Carnegie libraries AND mediatype:texts

[1] 2 3 4 5 6 7 8 9 10   Next   Last

A Book Of Carnegie Libraries - Theodore Wesley Koch
Downloads: 332

A Book of Carnegie Libraries - Theodore Wesley Koch
Book digitized by Google from the library of the University of Michigan and uploaded to the Internet Archive by user tpb.
Downloads: 129

A book of Carnegie libraries - Koch, Theodore Wesley, 1871-1941
Keywords: Carnegie, Andrew, 1835-1919; Libraries -- United States; Library architecture
Downloads: 345

A book of Carnegie libraries - Koch, Theodore Wesley, 1871-1941
The metadata below describe the original scanning. Follow the "All Files: HTTP" link in the "View the book" box to the left to find XML files that contain more metadata about the original images and the derived formats (OCR results, PDF etc.). See also the What is the directory structure for the **texts**? FAQ for information about file content and naming conventions.
Keywords: Carnegie, Andrew, 1835-1919; Libraries; Library architecture
Downloads: 53

Figure 4.22

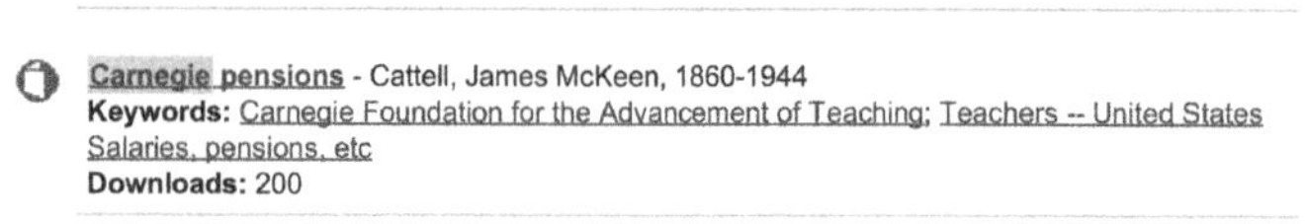

Carnegie pensions - Cattell, James McKeen, 1860-1944
Keywords: Carnegie Foundation for the Advancement of Teaching; Teachers -- United States Salaries, pensions, etc
Downloads: 200

Figure 4.23

Now let's look at your results. If you are following along in your web browser, look at your screen or use Figure 4.22 as an example.

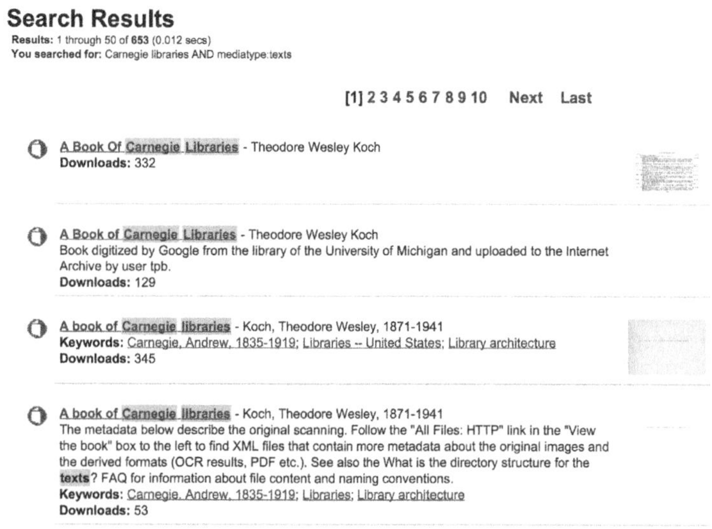

Notice that in your returned results you have more than 600 different hits on the terms **Carnegie** and **libraries**, with the search engine processing each word individually and then returning results. Notice Figure 4.23 as an example of a single returned resource.

This result includes nothing related to your query for information on Carnegie libraries, instead returning only a resource that has the search term **Carnegie** in it. The search engine made no distinction between the words being searched for—it identified only occurrences of each in the database. The results are not that helpful nor are they totally related to what we were actually searching for. This is indicative of the frustrations that can occur while using the Internet Archive. To get around this, it is possible when executing a basic search query to use delimiters and Boolean operators to refine and narrow our search results.

For now, let's redo our search for information on Carnegie libraries and use some delimiters that indicate a relationship between these two words. This time, search for Carnegie libraries with quotation marks around the phrase **Carnegie libraries**. The results are different, as noted in Figure 4.24.

Search Results

Results: 1 through 7 of **7** (0.012 secs)
You searched for: "Carnegie libraries" AND mediatype:texts

Figure 4.24

This result is a little closer to the mark than the first search and includes titles such as *A Book of Carnegie Libraries* and *The Carnegie Library of Pittsburgh: A Bit of History with Some Pictures*. But let's try one more method, one in which you can use Boolean operators.

For this next example, we are still looking for information about Carnegie libraries. However, our patron does not want any resources by the author Theodore Wesley Koch. How would you construct your search? One possible method of doing so would be this way: **"Carnegie Libraries" NOT Koch**. This tells the search engine to search for the terms "Carnegie" and "libraries" together but to exclude any resources that have the word "Koch" in them.

Looking at your results, you'll notice that you went from an initial set of seven results, of which five had Koch as one of the authors, to the two resources shown in Figure 4.25.

Notice also in the preceding search string that the category selection tool was

Figure 4.25

used to limit the search to only the texts portion of the Internet Archive's database. Remember there are also subcategories of texts on the project such as American Libraries, Canadian Libraries, and Community Texts to search, all of which can provide additional avenues to needed data.

How about another search using this approach? Let's say you have a patron come into your library looking for information in eBook format for Allan Pinkerton of the famous Pinkerton National Detective Agency. How should you help her find this information?

First, navigate back to the basic search screen and input the following terms, using the quotation delimiters as you did in your previous search. It will look like this: **"Allan Pinkerton."**

How many results did you get? As of early 2013, there were 16 results in the Internet Archive for this query. Now redo your search, only this time, limit your search to the American Libraries subcollection. Using this same search strategy, you are able to reduce your results down to 15, some of which can be seen Figure 4.26.

While for this particular search our lists of returned results were not too different than the standard quick search query, this does give you some sense of how limiting your searching with the collections tool can help save time. For more details on this specific option, as well as other Boolean operations that can be used on the Internet Archive, be sure and check the following link: http://www.archive.org/advancedsearch.php.

Figure 4.26

As a side note, if you are interested in learning more details about the search engine used at the Internet Archive, the following link can provide many additional search tips and information: http://lucene.apache.org/core/.

Browsing

While it is not the same as actively searching with keywords, Boolean terms, and other specific operators, browsing both physical and digital library collections can be an indirect form of searching, especially if a person has only a vague idea of what is being

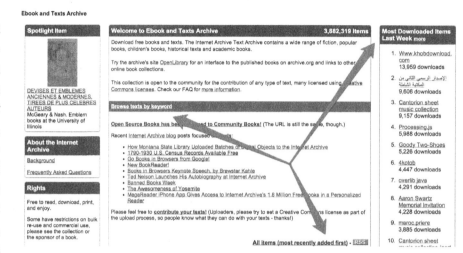

Figure 4.27

looked for, cannot describe it in specific terms, or has only a few details about the subject in question. If you normally work at the reference desk at your library, you know that this is often the case for many patrons looking through your own library's collection. Browsing can effectively help patrons determine what they are actually looking for. You can use the same

approach when searching the Internet Archive. To find out more, follow this link http://www.archive.org/details/texts and examine these sections: **Browse texts by keyword, Most Downloaded Items Last Week**, and **All items (most recently added first)**. (See Figure 4.27).

Browse texts by keyword

Figure 4.28

Browse Texts by Keyword

Figure 4.29

Figure 4.28 shows the browse by keyword link. Depending on what topics you're searching for, this option can be helpful. Click on the link and examine the results (shown in the following figure).

Notice in this screenshot that each link is actually a sublink to another level of available keywords. If you click on **The Library of Congress** link shown in Figure 4.29, you are immediately taken to yet another level of links (see Figure 4.30).

At this point, clicking on another link would take you to a list of titles on that particular subject. For example, clicking on the Library of Congress link and then clicking on **World's Columbian Exposition** returns the following results as shown in Figure 4.31.

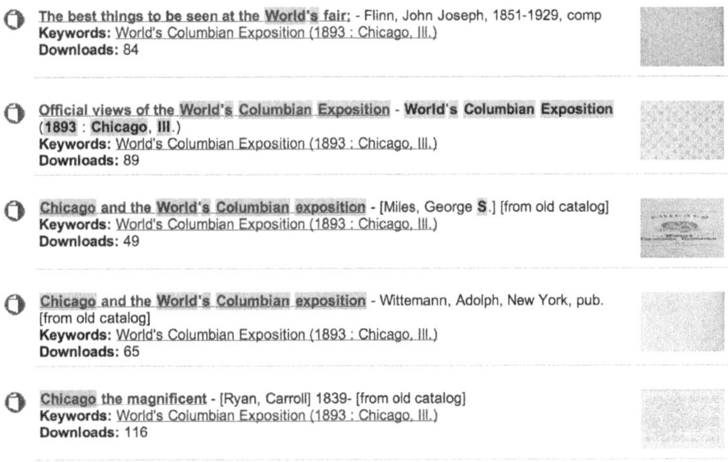

Interestingly, even though you conducted this search via the browsing option, the results include the back-end search conducted by the Internet Archive's search engine (see Figure 4.32).

Notice also in Figure 4.32 the Boolean operations in the background that demonstrate how the search was actually performed. Hidden from the patron, this shows the complexity and detail that actually goes into a simple search request.

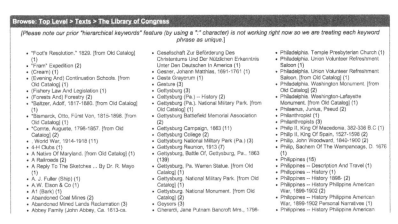

Figure 4.30

Figure 4.31

Search Results

Results: 1 through 50 of **124** (0.009 secs)
You searched for: mediatype:texts AND collection:library_of_congress AND subject:"World's Columbian Exposition (1893 : Chicago, Ill.)"

Figure 4.32

Most Downloaded Items

The next two search options that can be helpful are **Most Downloaded Items** and the **Most Downloaded Items Last Week**. While perhaps not useful for patrons looking for specific subjects or titles, browsing this way reveals interesting trends and popular titles, which

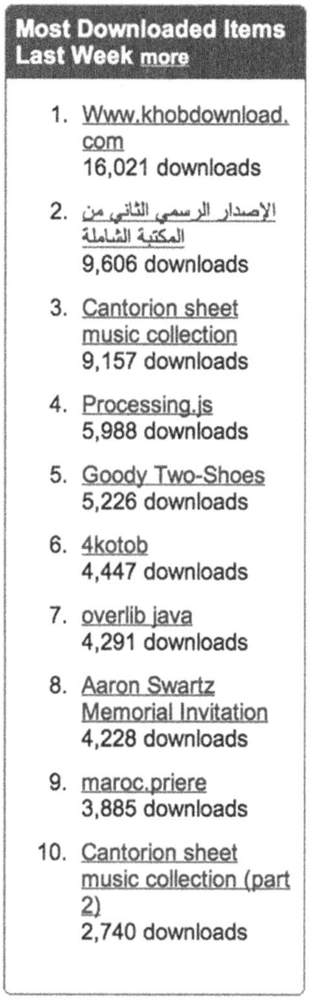

Most Downloaded Items Last Week more
1. Www.khobdownload.com
16,021 downloads
2. الإصدار الرسمي الثاني من المكتبة الشاملة
9,606 downloads
3. Cantorion sheet music collection
9,157 downloads
4. Processing.js
5,988 downloads
5. Goody Two-Shoes
5,226 downloads
6. 4kotob
4,447 downloads
7. overlib java
4,291 downloads
8. Aaron Swartz Memorial Invitation
4,228 downloads
9. maroc.priere
3,885 downloads
10. Cantorion sheet music collection (part 2)
2,740 downloads

Figure 4.33

is good if your patron is just looking for something to read online or transfer to their eReader. An example of this is a patron who found something on the most downloaded list originally and wants to find more titles in this same subject area. You can also search for number of downloads and click on the link to go directly to the resource in question. See Figure 4.33 as an example of this.

All Items (most recently added first) RSS

The last method of browsing to consider is the **All Items** link and the Really Simple Syndication (RSS) feed that accompanies it. Selecting this option takes you to a list of every eBook in the Internet Archive, with the most recently added items listed first. This can provide general background knowledge on a topic and can be useful if you are scanning for specific titles that might show up in the listings. While RSS is not as popular as other methods, this type of link is a great way for you and your patrons to stay up to date with the latest text additions to the Internet Archive.

Advanced Searching

For many patrons and library staff, basic searching of the Internet Archive is enough to help them find what they are looking for. However, there are times when more advanced searches are necessary. This is when the advanced search portion of the Internet Archive shines, with lots of useful options and the ability to go to a granular level. You can find this link at http://www.archive.org/advancedsearch.php.

Advanced Search
Any field:
AND Title:
AND Creator:
AND Description:
AND Collection:
AND Mediatype:
AND Custom field
AND Custom field
AND Custom field
AND Date:
AND Date range:
contains
is
All collections
All mediatypes
YYYY
MM
DD
TO
Search

Figure 4.34

The top component (Figure 4.34) is the primary method to use for searching. Of special note is the ability to specify ranges, media types, and collections. You can also stack multiple

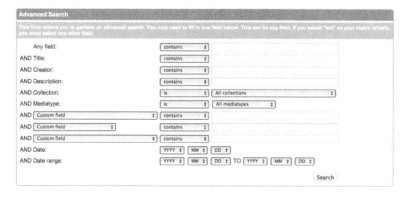

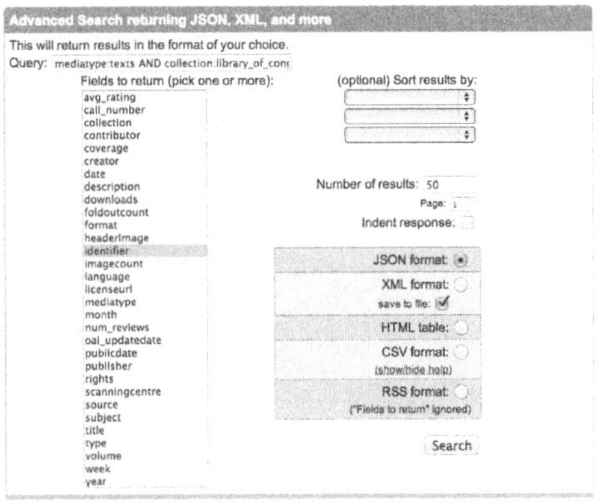

Figure 4.35

search requests inside the search box before actually conducting the search.

Figure 4.35 also shows methods of configuring search results, that will be explained below.

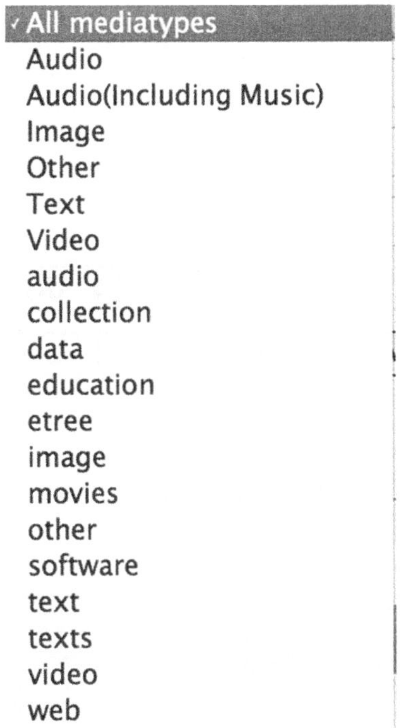

The ability to limit a search by media type and collection, as shown in Figures 4.36 and 4.37, enables flexibility, but can be quite involved. If your patron is not experienced in correctly applying these limiters to the search, this can lead to an overly complex search with few to no results and a very frustrated patron.

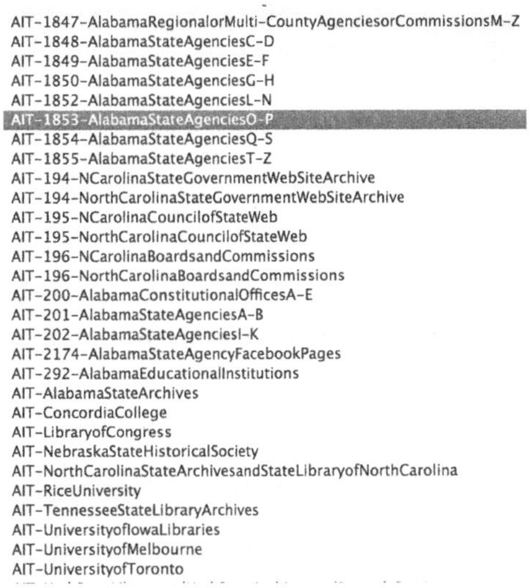

The second half of the advanced search page options, as seen in Figure 4.38 and Figure 4.39 provides a unique method to search and retrieve information. It's not the standard query seen on the site so far, but a very specific approach to searching that enables many fields to be explored, provides different sorting options, and even output format.

While it may be a bit beyond the typical patron search, this detailed output option can be a great internal tool for you or your staff when itemized records and analysis are needed. Figure 4.39 shows an example of some of the output that can be exported.

Now given what we've just learned, let's try a sample search and see these options in action. Consider a patron who is looking for information on the use of airplanes before World War I. In addition, he wants this output in XML format for a website he is currently

Figure 4.36

Figure 4.37

working on. As you talk to the patron, he also mentions that the multiple spellings of the term "airplane" during this time period included variants such as "aeroplane." Given this alternate spelling as well as your patron's information request, how would you begin your search on the Internet Archive? How can the advanced interface help you find results?

Start by navigating to the advanced search page at http://www.archive.org/advancedsearch.php and then entering the query as shown in Figure 4.40.

In this example, we have used the older spelling of "aeroplane"and have chosen delimiters such as media type, subject, title, and description. More than likely, these fields will have some sort of identifier that matches our search. The rest of the search is just a matter of filling in the search output options to limit results—such as XML, sortable field, and numbers of results.

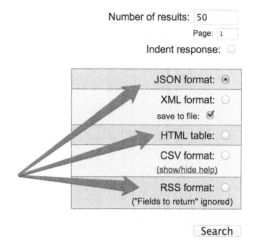

Figure 4.38

Figure 4.39

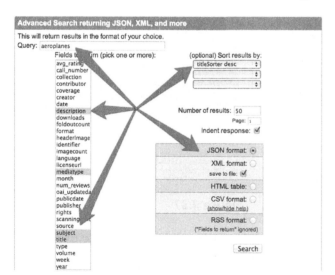

Figure 4.40

If you have been working with the example on your own web browser, how did your results come out? Take a look at the following screenshots to see my results.

Notice the output code followed by the keyword, title, and information from the sources found by the search, as noted in Figure 4.41 and Figure 4.42. While this particular output format, extensible markup language (XML), is not particularly conducive to reading, having this option is still good in some instances. It is likely that your patrons will want output formats in

```
▼<doc>
   ▼<str name="description">
      Book digitized by Google from the library of University of California and uploaded to the Internet Archive
   </str>
   <str name="mediatype">texts</str>
   ▼<str name="title">
      The Art of Aviation: A Handbook Upon Aeroplanes and Their Engines with Notes ...
   </str>
</doc>
```

Figure 4.41

more common formats such as **HTML table** or **CSV**. Ultimately, these options and the example search we just did illustrate the many methods in which the Inter-

```
▼<doc>
   ▼<str name="description">
      Thesis (B.S.)--Armour Institute of Technology, 1910
   </str>
   <str name="mediatype">texts</str>
   <str name="title">Test of slender wooden struts for aeroplanes</str>
</doc>
```

Figure 4.42

net Archive collection can be used in your library.

Viewing and Using Your Results

While searching is a fundamental part of any information request in the library, viewing, sorting, and weeding results ultimately help you find what you are looking for. So let's zero in on how to view and use the results of our queries. From sets of results to various tips, tricks, and techniques, knowledge of how to use results can help the Internet Archive remain a vital resource in your library's arsenal of information. Let's start off with a basic search. From there, we'll examine results and explore how to effectively use the tools provided.

Consider a patron who is looking for any information about the 1893 World's Fair that was held in Chicago. Open up your web browser and navigate to the Internet Archive. From there, you and the patron conduct the search, finding a title that you think will work: *The Historical World's Columbian Exposition and Chicago Guide*. Now that you have a resource, look at some individual results to see what options you have for working with it.

In Figure 4.43, you can see there is a lot of information to process. The top right corner of the page, as well as the menu, indicate that we're in the eBook and American Libraries section of the Internet Archive. The middle portion of the page gives you basic background information on the resource you have selected—including author, subject, publisher, and a short description of the work. Without having read any of the resource yet,

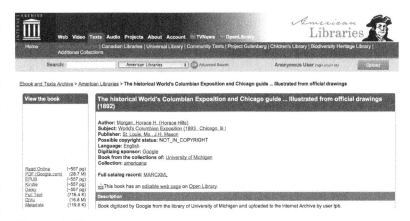

Figure 4.43

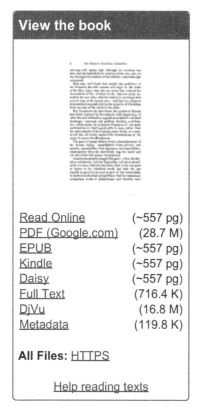

View the book

Read Online	(~557 pg)
PDF (Google.com)	(28.7 M)
EPUB	(~557 pg)
Kindle	(~557 pg)
Daisy	(~557 pg)
Full Text	(716.4 K)
DjVu	(16.8 M)
Metadata	(119.8 K)

All Files: HTTPS

Help reading texts

Figure 4.44

you and your patron probably have a pretty good idea whether this will give you the necessary information.

So what's your next step? How do you go in and use the resource that's been located? The **View the book** option to

```
../
historicalworld00unkngoog.djvu
historicalworld00unkngoog.gif
historicalworld00unkngoog.pdf
historicalworld00unkngoog_abbyy.gz
historicalworld00unkngoog_dc.xml
historicalworld00unkngoog_desc.html
historicalworld00unkngoog_djvu.txt
historicalworld00unkngoog_djvu.xml
historicalworld00unkngoog_files.xml
historicalworld00unkngoog_jp2.zip
historicalworld00unkngoog_marc.xml
historicalworld00unkngoog_meta.mrc
historicalworld00unkngoog_meta.xml
historicalworld00unkngoog_scandata.xml
```

Figure 4.45

the left is the key to accessing the title. As you can see in the screenshots (Figures 4.44 and 4.45), there are many ways to access the work, from reading it online to downloading various eBook formats such as ePub, Kindle, and DAISY. These options provide added flexibility as your library offers these resources to your patrons—with multiple formats, you can address a wide range of devices and file needs.

On a final note, to help your patrons who might be accessing these resources via desktop computer or laptop, you might occasionally see an option to get a resource via the regular HTTP connection. While not as commonly used as the traditional methods of access, HTTP access is just another method of accessing materials in the Internet Archive.

While we've mentioned downloading resources that have been found, what do you do if the patron just wants to view the title online? What options do you have? What's the best method of access? In many cases, the Internet Archive offers a more standard PDF option, but I would argue that your patron's best choice would be to use the **Read Online** option, which takes advantage of the BookReader software that the Internet Archive has made available for users. If you've never had a chance to use this method before, check it out, and you'll see that it's a very effective way to read online. How do you get started?

Click on the **Read Online** option, (as noted in Figure 4.46), and you will first notice that this book has been digitized by the Google

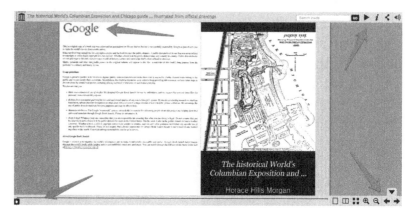

Figure 4.46

Books project. In fact, many of the titles on the Internet Archive have been scanned by Google and uploaded by end users. (This is also the case for

Figure 4.47

HathiTrust and many of the other online digital book sites. Especially with items thought to be in the public domain, this type of sharing is common.) Other important features to be aware of include the reading and viewing controls on the screen (see Figure 4.47).

In the top right corner are options to search inside the title, turn on or pause automatic page turning, bibliographic information about the book, book sharing options (that include links to the title and various embedding options), and finally the ability to hear the title read to you. While all of these options are interesting, a few specific choices can be useful in a library setting. For example, the **About This Book** option, as seen in Figure 4.48, gives basic information about the work—title, format options for downloading, and links to the Open Library (which we will talk about in the next chapter).

Figure 4.48

The sharing option, shown in Figure 4.49, can also be beneficial in a library setting, especially if you embed it in your website or link out to where the title is located on the Internet Archive. This is particularly useful when your library emphasizes a particular theme or collection (e.g., local history, the Great Depression, science fairs). Linking local resources with digital resources available on the Internet Archive is a great method of enhancing your local collection and offering your patrons more information on an almost infinite number of subjects. You can also use this approach to send email links to patrons who are not at the library but still need the information in question.

Figure 4.49

Other ways to view the book include using viewing selections such as single page, double page, and thumbnail views (see Figures 4.50 and 4.51). The thumbnail view can be especially advantageous with highly illustrated works or for quickly seeing what's in the title without going through page after page. You'll also find alternatives that give you the ability to shrink or enlarge the view and turn the pages manually, rather than the automatic method. This adjustability in viewing options can be handy when viewing titles on a variety of different sized devices, from laptops and desktop monitors to mobile devices.

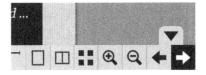

Figure 4.50

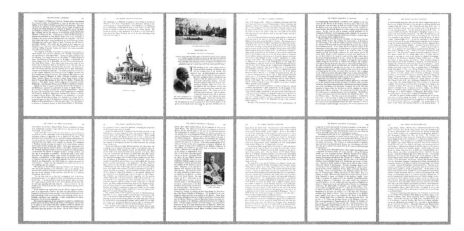

Figure 4.51

Finally, check out the timeline view at the bottom of the page (see Figure 4.52). This feature lets you know exactly where you are within the book, and it also helps when you are searching inside the work, revealing words or phrases you might have searched for. This can be particularly useful when viewing multiple citations or a large work.

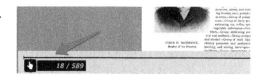

Figure 4.52

Special Tools for Libraries and Librarians

There's no doubt that the Internet Archive and other online book sites bring valuable resources to libraries, and they have in many cases developed special software and online tools that can speed the adoption of these online resources within these environments. Let's explore a few of these special features, including virtual library cards and DAISY-formatted titles as offered through the Internet Archive.

Virtual Library Card

Perhaps one of the most interesting features of the Internet Archive is the ability to get a free, online library card from the project, as seen in Figure 4.53.

While not a library card in the traditional physical sense of the cards you may offer your regular library patrons, this option brings many rewards, both to your patrons and your library, if you choose to create an account for your library. By doing so, in addition to viewing and using content, your library will then be able to upload content to the site, as shown in Figure 4.54.

By creating such an account, you can extend your collection to reach beyond your patron base and offer resources to

Log In

Email address

Password

☑ Remember me

Log in

Forgot your password?

Don't have a virtual library card? Register for free!

Figure 4.53

Share your Files

Please contribute books, audio, and video files that you have the right to share. The Internet Archive, a non-profit library, will provide free storage and access to them. (We reserve the right to remove any submitted material.)

Upload Files

Or choose an alternate upload method:

Classic Uploader	Internet Explorer users and print disabled (prefer to not use flash?)
Live Music Archive	For etree items
FTP	Large file alternative

Figure 4.54

surrounding communities—or really, anywhere else in the world. For locally produced content, such as library information, local history, or genealogy materials, this is a great low-cost way to share information.

DAISY-Formatted Titles

For most people, viewing and using resources available on the Internet Archive is an easy and uncomplicated experience. For those with vision issues or problems using a traditional computer interface, things can be a bit more challenging. To address this issue, your library can take advantage of several options offered through the project and the titles that can be accessed via the Digital Accessible Information System (DAISY).[10] This process puts titles in an audio format and opens doors to materials that would otherwise be unavailable to those with vision or other impairments, as shown in Figure 4.55.

Figure 4.55

These links show up as regular download options alongside other formats such as ePub and Kindle. For more information on particular titles, be sure to check out this link at the Internet Archive: http://www.archive.org/details/printdisabled. You can also try DAISY options at one of the subprojects of the Internet Archive, the Open Library. Links to its DAISY-formatted titles can be seen here: http://openlibrary.org/subjects/protected _daisy.

Things to Watch For

You've now seen what sorts of materials are available for use on the Internet Archive. You've also had a chance to see how searches are formulated and results returned. Overall, the experience of this online digital resource can be rewarding for both your library and your patrons.

However, when you consider where this resource fits into your library's digital strategy, it's not enough to just present the resource to your patrons by posting links on your website or announcing it in your library newsletter. You need to help them fully understand how to use the site, from searching it to using results. Librarians and library staff should actively train patrons, even if only a little, on how to use the many tools that are available online.

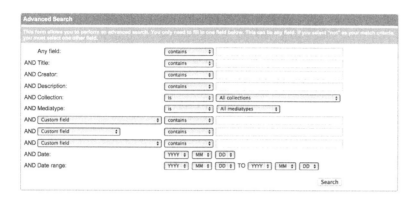

Consider some of the advanced searching options you've explored, such as what is shown in Figure 4.56.

Figure 4.56

It's not enough to just show patrons a feature like this without helping them understand the advanced limiting options. Not having the necessary knowledge makes for a frustrating experience. This principle extends to using resources they may find, especially eBooks that they want to transfer to devices. Plan ahead, if possible, to hold classes or create handouts to help your patrons take advantage of this amazing resource.

Important Points to Remember about the Internet Archive

The Internet Archive is a big site. As we've seen in this chapter, it's not limited to just digital books and magazines. It also contains movies, audio, podcasts, and more. It's a lot to remember. When working with patrons or even doing staff training or planning, it's important to keep your facts straight about the opportunities this site can bring to your library. Therefore, here are some important points to remember when using this resource. Use these as starting topics for your own research or share them with your staff and patrons.

More Than Just Web Pages: Origins of the Internet Archive

- Established in 1996
- Free use for everyone
- Member of the American Library Association
- Sharing and advancement of knowledge for everybody

Site Structure, Materials, and Components

- Easy to search layout—multi-paned information
- Subcollections options
- Includes audio, video, podcasts, software, and other formats

Searching the Internet Archive

- Both basic and advanced searching is available
- Boolean searching is included
- Includes specialized technical exports (JSON, CSV, etc.)
- Can browse by subcollection

Viewing and Using Your Results

- Search results can be directly downloaded or just read on the screen
- BookReader options contain controls for on-screen reading
- Results include various levels of bibliographic detail

Special Tools for Libraries and Librarians

- Free electronic library cards/accounts enable sharing and uploads
- DAISY-formatted titles are available for use by your patrons

Things to Watch For

- Given the extensive nature of the Internet Archive, it's important to remember that your patrons need to be trained.
- Consider a complete training approach, not just signage or handouts

Questions for You to Try

Origins of the Internet Archive

1. Given the tremendous amount of materials available on the Internet Archive, which types of titles do you feel would be the easiest to integrate into your own library? Why? Which resource would be most difficult to use with patrons?

Site Structure, Materials, and Components

1. Given the site structure of the project, how would you recommend using the site for someone who has never used it before? Would you recommend a specific material type search over all the materials in the archive or only a few? Why?

2. Find a topic that's interesting to you. Now, using the Internet Archive, try to find two different sources of material on that topic (e.g., for the history of Cleveland, you could search for video, audio, or eBooks). Write down the sources you found and the process by which you found them.

    Source #1 _____

    Source #2 _____

Searching the Internet Archive

1. You're in charge of storytime one Wednesday morning and the parents of one of the children come up to you with a question. They're looking for a book of fairy tales written by Hans Christian Andersen. However, they're specifically looking for one story in the book: "Little Claus and Big Claus," and your library does not have a print copy of the tale. Using your knowledge of searching the Internet Archive, how would you find this story?

2. Given the advanced search functions of the project, name some of the custom fields available for searching. Which would be used most often? Which ones would not? Why?

Viewing and Using Your Results

1. You're working at the reference desk when a patron comes in with her Kindle. She wants to find comic books about the Lone Ranger for her device. Using the Internet Archive, how would you help her?

2. It's been a tough week, and just as you get ready to walk out the door, a patron comes up to you looking for information about 1930 census records from Florida. Because you really want to go home and relax, what's the fastest method to help your patron use the Internet Archive? Are the census records themselves searchable?

Special Tools for Libraries and Librarians

1. What are DAISY books? What extra tools does one need to be able to use them?

2. What are some of the additional text collections that are available for use on the Internet Archive? Try two different collections. Do you think it is effective to have these specialized collection notations, or would it be better to have a single large collection? Why?

Notes

1. Internet Archive, http://archive.org/details/texts.
2. Internet Archive, http://archive.org/about/.
3. Internet Archive, http://archive.org/about/.
4. Internet Archive, http://archive.org/about/faqs.php#296.
5. Internet Archive, http://blog.archive.org/2011/09/17/3-million-texts-for-free/.
6. Open Publication Distribution System, http://opds-spec.org/.
7. Internet Archive, http://www.archive.org/details/The39Steps.
8. Internet Archive, http://www.archive.org/details/prelinger.
9. Internet Archive, http://www.archive.org/post/312815/digital-lending-library.
10. DAISY Consortium, http://www.daisy.org/.

Resources

Given the wide scope and expansive digital collections of the Internet Archive, it can be overwhelming when you are first using the site. The resources in this section will help you get a more complete picture of what the project contains. Categorized by topic, you'll find links to many of the resources. By scanning this list, you can quickly zero in on what interests you and your library. It is by no means complete, so add your own links and share them with other staff.

News and Reviews

ENews Park Forest, "Internet Archive Reaches 3 Million Items with Rare Galileo Texts from the University of Toronto Libraries," http://www.enewspf.com/latest-news/science-a-environmental/27312-internet-archive-reaches-3-million-items-with-rare-galileo-texts-from-the-university-of-toronto-libraries.html.

Keller, Jared, *The Atlantic*, "Moving towards a Physical Archive of the World's Books," *The Atlantic*, June 7, 2011, http://www.theatlantic.com/technology/archive/2011/06/moving-towards-a-physical-archive-of-the-worlds-books/240045/.

Rapp, David, "IDPF Digital Book 2011: The Internet Archive's Potential 'Library Option,'" *Library Journal*, May 24, 2011, http://blog.libraryjournal.com/ljinsider/2011/05/24/idpf-digital-book-2011-the-internet-archives-potential-library-option/.

Technology and Special Tools

DAISY-formatted books for people with impaired vision: http://www.libraryjournal.com/article/CA6728034.html.

Internet Archive Blogs, "Book Scan Wizard Software Now Supports Internet Archive Uploads!" http://blog.archive.org/2011/03/14/book-scan-wizard-software-now-supports-internet-archive-uploads/.

Internet Archive Blogs, "How Archive.org Items Are Structured," http://blog.archive.org/2011/03/31/how-archive-org-items-are-structured/.

Internet Archive, "FAQ's," http://www.archive.org/about/faqs.php.

Excellent resource for almost any question about the Internet Archive you might have.

TeleRead (Internet Archive Book Lending): http://www.teleread.com/library/internet-archive-launches-in-library-ebook-lending-program/.

Chapter 5

The Open Library

Origins, Sites, and Catalogs

Figure 5.1

Our focus now turns to another digital online book site known as the Open Library. While similar in many respects to the other sites we've seen already, the Open Library is substantially different, as it is more of an information hybrid than a strict storage resource for digitized titles and other materials. While it does offer digital materials for your library and your patrons, you can also use, edit, and add to the site's online catalog. In this chapter, you will take an in-depth look at the Open Library, where it came from, how to use it, how to search it, and methods to make this an invaluable part of your library. But first, consider a scenario in which use of the Open Library might be helpful.

Too Many Places!

Seeing she was already late for lunch, Merena pushed the ever-growing pile of patron requests to the corner of her desk and stared back at her screen, fingers dancing over the keyboard. She'd found quite a few titles this morning but had just printed off a new batch of requests for her afternoon shift at the reference desk. She put the keyboard aside and grabbed her lunch as the printer churned out the last of the request slips.

(continued)

(continued)

She couldn't help but think about the newest task that had been assigned to her, being responsible for the library's new eBook requester program. She still was not convinced this was the best course of action, but the library's administrative team seemed to think it was the answer to everything.

The program was to run like this: Any patron could request eBook titles, even if they weren't in the library catalog, and the staff would fulfill the request via a variety of sources, both free and through vendors such as OverDrive and Amazon. When the staff found the title, the patron was notified, and the librarian would help them procure the title. It was an unorthodox service, and Merena wasn't totally sold on it yet, but the patrons who had tried it really liked it, even though some struggled with getting the digital items on their devices. Merena sighed as she remembered being swamped with six people at once last week, all trying to figure out how to get eBooks on their different readers. What a mess that had been!

The biggest issue Merena faced in all of this was one of a practical nature. Having to go to various sites to track down the titles and then finding the format the patron had requested was extremely time consuming! Most of the common items—bestsellers, popular nonfiction, and trade books—were easy to find, but the esoteric stuff was a challenge, and when combined with her regular duties, it took way too much time. Merena wondered if there was some other way to do this. She just didn't have enough time to do this and her regularly assigned duties!

The Issues

While the preceding scenario is fictional, it aptly illustrates some of the ongoing issues faced by librarians deciding on any digital book strategy. As you probably already know, there are no easy decisions related to digital collections because there are really no standards as to what a digital collection should be. Beyond this, there are the everyday questions that consistently seem to crop up, ranging from which eBook formats staff will help patrons with to helping patrons with their various digital devices.

Vendors provide some solutions to these ongoing issues, but quite often, proprietary vendor-based solutions are restrictive in their implementation and are costly to the library. Switching to only free online resources could be a consideration, but they must be applied on a consistent and thought-out basis, not just thrown into use or integrated poorly into existing physical collections.

However, the Open Library project might partially fulfill the library's needs. Unlike some of the more traditional resources covered in previous chapters—the Google Books project, HathiTrust, and others—the Open Library project isn't just a digital resource site; it's also a catalog that is open for anyone to contribute to. Almost wiki-like in its approach, with a high level of quality and openness, it's an excellent digital resource that you really should consider.

Origins and Goals

Figure 5.2

So where did the Open Library come from? What are the project's goals? In looking at the project's website, you'll find that it goes back to 2007 and a group of talented individuals that include the late Aaron Swartz,[1] of RSS and Reddit fame; Brewster Kahle; and Karen Coyle. These people, along with outside partners such as the California State Library and the Kahle/Austin Foundation, established a shared goal of maintaining "one web page for every book ever published." Hence, the Open Library!

The second goal of the Open Library, as also noted on the site, is to maintain an online, searchable, and accessible catalog in which to find both digital and nondigital materials. This singular focus, along with the help of many contributors, has enabled the project to grow exponentially. Today's Open Library continues to expand, at this point offering more than a million free eBook titles and more than 20 million book records,[2] making it one of the top digital resource destinations on the Internet.

Freely available for everyone at http://www.openlibrary.org, the project continues to evolve, adding records and other digital items, and contributing to other projects that enhance and extend interaction with the web catalog (the Open Library works with both OverDrive and OCLC). In fact, this pace of change and open acquisition, as noted on its blog,[3] has made the Open Library extremely valuable in the realm of online library resources. In short, a natural candidate to be used in your library's ongoing digital strategy!

For Your Library?

So what are the practical implications of using the Open Library project to meet your library's everyday information needs? It is likely that many questions come to mind. How does it work? Will your patrons understand it? Are its resources useful? Does the Open Library really deserve a spot in your litany of digital resources, or is it just another website? The simple facts are that the Open Library is anything but just another website. While you might choose to implement this site strictly on the merits of the digital resources it provides, you should consider other features as well, from the multiple eBook formats available for download to how easy the online cataloging can be used. There are many digital sites from which to download books, but few can match the open and easy-contributing nature of the Open Library.

Let's take a practical example for a moment, one that can help illustrate everyday use of the Open Library. Does your library participate in the interlibrary loan program (ILL)? If so, then you know that participation takes both staff time and a portion of your budget, from pulling and processing the requested items to checking them out and preparing them for shipment. What if there were ways to let your patrons borrow items without this cost?

With the Open Library's digital book lending program, this becomes possible. As noted by the project,[4] this unique approach to lending eBooks can save your library money over the traditional ILL model of lending and borrowing physical items from other libraries. Will it ever replace traditional ILL? Probably not totally, but in today's library world, it's a great supplementary service to offer your patrons.

Site Structure, Materials, and Components

While it may seem natural to lump the Open Library in with all of the other digital book sites we've examined so far, to do so would overlook the special aspects of open use and access that make the Open Library unique. Users can utilize the digital resources available on the site, but they can also give something back and contribute to the project in many ways, from uploading book information and cover scans to even cataloging individual materials. In light of this, let's see exactly how the site is put together, from navigation to types of materials and more.

Basic Navigation

Let's start our investigation by looking at the basic site navigation. Go to http://www.openlibrary.org and examine the homepage. If you're not following along with your computer at this time, consider the following series of screenshots.

From the homepage, as noted in Figure 5.3, you can begin your search for materials in a variety of ways. If you're in a rush or are not sure how to search, the search box on the top right of the Open Library's pages allows you to begin with a basic or advanced search for materials.

A similar box is available on the bottom right of the page, as seen in Figure 5.4. You might notice the option underneath the boxes to search for just digital materials. When working with your patrons, make sure they are aware of this feature. It will help to avoid possible confusion about what this option actually does and how it differs from the regular search.

Figure 5.3

This option can serve as a great reminder about the nature of the Open Library as well as its goals and mission, that is that the project is a place to search for, find, and use **both** digital and analog-based resources. Unlike the singular eBook nature of the other sites we've profiled so far, this duality makes this project so much more valuable for your library.

Figure 5.4

Advanced Searching Options

While other digital book sites offer advanced searching on a separate page or as a distinct part of the site, the Open Library makes advanced searching options easy to use with a single click on the **More search options** link, which is under the regular basic search box. Doing so brings up a pop-up window of additional options (seen in Figure 5.5A). Along with the standard choices such as title, author, ISBN, and subject, you will notice other categories such as **Person**, **Place**, and **Publisher**. The inclusion of these categories is very much in line with Open Library's unique approach to cataloging titles, emphasizing the unique aspects of each material as well as many searchable record fields in which to find them.

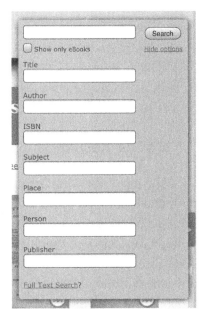

Figure 5.5A

In further exploring the Open Library site, and as noted in Figure 5.5B, you will notice a **Full Text Search** option in the advanced search box. This option is similar to HathiTrust's full-text searching option and the Google Books project's text-searching capabilities. With this feature on the Open Library, it's easy to target queries for specific phrases or keywords across the entire catalog of Open Library materials.

However, with this method of searching (and as we have noted about the other projects covered so far), you are likely to get too many results and false hits, forcing you to waste time on resources that are not appropriate. In short, while this is an extremely powerful feature, use it with care, experimenting with the options before helping your patrons learn to use it. Make sure patrons are aware of the drawbacks related to searching by this method.

Looking at the Open Library website once again, notice at the top left and bottom left of each page quick links to either subject or author search, an example of which is shown in Figure 5.6A. Clicking on

Figure 5.5B

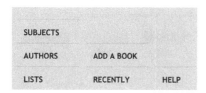

Figure 5.6A

either one of these links brings up an additional page of options and information related to each type of query, as noted in Figure 5.6B.

Depending on how skilled your patrons are at searching, the many methods of search available on the site may be somewhat confusing. If that's the case, plan on spending some extra time with them, reviewing and explaining the available options and how they work. Alternatively, you could produce signs or handouts with screenshots and other information to help explain. Remember this option if you choose to offer any sort of internal staff training.

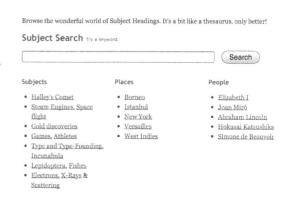

Figure 5.6B

It's the Results That Matter!

The results of your Open Library queries are returned via list, and you have options to sort by publish date, editions, and more. Refining your search is easy, as the right side of the page presents filtering options such as year, times, places, and even persons. Links found in these filter options can help you quickly expand your search or search for something completely different. Overall, the effect is similar to how the HathiTrust project allows you to expand your search options. But the Open Library does present it in a new way, one that is not often seen on the other sites we've examined so far. We will discuss these options in depth later in the chapter.

Lists, Lists and More Lists!

Similar to the Google Books online bookshelf and the HathiTrust Collections feature, Open Library's **Lists** function helps users list items from the project on specific subjects, authors, and favorite topics.

Figure 5.7

Many people are big fans of lists, and this Open Library feature can be used as part of your library's public service to your patrons to help keep them informed throughout the year on topics of interest. Take, for example, familiar topics that might be popular in your library such as gardening, art, or historic American authors. While it's possible to redo your search every time for materials like these, having lists already preformatted with results on the Open Library can save time and be a great way to draw attention to other circulating materials or even alternative digital collections the library makes available. It's important to note, however, that at this point lists are not yet searchable in the Open Library, but if a title is brought up, you can tell if it is on another list. This doesn't reduce the functionality, but it is something to be aware of.

Materials Offered

What sort of materials can you expect to find at the Open Library? While many of the titles are the familiar popular novels, public domain works, and nonfiction titles available elsewhere, the Open Library offers access to some unique resources as well, including items such as comic books, pamphlets, Scholastic Readers, and even ancient historical texts. With titles such as *Captain America* and *The Magic School Bus Rides the Wind*, your younger patrons might be impressed.

It's worth emphasizing again that the Open Library does not actually *have* any digital resources. Unlike the other projects we've seen so far, because the project is part of the Internet Archive, the Open Library relies on that project to store and provide access to the digital titles used in its catalog. However, don't let this deter you or your library from the contributions that the Open Library can bring to your own collection and how it can address your patrons' information needs.

Any Catalogers Here?

While your patrons probably don't think about them much, accurate cataloging records are of utmost importance to any library. Bad cataloging means people cannot find the titles they are looking for. If a bibliographic record is incomplete or missing vital fields, it directly affects the success of the search at hand. Because cataloging can be such a challenge, one of the most intriguing aspects of the Open Library is that it offers just this opportunity—anyone can upload, edit, and change materials records in the database! If you or your patrons find something that is incorrectly cataloged, you have the access to go in and change it!

In fact, this was one of the goals of the project—to make a catalog of all books that **anyone can edit** and that is flexible enough to include all sorts of descriptors and cataloging practices. In practice, the results are pretty amazing! Let's look at this sample entry form that is presented when users contribute records to the project.

As you see in Figure 5.8, entering title information is easy, with a minimum of jargon or ILS restrictions. This is vastly different from transferring records into most library ILS systems, which quite often contain vendor-specific record input schema or proprietary methods of doing so.

Figure 5.8

If you are new to the cataloging process or just need a bit of additional information, the Open Library offers a lot of help and other practical information. For more background and a great example, watch the following video from the Open Library blog, which talks about merging different author records: http://blog.openlibrary.org/2010/09/21/merge-authors-the-screencast/.

Beyond adding new entries to the catalog, users can also edit existing records on the system and export cataloging records in a variety of formats. Take a look at Table 5.1.

Table 5.1 Open Library Cataloging Record Types

Record Type or Format	Used In
RDF	Includes metadata used by the projects
JSON	Coding/API calls
Wikipedia	Wikipedia page entries/citations

While this is just a quick and simple introduction to record editing and exporting, be sure to check out the developer pages on the Open Library for more information (http://openlibrary.org/developers/api). You will find more detailed explanations, sample formats, and more. It is a good method of getting the complete story on the many record options available.

You should also know that the Open Library also makes available complete downloads of its entire cataloging records (see http://openlibrary.org/data#downloads). For more interesting comments on the background of data formats currently used in the Open Library, check out http://blog.openlibrary.org/2011/04/11/minimum-viable-record/. The information on these pages should be enough to get your catalogers and library staff up and running quickly.

Figure 5.9

Searching the Open Library

With millions of print and digital resources available through the Open Library, it's essential that both you and your staff become skilled in effectively searching and taking full advantage of all the project has to offer. From simple browsing and basic searching to advanced searching options with subjects, ISBNs, and more, you'll find many tools to help you quickly zero in on the materials you need. In this section, you'll explore the four most common methods of search used with the Open Library:

- Basic searching skills
- Advanced searching skills

- Browse tools

- Search inside

As you become more familiar with how searches are structured on the site, you'll find that it's relatively easy and intuitive, requires a minimum of fuss, and provides lots of great results. While similar in some respects to other online book sites already profiled, the Open Library's tools offer some unique methods that can really transform your search. Let's get started!

Basic Searching Skills

A variety of methods can be used to search the Open Library, but basic search is fundamental to the project. To get started looking for specific titles, authors, and subjects, you have two options. The first is the quick-search box located at both the bottom and top of the right side of the home page at www.openlibrary.org. This is perhaps the best method for general searching or just dashing off a quick query to get a sense of what is present. If you have additional details for your search (e.g., title, ISBN), you might want to start with the additional search options. In Table 5.2, you'll find the complete list of what is available.

Table 5.2 Open Library More Search Options

Title
Author
ISBN (includes variants)
Subject
Place
Person
Publisher

Any Variations?

One interesting way to search the Open Library (see http://openlibrary.org/search/howto for more details) is by prefacing your basic query elements with an indicator in the search box. For example, let's say you have a patron looking for information about victory gardens during World War I and World War II. You could use the indicators in the search box to construct the following search: **Subject: Victory Gardens**

If the patron decides she wants information on gardening only during World War II, you can stack your search terms in the box like this: **Subject: Gardening first_publish_year: [1939 TO 1945]**

As noted on the site documentation, it's even possible to construct Boolean searching phrases such as this: **World War, 1939-1945 AND (gardening)**

While these are not everyday methods, being able to search like this on the basic level can help you become more effective in your information query. You might also note that if you're searching for a phrase such as **Carnegie libraries**, the use of quotation marks give you more consistent results than the default term without the quotation marks.

- **Read online**

- PDF
- Plain text
- DAISY
- ePub
- DjVu
- MOBI
- Send to Kindle

Figure 5.10

Don't Forget eBooks!

It's important to remember that if your patron is looking for digital resources, you should check the **Show only eBooks** option. Not checking this option will result in lists of results that contain titles in both paper and digital format. Note Figure 5.10 for representative eBook formats available in the Open Library.

Advanced Searching Skills

Using the basic search box is great for dashing off a quick query or two and can be quite powerful, but often you are looking for a specific item or piece of information, such as a book title, author, or subject that can be represented by a keyword. In this case, the advanced search options available on the site are the best place to start. To do an advanced search in the Open Library, simply click on **More search options** directly underneath the quick-search box, as noted in Figure 5.11. You will then see a pop-up window filled with many more search options (e.g., title, author, ISBN, subject). At this point, all you need to do is enter the query terms and begin your search.

Figure 5.11

For now, let's perform a search to see how things work. Consider a patron looking for titles in the *U.S.A.* trilogy from the author John Dos Passos. Selecting the advanced search options, fill in the author box with **John Dos Passos** and the title box with **U.S.A.** to begin the search. Your returned results include various editions of the work in question, as shown in Figure 5.12.

Note some of the specifics of this search. It's possible to enter the author name either way—last name, first name **or** first name, last name. Also note that we did **not** select the **Show only eBooks** option so that all types of titles were shown, giving your patron a wider selection to choose from.

You will also notice two interesting search options when doing advanced searching on the site: **Place** and **Person**. These can be helpful depending on what you are looking for.

For example, consider a patron looking for information on the famous author James Thurber, as well as any information about Thurber's family history in Columbus, Ohio. Using the advanced search method discussed previously, you can type his name in the Person field, type **Columbus Ohio** in the Place field, and perform the query. Notice that you get four results, one of which is *Of Thurber and Columbustown*. Contrast this with a standard keyword search of James Thurber, which has many more results. If you want more specific titles for whatever it is you or your patron are searching for, this is a great method of winnowing results down to a manageable level.

In addition to the basic and advanced search boxes, there are other ways built into the Open Library for searching specific authors and subjects. On the top and bottom of the left side of the site's pages, you can

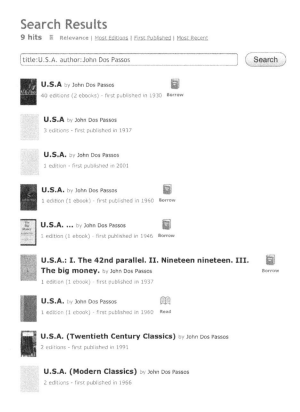

Figure 5.12

click on either the **Subjects** or the **Authors** link, which will bring you to specific pages for each of these searching options. These pages use the same search mechanisms as the rest of the site. However, there are some unique twists that can really come in handy. Let's do a sample search to help illustrate.

Say you have a student who needs to write a paper on Ernest Hemingway and is looking in the Open Library for books written by him. Using the specific subject or authors page links, enter your search term **Ernest Hemingway** and check the results. Your returned list should include Ernest Hemingway at the top, so click on his name. From there, you are brought to a second page, which offers information about his life, both personal and literary, followed by a list of works that are accessible through the Open Library database. Excellent results!

Now, look at Figure 5.13A. What you will see are many additional methods of finding information about this author. Specifically, you can search subjects, places, people, times, and lists (as noted in Figure 5.13B). While it ultimately depends on what you are looking for, this option really accelerates research and saves a tremendous amount of time. Instead of many unfocused results, it's possible to quickly zero in on the specifics!

PLACES
Spain, Paris (France), Kenya, Cuba, United States, France, Paris, Caribbean Area, Caribe (Región), París (Francia), Italy, Africa, Bahamas, Bimini Islands (Bahamas), Caribbean Sea, East Africa, Ficción, Florida, Gulf of Florida, Michigan, Milan, Pamplona, Riviera (France), Spanien, The Battle of Caporetto

PEOPLE
Ernest Hemingway (1899-1961), Antonio Ordóñez Araujo (1932-), Luis Miguel Dominguín (1926-), Ernest Hemingway, A. E. Hotchner, Antonio Ordóñez Araujo (1932-1998), Ernest Hemingway (1898-1961), General Francisco Franco, John C. Schweitzer, Maxwell E. Perkins (1884-1947)

TIME
20th century, Civil War, 1936-1939, 1920's, Early 20th century, 1920s, 1930's, 1940's, 1950s, 1951-1980, Alfonso XIII, 1886-1931, Spanish Civil War, 1936-1939

4 Lists See all

Authors
from Ophelia Hu

Favorite Writers
from Lane Willson

authors
from Peter Ding

Links (outside Open Library)

* nobelprize.org
* timeleshemingway.com
* Wikipedia entry
* Wikipedia link for Ernest Hemingway

Figure 5.13A

As you can see, you can immediately begin typing in your search query and looking at the results. However, before you do that, notice the bottom of the page (see Figure 5.15).

Now that you've performed an author search, let's perform a sample subject search so that you can see the benefits of using this method as well. Let's say you have a patron who comes to the library one day looking for information

SUBJECTS
Fiction, History, Correspondence, Protected DAISY, Accessible book, Ficción, World War, 1914-1918, American Short stories, Biography, Social life and customs, Translations into Vietnamese, Americans, Authors, Bullfights, In library, American Authors, American Novelists, Drama, Fiction in English, Guerra Mundial I, 1914-1918, Spain Civil War, 1936-1939, Big game hunting, Fishers, Homes and haunts, Hunting

Figure 5.13B

on how to get started with the hobby of gardening. While he would prefer an eBook for his iPad, he tells you that any information would be helpful. Navigating to the Open Library and clicking on the link for a subject search brings you to the following page shown in Figure 5.14.

Figure 5.14

Links to special books found within the Open Library such as those found on the Digital Accessible Information System (DAISY), the free eBooks, and the lending library option enable you to find titles for your patron in his or her preferred format.

Accessible book - Over 1,000,000 free eBooks, available to all in a variety of formats

Protected DAISY - Over 250,000 modern works, available for the U.S. print-disabled community

Lending library - About 10,000 eBooks available to anyone to borrow, 1 copy at a time, for 2 weeks

In Library - Find out more about our In-Library lending program.

Figure 5.15

Subject Search
111 hits

gardening	Search

- Gardening   3,723 **books**, subject
- gardening   3,610 **books**, subject
- Landscape gardening   1,565 **books**, subject
- Vegetable gardening   1,169 **books**, subject
- Organic gardening   415 **books**, subject
- Flower gardening   407 **books**, subject
- Herb gardening   395 **books**, subject
- Container gardening   223 **books**, subject
- Indoor gardening   209 **books**, subject
- Greenhouse gardening   122 **books**, subject
- Wild flower gardening   98 **books**, subject
- Native plant gardening   97 **books**, subject
- Color in gardening   67 **books**, subject
- Window gardening   58 **books**, subject
- Low maintenance gardening   48 **books**, subject
- Gardening to attract wildlife   46 **books**, subject
- Gardening to attract birds   46 **books**, subject
- Gardening in the shade   41 **books**, subject
- Gardening in fiction   41 **books**, subject
- Patio gardening   39 **books**, subject
- Balcony gardening   33 **books**, subject
- Artificial light gardening   32 **books**, subject
- Gardens and gardening   32 **books**, subject
- Butterfly gardening   31 **books**, subject
- Gardening, [from old catalog]   31 **books**, subject
- Winter gardening   26 **books**, subject
- Roof gardening   26 **books**, subject
- Desert gardening   22 **books**, subject
- Vegetable gardening, [from old catalog]   21 **books**, subject
- Stone in landscape gardening   17 **books**, subject
- Seaside gardening   13 **books**, subject
- Gardening equipment industry   12 **books**, subject
- Raised bed gardening   12 **books**, subject

Figure 5.16

Landscape gardening   1,567 **works** / 362 ebooks published between 1670 & 2013.

≡ Sort by: # of Editions | Most Recent Publish Date

Figure 5.17

Figure 5.18

This is a great method for patrons who are looking for additional titles, especially if they are familiar with the DAISY format.

For now, however, let's go back to your subject search of gardening and see what sorts of results are returned from a simple query. Note that if your patron was looking for specific types of gardening—such as vegetable, herb, or flower—these keywords could be used as well. Returned results are shown in Figure 5.16.

Notice the major divisions within the topic of gardening. These can help your patron quickly zero in on specific types of gardening that may appeal to him. For this example, let's choose landscape gardening. There are more than 1,500 returned titles, so click on the link and see what the results look like.

As shown in Figure 5.17, the results are impressive, ranging from publishing history to related subjects, authors, and more. It's almost guaranteed your patron will be impressed. More importantly, in the real world, it's likely **your patrons** will find the answers they were looking for! See Figure 5.18 for more details.

Browse Tools

While direct search is an important skill to have and use, it's possible to get equally good results just by browsing what is available on the Open Library, which you might already know about from helping patrons in your own library. If your patron is not sure what she is looking for, as far as a specific title, author, or even subject, then browsing the available resources on the project is a great method. So how do you get started?

Browsing the Open Library can be done in a few different ways. First, it can be done through a regular search in which results include options on the right side of the page for publisher, places, dates, persons, and so on, as noted in our previous searching on Ernest Hemingway. These are great places to start browsing for items related to your original search and perhaps the quickest.

The second method involves examining your list of returned results and using the titles and other information as a starting point for more research. For example, let's say your patron is looking for books or other information on Johnny Appleseed. Doing a subject search for the term **Johnny Appleseed** returns a list of subjects (see Figure 5.19). From here, you could browse the individual subject list for titles, looking for whatever the patron wants. Don't overlook the option of browsing the lists as well. With many collections and lists of different topics, your patron might just find what she is looking for!

Search Inside

One of the most impressive search options offered by the Open Library is the ability to search inside digital resources for information on whatever topic is being looked for. While this same option is offered on the other digital book sites, the Open Library's implementation is particularly helpful. It's called **Search Inside**, and the easiest way to use it involves the quick-search box labeled

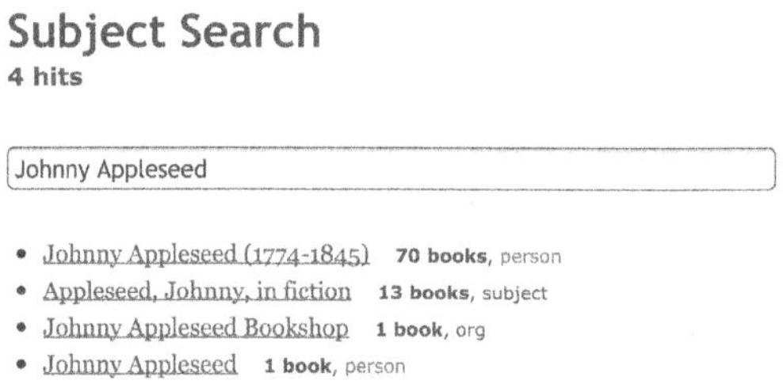

Subject Search
4 hits

Johnny Appleseed

- Johnny Appleseed (1774-1845)   **70 books**, person
- Appleseed, Johnny, in fiction   **13 books**, subject
- Johnny Appleseed Bookshop   **1 book**, org
- Johnny Appleseed   **1 book**, person

Figure 5.19

Full Text Search found on the top right and bottom of the project. Selecting these links takes you to this URL: http://openlibrary.org/search/inside. Note that you can also just enter this URL directly also.

How does this work? As you can see in Figure 5.20, you simply enter your search terms in the box and click on the search button. While you can use Boolean search methods,

Search Inside

[   ] (Search)

Figure 5.20

sometimes just looking for the text phrase works as well. Let's try a sample search to help illustrate this process.

Consider a patron looking for information on the history of the U.S. Atomic Energy Commission. Would the **Search Inside** function be helpful? Let's see what happens. First, navigate to http://openlibrary.org/search/inside and enter your search query of **Atomic Energy Commission**. Partial results can be seen in Figure 5.21.

Notice that in the results, you see a bit more about each title, options for reading, and a quote from the full text that shows a snippet of your search terms.

Figure 5.21A

Figure 5.21B

The potential drawback of the **Search Inside** function is the massive number of results that are sometimes returned—a quick search for **Atomic Energy Commission** returned over 50,000 hits. If you get too many results, refining your search terms either by adding additional words or changing your initial query will often reduce the number of results to a more manageable number. Note as well that the judicious use of quotation marks, especially for phrase searching, is particularly effective, much as we've seen for the previously mentioned online digital book sites.

With this in mind, let's go back and use the **Search Inside** function to look for information on the Atomic Energy Commission, only this time, we'll use quotation marks to indicate to the search engine that we are looking for a phrase. As seen in Figure 5.21B, searching this way results in a substantial change and produces results that are much more focused.

Viewing, Using, and Interpreting Your Results

Now that you're familiar with searching the Open Library, let's move on to viewing, using, and interpreting the results of your queries. Knowing how to effectively use returned results from searches done on the Open Library project catalog is an essential skill and one that you need to be familiar with. In this section, you'll examine the results of your searches as well as the individual elements that make up those results. And of course, along the way, you'll learn how it all relates to your patrons. You'll also learn some tips, tricks, and techniques that you can employ when using this in your everyday library duties.

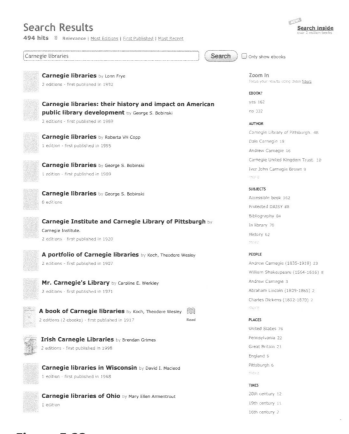

Figure 5.22

The Returned List

The initial results of your queries on the Open Library can be returned in different ways, depending in part on how the search was initially constructed and conducted. Let's go back to our standard search for information on Carnegie libraries. To start, go to the project homepage and enter a quick search in the basic search box—use the phrase **Carnegie libraries** without any specific limiters or changes. After typing in your search term, you'll see results similar to what is shown in Figure 5.22.

In this sample search, what are the major components of the results page? There are four distinct components for us to consider:

- List of titles
- Search modifiers
- Information strip
- Search box

Let's investigate each of these.

List of Titles

Obviously, the most important parts of the page are your results. After all, it's what you're looking for! However, it's what each result contains that can be the most helpful. First, you'll see cover images. Not all results will have them, but some of them will. If you are looking for a particular edition that might carry a specific cover or image on the cover, this is helpful. Other things you'll see on the list are the title, author, publish date, number of editions, and, if it exists, an additional small icon indicating the title may be read online. Notice in Figure 5.23 the icon for *A Book of Carnegie Libraries*, which indicates this is an online resource.

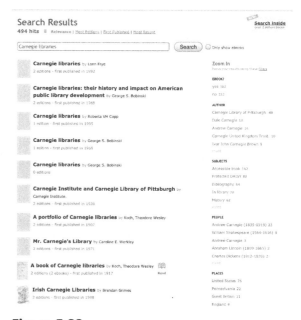

Figure 5.23

Search Modifiers

If you are not encouraged by your list of results, or the results are wildly inappropriate or out of range, you might assume the entire search should be redone. While that's certainly an option, before you resort to starting over, consider the search modifiers to the right of the returned results list as noted in Figure 5.24. Additional categories such as times, places, persons, and subjects often enable you to jump to the correct information or at least find some additional search terms that will help you get better results. For more details on restructuring your search this way, try the following informative link: http://openlibrary.org/search/howto.

Search Results

494 hits   ☰ Relevance | <u>Most Editions</u> | <u>First Published</u> | <u>Most Recent</u>

Figure 5.25

Information Strip

While the name I've given to this component is somewhat arbitrary, the information located in the information strip is not. Given any list of returned results, you can use the modifiers located here to see how many "hits" were returned and then sort your results via relevance, most editions, first published, and most recent—as you see in Figure 5.25.

Search Box

Finally, let's not forget the search box. You've already explored the Open Library's search box, and having it available in this page of returned results gives you a safety valve. If your initial research turned up nothing or gave results completely outside of what you were looking for, you can quickly redo your search from this point without having to go back to the initial search page. Note the option to look for only eBook titles.

Figure 5.26

Zoom In
Focus your results using these <u>filters</u>

EBOOK?
yes 162
no 332

AUTHOR
Carnegie Library of Pittsburgh. 48
Dale Carnegie 18
Andrew Carnegie 16
Carnegie United Kingdom Trust. 10
Ivor John Carnegie Brown 9
more

SUBJECTS
Accessible book 162
Protected DAISY 88
Bibliography 84
In library 70
History 62
more

PEOPLE
Andrew Carnegie (1835-1919) 23
William Shakespeare (1564-1616) 8
Andrew Carnegie 3
Abraham Lincoln (1809-1865) 2
Charles Dickens (1812-1870) 2
more

PLACES
United States 76
Pennsylvania 22
Great Britain 21
England 9
Pittsburgh 6
more

TIMES
20th century 12
19th century 11
16th century 2

Figure 5.24

Viewing Individual Results

Now that you've examined lists of returned results and how to manage them, let's take some time to look at individual results. What do these look like? What are the specific components that make up these individual results? How do you take these elements and use them in solving your or your patron's information query? To demonstrate the process, let's do some more sample searching that is concentrated on an individual title. We'll then show you each piece as it's presented on the screen.

Figure 5.27

Let's say you have a patron looking for information about the San Francisco earthquake and fire of 1906. After you direct the patron to the Open Library and do some initial searching, you come across a title that looks like it meets the patron's needs perfectly: *A History of the Earthquake and Fire in San Francisco*. Clicking on the title in the list of results, you are transported to the page for the book (see Figure 5.27).

What do you need to know about this page? What does it tell you about this particular title? Let's consider each part individually.

First, as noted in Figure 5.28, there's the title section. From here, you can see the title, author, edition, and even the last time this particular page was edited on the Open

A History Of The Earthquake And Fire In San
Francisco: An Account Of The Disaster Of April 18, 1906 i edition
By Frank W. Aitken

Figure 5.28

Library. Note that the author and edition information are linked, enabling you to click and find out more details, either about the author or the edition.

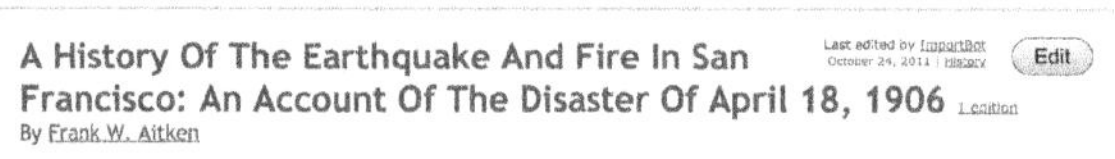

When you review the information about this particular edition, you will find almost complete bibliographic details, including call number, number of pages, and various identification numbers, ranging from the OCLC identifier to the Library of Congress control number. Note as well the Internet Archive inventory number. As noticed in Figure 5.29, having this level of detail is important, especially if you need a physical copy of the item. Jumping back to your original results page for this title, you'll see the same level of detail (as shown in Figures 5.30 and 5.31).

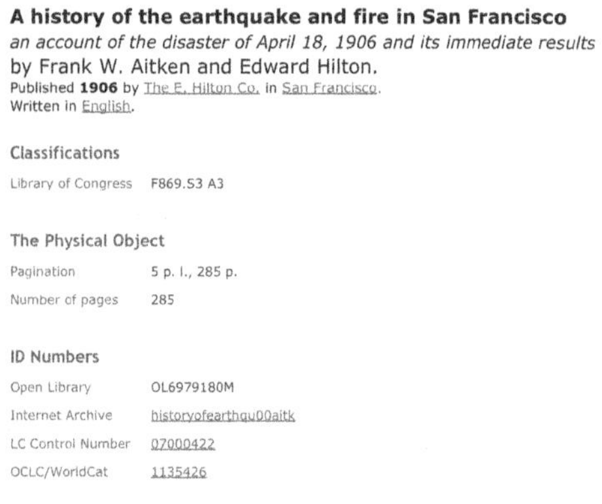

A history of the earthquake and fire in San Francisco
an account of the disaster of April 18, 1906 and its immediate results
by Frank W. Aitken and Edward Hilton.
Published **1906** by The E. Hilton Co. in San Francisco.
Written in English.

Classifications

Library of Congress   F869.S3 A3

The Physical Object

Pagination   5 p. l., 285 p.
Number of pages   285

ID Numbers

Open Library   OL6979180M
Internet Archive   historyofearthqu00aitk
LC Control Number   07000422
OCLC/WorldCat   1135426

Figure 5.29

Moving on to the right side of your results page for this title, is there any additional information that you can gather? Look at Figure 5.32, and you'll see cover information, the option to add this title to a list you may have created, the option to purchase the book, and multiple ways to view this resource online or in various eBook formats. This multiformat option, which we saw initially in the chapter on the Internet Archive, is one of the most useful features

Figure 5.30

Figure 5.31

of the Open Library. Because you and your patrons are using so many types of devices, this format flexibility is great. And don't overlook the outbound links to WorldCat,[5] which can be helpful in locating physical copies that might be near your library.

Viewing Titles Online

There is no doubt that device-specific digital content brings flexibility to your library, but sometimes you or the patron may just want to read online through the web browser. The Open Library, via the support structure of the Internet Archive, offers a quick method of doing so, as you can see in Figure 5.33.

This innovative web browser reader, known as the **Book-Reader**, while similar in some ways to other on-screen digital book readers we have already seen, has some unique and innovative features. At the top right corner of the reader are various controls for searching the resource, sharing the title you've found, turning the pages automatically, and reading out loud (see Figure 5.34).

Figure 5.33

Figure 5.34

Figure 5.32

The sharing options give you the ability to link to a particular title or page, or even embed the book in a webpage (see Figure 5.35). This linking can be useful, especially if there is a special program or local collection at your library that could be used in conjunction with titles found through the project. The same approach could be used for other library services as well, including class visits from local schools, summer reading programs, or other special library programs and services you may want to emphasize.

The read out loud feature, although perhaps not appropriate for the open areas of the library, can be useful to patrons who have vision difficulties or other conditions that prevent them from accessing the book through the browser.

Figure 5.35

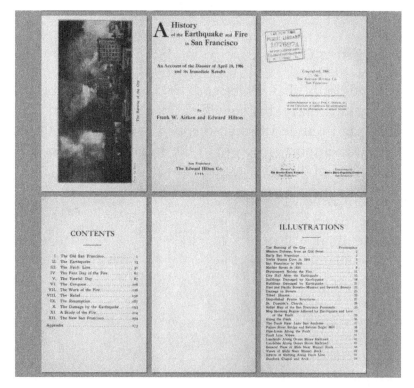

Figure 5.36

As you can see in Figure 5.36, page-viewing options abound. From thumbnails to zooming in and out on particular pages, this flexibility makes things easy to read. Don't forget the many search options as well. As you can see in the top right corner of the title, the BookReader software has the **Search Inside** capability, which enables you to query for specific words or phrases within the title. If you do use this option, your search results are illustrated on a timeline in the bottom of the BookReader software, as shown in Figures 5.37 and

5.38. These features can help patrons who might be looking for heavily formatted/illustrated titles or specific portions of text.

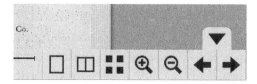

Figure 5.37

Finally, don't forget to mention to your staff and patrons that when searching, viewing, and further exploring these individual results, not all titles or resources mentioned in the Open Library are available in electronic format, either due to copyright restrictions or other limitations imposed by the resource provider. In

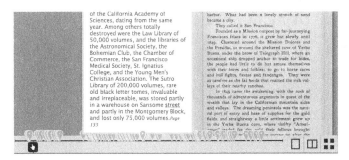

Figure 5.38

these instances, one might need to go back to the individual results page to find access through another library or bookseller.

Special Options and Other Projects

Innovation, improvements, changes. These terms can be said to aptly describe the many subprojects and special collections offered by the Open Library. Let's see what we can find. As we do this, you might want to consider the possibility of adapting some of these to be used in conjunction with what you or your library might currently be offering your patrons and community.

DAISY!

No, it's not just a flower. DAISY-formatted titles, as seen on the Open Library offer a great opportunity for many of your patrons who want to read but are struggling with health or vision issues that prevent this. What exactly is DAISY? According to the DAISY consortium website,[6] DAISY stands for Digital Accessible Information System, and it offers digital methods for reading books aloud, replacing or supplementing audio versions that you may already use in your library.

Endorsed by the National Library Service for the Blind and Physically Handicapped (NLS), this new form of access consists of encrypted book files and software to play audio of them. For more information on DAISY and the NLS, check the following link: http://www.loc.gov/nls/. You can also find information about implementing it on the Open Library at this link: http://openlibrary.org/subjects/protected_daisy#ebooks=true. It's important to note here that Open Library digital items that are available in DAISY formats have a special DAISY access icon (see Figure 5.39).

From a practical everyday standpoint, how could your patrons benefit from this service, especially if you have access to these titles via your library's online catalog? Think about your outreach services to those in the community. Many new doors might be opened to help your library become more valuable to your patrons as you address everyone's information needs!

Figure 5.39

Using the API

We've already discussed the application programming interface (API) options available via other online book sites, and you can rest assured that the same options are available for users of the Open Library. Providing more than just a single option, the Open Library offers a wide variety of APIs, from books to book covers and more. If you are technically inclined, the API option offers some great benefits that you can take advantage of for your library.

Using this option, your patrons can search your library's catalog, retrieve book covers, and even check to see if the Open Library has available copies—which is helpful in case your library's copy is checked out. With a recent development, you can even browse lists of titles on the Open Library website. For more direct information, check the following link: http://openlibrary.org/developers/api. This link also includes code examples and demonstrations of what possible results will look like.

Lending Library

One of the biggest issues in integrating any type of eBook into your library collection involves how to get the titles into your patrons' hands. Purchasing (or renting) eBooks with your own budget is certainly an option, and many libraries do this. However, the costs can be prohibitive in these days of highly restricted budgets. If you are looking at implementing this, first consider the options available via the Open Library.

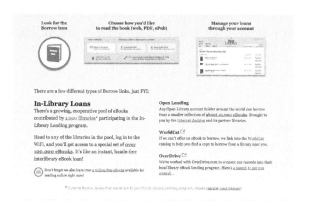

Figure 5.40

The project, in conjunction with the Internet Archive, now offers an innovative eBook lending program that you can use at your library. Via partnerships with libraries all across the country, your patrons can access the Open Library and check out eBook titles of all types, as noted in Figure 5.40. To get started, look for program details at these links: http://www.archive.org/post/349420/in-library-ebook-lending-program-launched and http://openlibrary.org/borrow/about.

Let's look at a practical example of how this could work for your library. Assume you have a patron looking for information on the topic of historical and famous French artists, art, and painters in particular. Unfortunately, your local collection, while possessing items on the subject in general, does not go into enough depth to meet the patron's needs. While it's certainly possible to steer your patron to a different library or the Internet and a favorite search engine, how could using the Open Library help instead?

Navigating to the project site, and using various keyword and phrase searches, after a while you find for your patron a particular title called *The Masterpieces of French Painting from the Metropolitan Museum of Art, 1800–1920*. At this point, using the Open Library free-to-acquire public account, your patron could check out this eBook and be reading it on his device of choice in a matter of minutes. What are the specific details in how this process works?

Because we've already located our title, the next step is for the patron to log in to the Open Library. If they already have an account, this is easy, but if they don't, you just need to walk them through creating their account, coming back to this title page, and then signing in. Once logged in, your patron will have the option to read the title within the browser screen using the BookReader software, download a PDF copy to his device of choice, or download an ePub-formatted title. Note that for this particular book, your patron will also have to install a small additional piece of software called Adobe Digital Editions[7] to read the title. This is the same software that you may already use in your library for DRM or vendor-based eBook titles, and it has gained wide acceptance in the library world. Once this is done, your patron will have the information he needs, and your library has been successful!

While what we have seen is just one small example, imagine multiplying this many times a day! By finding this resource for your patron via the Open Library, your library has saved money (instead of having to purchase or borrow the title in question), and your patron comes away with a favorable impression of the library!

Important Points to Remember about the Open Library

Now that you've explored the Open Library at least initially, you've hopefully found the information enlightening, useful, and applicable. The project is amazing, especially if we contrast its approach with the other eBook sites already mentioned. From the many formats offered to the ease of use in searching and utilizing the digital resources, it's a worthy addition to your collection! What follows are some important points to help you remember the Open Library project. Use these as starting points for your own training and patron education needs.

Origins, Sites and Catalogs

- The Open Library is a project of the Internet Archive, the California Digital Library, and other strategic partners

- In addition to digital books and other materials, the Open Library is an online user-extensible catalog, similar in many ways to your local ILS

- Book lending is available and includes partnerships with both OverDrive and OCLC

- Individual users can log in and create, update, and otherwise edit existing source material pages

Site Structure, Materials, and Components

- Both basic and advanced searching options area available for use

- User-created collections, known as lists can help you quickly gather and collate similar materials

- Material formats are both physical *and* digital!

- Digital formats include a multiplicity of options, from ePub to plain text, HTML, and vendor-based formats

Searching the Open Library

- Basic and advanced searching options include traditional author, title, and subject options

- Boolean logic and indicator searching is supported, as are with nested queries

- Specific search options exist for both subjects and authors

- The Open Library offers in-material searching via the **Search Inside** option

- Linked and related searching options are available within specific results

Viewing, Using, and Interpreting Your Results

- Search results can be ranked via relevance, publish date, number of editions, and other options

- If allowed, individual results can be downloaded in a wide variety of formats including Kindle-supported files, ePub, text, HTML, and other formats

- Results can be read online through the web browser using the Internet Archive's Book-Reader software

Special Options and Other Projects

- DAISY-formatted digital books can be downloaded for free by your patrons

- Various data and book API options exist to either develop an interface to the Open Library or to pull down book data and other information

- Lending library options exist for many libraries across the country

Questions for You to Try

The Open Library, in partnership with the Internet Archive and other organizations, is one of the few resources that go well beyond providing standard digital eBook materials. From its online user-editable catalog to the **Search Inside** function, this tremendous resource can be of great value to you, your library, and your patrons. However, the Open Library can also be confusing, especially if you have little experience searching and otherwise using the site on a daily basis.

If you'd like to increase your knowledge of the Open Library, use the following questions to test yourself and become more familiar with the project. Take a few minutes to see if you can answer the questions. Answers can be found at the back of the book, so if you get stuck, feel free to sneak a peek. Note that there are many ways to answer to these questions, and you might have an alternative method of getting the same results. That's perfectly fine because the goal here is to help you familiarize yourself with the site.

Site Structure and Materials

1. Considering the design of the Open Library website, what would be the best method of conducting a subject search for a patron looking for any sort of information on the Cuban Missile Crisis?

2. One of the biggest strengths of the Open Library is the ability to have the Internet Archive provide many of the digital materials mentioned in its catalog. With this in mind, find two to three digital resource materials for a patron looking both for ePub and Amazon Kindle–based formats. Second, find a DAISY-formatted source. Why would or wouldn't your patrons be able to use this particular format if they wanted to?

3. How are OverDrive and OCLC used within the Open Library and the Internet Archive? Do you think the inclusion of these commercial and nonprofit organizations helps or hinders the Open Library project? Does this influence how your patrons will search for and use titles they may find on the Open Library?

Searching the Open Library

1. Using any combination of search techniques, find a list of titles from the author Evelyn C. White about the famous African American Pulitzer Prize winning author Alice Walker. How many did you find? Are there any special formats available?

2. You're working at the reference desk, and a student comes to you looking for downloadable digital resources on oil spills. Your online journals database is not accessible,

which leaves the Open Library as your sole source. How would you conduct the search and why?

3. Using the **Search Inside** function of the Open Library, look for a list of titles about Judy Garland. Why do some titles turn out to be false hits? Is there a better method of using the **Search Inside** function for information on a particular topic?

4. In this chapter, you've learned about linking options within lists of records or individual results. These are clickable links to other resources that can help you either expand what you're looking for or quickly zero in on a particular bit of information. Are these functions helpful? Give two examples you have found of these links being useful for you or a patron.

Viewing, Using, and Interpreting Your Results

1. Using your answers from question 1 in **Searching the Open Library**, how could you help a patron locate a copy to purchase?

2. Search for the *Iliad* on the Open Library. How many editions are available to read online or download? What if your patron wanted to read a copy on her Kindle—what's the best method of doing so from within the Open Library?

3. Your patron comes to you just as your library is closing, looking for a particular title by Carl Sandburg. The only part of the title he remembers is *Slabs of the Sunburnt West*. Find the title and then explain how you would show your patron he could read this title online through his web browser at home. Are there any other formats available that he could use?

Notes

1. Aaron Swartz, http://www.aaronsw.com/.
2. Open Library, http://openlibrary.org/about.
3. Open Library, http://blog.openlibrary.org.
4. Internet Archive, http://blog.archive.org/2011/06/25/in-library-ebook-lending-program-expands-to-1000-libraries/.
5. OCLC WorldCat, http://www.oclc.org/worldcat/.
6. Daisy.org, http://www.daisy.org/about_us.
7. Adobe, http://www.adobe.com/products/digital-editions.html.

Resources

Now that you've had the opportunity to learn about the Open Library, spend some time on the site learning more, use these digital materials and technologies, and offer them to your patrons. The following resources can help you get started with implementing the project at your library and helping your patrons.

Origins, Sites and Catalogs

Literary Tourist, "Brewster Kahl Talks about the Open Library Project," http://literarytourist.com/2006/02/brewster-kahl-talks-about-the-open-library-project/.

Raw Thought (Aaron Swartz), "Announcing the Open Library," http://www.aaronsw.com/weblog/openlibrary.

Site Structure, Materials, Components, and Search

LibraryJournal.com, "Internet Archive Offers One Million Works for the Blind and Print Impaired," http://www.libraryjournal.com/article/CA6728034.html.

Openlibrary.org, "In Library Lending," http://openlibrary.org/subjects/in_library#ebooks=true.

Open Library Blog, "New BookReader," http://blog.openlibrary.org/2010/12/09/new-bookreader/.

Reviews, News, and More!

LibraryJournal.com, "The Open Library Is Opening Room for Debate," http://www.libraryjournal.com/lj/newsletters/newsletterbucketacademicnewswire/885595-440/the_open_library_is_opening.html.csp.

Wired.com, "Africa's Past Landscapes Revealed in Historical Travel Accounts," http://www.wired.com/wiredscience/2011/09/travel-writing-conservation/?pid=2064&pageid=72411.

Chapter 6

But What about the Others?

There Are Many, Many More!

Having had a chance to examine and use the **Big Four** online digital book sites, in this chapter you will learn about some of the other unique digital book sites that are also available. Adding depth and breadth to your library's collection for patrons and staff alike, you will find these sites, although smaller, are not limited to just classic fiction or the more familiar authors' works. In fact, you can find a wide variety of reading resources, from bestsellers and popular classics to governmental information and more. A whole spectrum of digital resources is waiting to be found for your library and patrons' use.

In this chapter, you'll examine some of these other sites, gaining background information on them as well as an overview of how each works. The chapter then concludes with everyday practical examples of how you can use these sites to answer common reference and other patron questions. But before we get into the specifics, however, let me introduce you to a librarian named Frank.

Still Can't Find It!

It was going to be a long day. The kid was heading for the reference desk, and Frank, currently on duty for the morning shift, wished he could duck out, go back to the stacks, and

(continued)

(*continued*)

hide. This kid was driving him crazy! He'd been in seven times this week, continually coming to the reference desk and asking about a science fiction series he had learned about in an online fan fiction forum. Frank had checked the library catalog and even asked the librarian responsible for the interlibrary loan program about the title in question, but the particular series was too obscure, didn't exist, or had never been bought by the usual range of libraries that they borrowed from. Even Amazon didn't stock the title. A science fiction fan himself, Frank hated disappointing the kid, but at this point he wasn't sure what else to do.

Just as the kid was about to reach the desk, Frank saw the pamphlet he had placed in the Ready Reference file. He'd picked it up at a conference on eBooks last week, and he thought he remembered something in it that mentioned a site that specialized in science fiction eBook downloads. Frank opened the pamphlet and saw the name again: the Baen Free Library. Maybe he could help the kid find what he was looking for after all!

Many Others

Frank's story is a scenario based on real situations faced by many librarians and staff today. We've all been there with our patrons looking for a title, a source of information, a bit of data—and have not been able to find anything. But with the advent of online digital eBook resources, we now have a better chance of finding that elusive answer.

However when doing so, it's easy to think only of the bigger sites like Google Books, HathiTrust, or even the Internet Archive when considering how to solve our patrons' information needs. But we shouldn't get tunnel vision and overlook the many more options that also exist with these other sites, which often contain a veritable treasure trove of unfound resources that would be equally useful.

It's not just content that makes these smaller sites invaluable for your library. Not bound by convention or standard structure, many of these other sites offer unique methods of delivery or presentation for the materials they do contain. Let's examine one site in particular: DailyLit.

While it contains some of the same resources that you can find at Google Books, Hathi-Trust and others, DailyLit also provides access to these digital resources in innovative ways these large sites have yet to employ, in particular utilizing email and RSS as the primary delivery method. Given today's on-the-go lifestyle, what a better method of opening access—information when and where you want it! While patrons may not have time to sit down with you at your public PC area and spend time exploring Google Books,

Figure 6.1

they probably do have time to check their email while on a break at work or at soccer practice with the kids.

Consider as well Project Gutenberg, one of the first and foremost eBook resource sites on the Internet. Well known for public domain content and easy availability, this project also features innovations such as topical bookshelves and the unique **Sheet Music Project**, which contains vast amounts of digitized sheet music just waiting to be used. Technology and library pundits often overlook smaller improvements and innovations such as these, yet they can be a boon to libraries looking for this type of information.

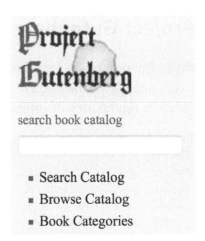

Figure 6.2

Of course, as inventive and nimble as these smaller sites are, they sometimes lack the extensive software and usage options found on the larger sites. It seems to be a balance of sorts, that is, innovation versus resources. And that's an important distinction that you, your staff, and your patrons should be aware of. As you examine each of the smaller sites profiled in this chapter, be sure to take the time to work with each one, becoming aware of the advantages and disadvantages, in delivery as well as overall balance and availability of online titles. If you're thinking about offering these sites to your patrons and making them part of your ongoing digital strategy, consider offering classes or one-on-one instruction so that your patrons (and staff) can learn how to use them successfully.

Take a few moments to examine Table 6.1. It contains the name, uniform resource locator (URL), and typical eBook formats of the sites we will be discussing in this chapter. By no means complete, it gives you a glimpse of what you can expect as you review each one. Also, don't forget the resources listed at the back of the chapter, where you'll find some excellent links and added information that can help as well.

Table 6.1 Other Digital eBook Sites

Site	URL	eBook Format
Project Gutenberg	http://www.gutenberg.org/	Online viewer, PDF, ePub, text
ManyBooks	http://www.manybooks.net/	Online viewer
Daily Lit	http://www.dailylit.com/	Email, RSS, other
ibiblio	http://www.ibiblio.org/	Online viewer, PDF, text, many formats
Baen Free Library	http://www.baen.com/library/	PDF, text, many formats

For now, let's get started and look at the individually profiled resources!

Project Gutenberg

Probably one of the best-known and popular sites for digital resources and eBook downloads outside of the bigger sites already mentioned, Project Gutenberg maintains a special place in the history of online book sites. From its origins in the early days of the Internet to its presence today, this site is firmly entrenched as one of the first places to go for information and eBooks. Today, Project Gutenberg continues to add resources and innovate new ideas, increasing everyone's access to knowledge.

Figure 6.3

In this section, you'll learn about the origins of Project Gutenberg as well as its scope. From there, you will learn the basics of searching as well as methods of integrating these resources into your everyday library work.

Background

Known well by most people in the library profession, Project Gutenberg's origins can be traced back to the early 1970s and the late Michael Hart, according to information found on the project's site. Freely available online at http://www.gutenberg.org, Project Gutenberg offers over 40,000 free titles.[1] The project's mission statement fits right into the heart of the digital eBook content covered so far in our research: "To encourage the creation and distribution of eBooks."[2] This philosophy of of free use combined with the many ways one can search, download, and use the available titles are what make this project great.

Scope

So what types of resources can you find at Project Gutenberg? According to information found on Project Gutenberg's website,[3] the three main categories of digital resources include:

- Easy reading, known on the site as "Light Literature"

- Scholarly resources and more, known on the site as "Heavy Literature"

- Reference materials, known on the site as "References"

Within these three categories, you can find titles as well known as the *King James Bible* to more esoteric works such as *The Old English Physiologus*. You can also find works of well-known authors such as Wodehouse, Grahame, and Austen. Of course, you can also rediscover thousands of other fiction and nonfiction authors and titles waiting to be found and read again!

Search and Results

Given this vast array of resources available at Project Gutenberg, what's the best way for you and your patrons to find information? There are many ways to use the site. You can start by simply looking for a book (i.e., browse the catalog for titles), or you can view bookshelves of materials grouped by subjects such as poetry, adventure, Harvard Classics, and more. However, the best method is utilizing the search options offered by the project.

Let's illustrate this by performing a quick search on the site for the classic author, Mark Twain, as seen in Figure 6.4.

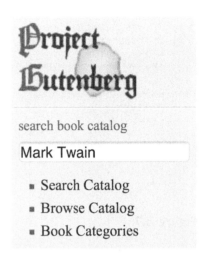

search book catalog

Mark Twain

- Search Catalog
- Browse Catalog
- Book Categories

Figure 6.4

Using the search box located on the top left of the site, and putting in your query of **Mark Twain**, your returned results include an author listing, multiple subject listings, and more than 200 profiled titles, as seen in Figure 6.5.

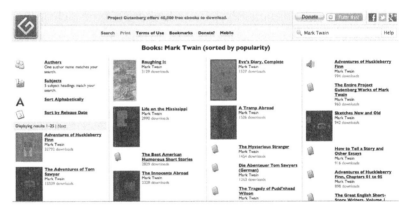

Figure 6.5

Now revise your search to the other name we know this popular author by: Samuel Clemens. Your returned results now reveal 217 different listings, with options to sort results by popularity, alphabetically, or even by release date, as shown in Figure 6.6. Note that it's also possible to see how many downloads there are, which is a good indicator of the type of resource that you might be looking for.

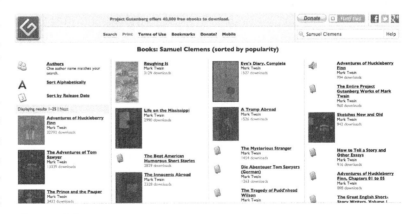

Figure 6.6

When you click on any of these titles, you are taken to the page for the selected edition (see Figure 6.7).

Figure 6.7

Figure 6.8

At this point, if a specific title has been selected, you have other options to consider, including reading the title online or downloading it for later use by choosing a wide variety of available eBook formats. Project Gutenberg's many selections of file types are great for library patrons, especially considering the many different eReaders and formats currently on the market.

As you can see from Figure 6.8, some of these popular formats include HTML, Kindle, ePub, and even plain text. You might even notice a few older and more obscure formats as well.

Figure 6.9

In addition to the quick search box that's located on every page of the site, Project Gutenberg offers alternative (and quite detailed) searching methods. For this approach to searching, you can go directly to the online catalog by clicking on **Search Catalog**.[4] Once there, you will see options to search by popularity, the latest added titles, or even random works if you or your patrons are feeling adventuresome. Look at Figure 6.9 for an example of the main search page.

As you examine the page, notice the main search box at the top right. This is where your detailed investigations can begin. It is easy to use, and you can type words or phrases to begin looking for titles or information. Use the **Help** button to see all of the detailed methods in which you can search, including author, title, subject, category, and even Boolean operators.

Consider, for example, a patron who comes to your reference desk and needs eBook titles about Sherlock Holmes for his iPhone. Let's see what titles are available to help him out. Navigate to the project, go to the search box at the top right of the page, and type the following: **s. Sherlock Holmes**. See Figure 6.10 for example results.

The results of your search are sorted by popularity but also include options to look at different subjects, sort by date, or sort even alphabetically. Selecting any of these other topics will give you the same results but will show them in different ways. Notice as well the different types of materials available on the site, seen by the icons

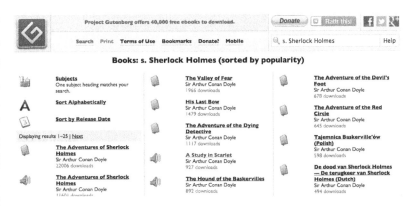

Figure 6.10

in front of each title. For the most part these are eBooks, but there are audio formats as well. This is a great option for you to consider for your library, and it would be easy to integrate into your regular spoken book or audio collection as an additional resource.

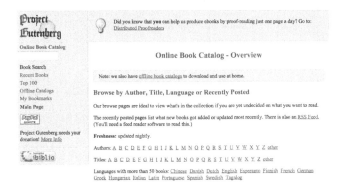

Figure 6.11

Browsing the project's catalog is another way to search for titles. You can find it online here: http://www .gutenberg.org/catalog. Similar in many ways to the regular **Book Search** option, the page is arranged a bit differently, as shown in Figure 6.11. In particular, notice the A-to-Z arrangement of author and title, language categories, and listings of the latest additions to the database. While perhaps not as searchable for specific needs, this is a great option for patrons who just might be looking for something new or unusual to read.

Tools and Other Options

While it's certainly easy to think of Project Gutenberg only as a great resource for eBooks and audio as shown earlier, there are some special parts to the site that you should not overlook either. These include:

- Offline catalogs
- "Top 100" titles
- MARC
- Online bookshelves

Let's look more closely at each of these.

Figure 6.12

Offline Catalogs

It's easy to open a web browser or mobile device and navigate to Project Gutenberg to search for a particular subject, author, or title, but sometimes going online isn't an option. If you are ever faced with this situation, Project Gutenberg offers a great feature called offline catalogs. As seen in Figure 6.12, the link is available at http://www.gutenberg.org/wiki/ Gutenberg:Offline_Catalogs. Here you can find online websites that offer complete backups of the project as well as the GUTINDEX. The GUTINDEX provides a complete listing of all titles in the database and includes information about each. The index is also available by year.

Figure 6.13

Top 100

Everyone loves a good story or a new book to read. With this in mind, you might consider emphasizing to your patrons the listing of the top 100 titles on Project Gutenberg, as noted in Figure 6.13. You can find the link at http://www.gutenberg.org/browse/scores/top. Clicking this will take you to the top 100 eBooks and authors from the previous day, week, and even month. If your library wants to emphasize a particular eBook concept, perhaps a subject or topic that your patrons are interested in or that seems to be trending, you can use this method to get started. If you are a special or business library, this could be a way to reinforce your local collection. For patrons, it's a great way to browse and see what others are reading and downloading.

MARC

MARC records still form the foundation of any modern library catalog. Your catalogers use them every day, and the backbone of your library's ILS rests on them. With this in mind, it's easy to add Project Gutenberg's MARC records into your library's own system for use. MARC downloads provide a great way to quickly enhance your current catalog, or they can be used in conjunction with other library projects you may be working on.

To get started, you can use the offline catalogs link[5] or just access the records directly at http://www.gutenberg.org/feeds/catalog.marc.bz2. If you decide to use this feature, note that the MARC files will be in zipped format, and you will need to uncompress them before you use them. Once done, these records can be viewed with any text editor or your favorite MARC editor (e.g., MarcEdit[6]) if you prefer (as shown in Figure 6.14). An alternate method of importing these records also exists, utilizing the data via the XML/RDF formats (see http://ebooks.adelaide.edu.au/meta/pg/ for a detailed explanation). While not as common as MARC, XML and other formats help to address changes in cataloging and indexing that libraries are just now coming to grips with.

```
035  __  (PGUSA)32572
040  __  PGUSA ‡b eng
042  __  dc
100  1_  Andersen, H. C., 1805–1875 ‡q (Hans Christian)
245  10  Hans Andersen's Fairy Tales
Second Series ‡h [electronic resource] / ‡c by H. C., 1805–1875 Andersen; edited by J.H. Stickney;
illustrated by Edna F. Hart
260  __  ‡b Project Gutenberg, ‡c 2010
500  __  Project Gutenberg
506  __  Freely available.
516  __  Electronic text
700  1_  Stickney, J.H., ‡e Editor
700  1_  Hart, Edna F., ‡e Illustrator
830  _0  Project Gutenberg ‡v 32572
856  40  ‡u http://www.gutenberg.org/etext/32572
856  42  ‡u http://www.gutenberg.org/license ‡3 Rights
```

Figure 6.14

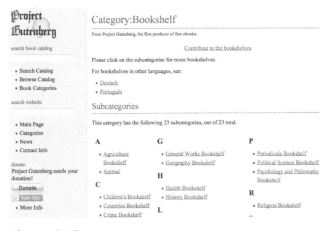

Figure 6.15

Online Bookshelves

If you've ever worked at a reference desk, you know that browsing the shelves is an essential process in assisting patrons with their information needs, especially when the resource a patron is looking for is already checked out or is missing. Project Gutenberg offers a similar approach via online bookshelves for browsing. Available at http://www.gutenberg.org/wiki/Category:Bookshelf, the bookshelves offer categories for searching as well as individual pages on a variety of topics.

Similar in some ways to the collections features of HathiTrust and the online bookshelves offered by Google Books, this bookshelves option within Project Gutenberg often includes much more information, with lists of topics and outbound links to related subjects in the Project Gutenberg catalog. With collections on subjects ranging from science and technology to wars, language, and even periodicals, this is a great way for you or your patrons to quickly find resources on a single topic. Click on the starting link, and you will be taken to any of the sublinks you choose. From there, you can navigate to more specific resources as needed.

As an example, let's do a topic search for books or resources on adventures and adventuring. Navigate to the **Bookshelf** page or simply click the **Book Categories** from the site menu. Once there, click on **Adventure**. As you will see, well-known authors such as Jack London and Robert Louis Stevenson appear, as do popular titles ranging from the classic *Count of Monte Cristo* to Edgar Rice Burroughs's famous Tarzan series and others. Notice as well the integration of social media resources such as Facebook, Twitter, and Google +. If your library is using these social media sites, this is a great method to bring patrons back to your own public pages and even your online catalog.

For now, let's select a title from our list of books on adventure. Notice the individual listings for the title you have picked. You will see various formats to choose from as well as bibliographic information and a QR code listing. Used by many in the library world, the QR code, if scanned with a patron's mobile device, takes the user directly the mobile version of Project Gutenberg and the specific title. Using QR codes in conjunction with your own library's mobile projects is a great way to go that extra mile for your patrons, and it would be easy to integrate these codes into any sort of library program or collection development process. For more information about the use of QR codes in your library, try the following link: http://www.libsuccess.org/index.php?title=QR_Codes.

Mobile Version

Today's patrons are more on the go more than ever, and as such they expect their library to be available on the go as well. With this in mind, Project Gutenberg has an easy-to-use mobile site that you can tell your patrons about. As noted in Fig. 6.16A, it has options to view the latest additions as well as popular titles. The site worked well on my iPad as well as my smart phone. Searching the mobile site is easy, and you can use the same advanced searching process that you

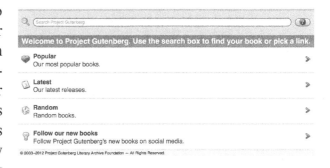

Figure 6.16A

do on the full site. To get started using the mobile site, simply navigate to http://m.gutenberg .org. Do some sample searches and view the available options to acquaint yourself with how things work.

Once you've done this, step back and think about how your patrons would perform this same process. What sort of training would help them in the use of this mobile catalog? How could your library assist in this process? Look at individual results of your own searching on the mobile site, and note in Figure 6.16B the individual title pages that are listed in the mobile catalog. Including the subject headings as well

Figure 6.16B

as the additional topic links toward the bottom, it is easy to get a variety of formats for reading as well as jump to other related titles by subject, author, and so on. How could your library assist patrons who might be unfamiliar with this process?

Figure 6.17A

DailyLit

DailyLit is another innovative site you should be aware of as well. While certainly not on the same scale as HathiTrust or some of the other larger sites profiled so far, DailyLit has an innovative approach and many interesting eBook titles for yourself and your patrons. In this section, you'll find out what makes this site so successful as well as how to search it, under-

stand your results, and then use it in your library.

About

Founded by Susan Danziger and freely available to all, DailyLit offers a great mix of both current and classic fiction that is easily accessible across all types of mobile devices and computers as noted in Figure 6.17B. Although recently acquired by Plympton (http://plympton.com/) in early 2013, DailyLit has a unique approach to viewing and reading books and other resources. As noted in on the DailyLit blog,[7] books chosen by users are delivered in bits and pieces over email or RSS on a schedule of the user's choosing, unlike the more traditional method of downloading an entire title at once.

Figure 6.17B

Getting started is easy. Navigate to the home page at http://www.dailylit.com. Once there, you can search for titles, authors, and even subject categories. After you find an interesting title or two, register to use the service and then subscribe to the title(s) you have found. Once done, your selection(s) will begin to appear in your email inbox or RSS reader on the starting date that you have set. Not just a singular option, notice in Figure 6.18A that these settings are completely customizable, including options for the length of the book section delivered as well as day of the week and time.

While at first glance this seems like a great way to catch up on some personal reading, you might be wondering how DailyLit would ever apply to library use. After all, it is a smaller site with fewer titles and fewer options than the bigger digital book sites we've already profiled.

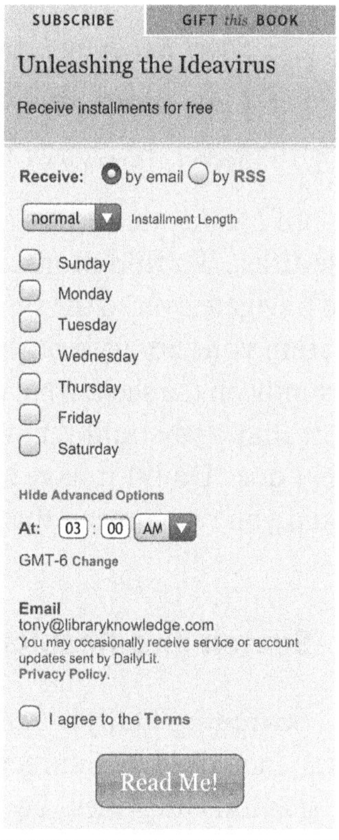

Figure 6.18A

Be that as it may, the real usefulness of DailyLit becomes apparent when you see it as an easily accessed resource that can back up your local paper-based collection. Delivered on your patrons' schedules and containing both current and classic fiction, this is a resource that could easily be brought into your library's workflow. Beyond using it as a digital resource, think about other ways DailyLit could be applied to programs and other group events at your library. Do you have book groups meeting? How about school classes? DailyLit is also natural fit for busy professionals and even students reading required titles for class.

Scope

What sort of digital materials can you find on DailyLit, and how many titles are currently available? As of early 2013, DailyLit had more than 950 titles listed on the site, which provide a wide variety of reading for your patrons to enjoy. Titles include:

- *The Wisdom of (Steve) Jobs*[8]
- *Seth Godin: Unboxed*[9]
- *With a Little Help* (Cory Doctorow)[10]

Classic works found on DailyLit include:

- *Short Reads by Edgar Allen Poe*[11]
- *Little Women*[12]
- *Secret Adversary* (Agatha Christie)[13]

Of course, this is just a small sample of all available titles. To find more, take a few moments now and navigate over to the site. What can you find? Considering your library's physical collection and what is currently on the shelf, what electronic titles are on DailyLit that you could recommend for your patrons? What does DailyLit have that your library does not? Could you recommend this site to your patrons?

Search and Results

Searching DailyLit can be done in a variety of ways, including by indirect browsing or just viewing the site and categories. To browse by title, author, or some other category, simply click the links available on the site's homepage at http://www.dailylit.com.

Robin Hood: How Robin Hood Became an Outlaw: Chapter 1
by J. WALKER MCSPADDEN

5 Installments—Entirely free (Preview)

MEMBERS' RATING: ●●●●● from 7 Ratings and 3 Reviews

TAGS: Adventure, Classics, Short Stories

Figure 6.18B

Figure 6.19

Categories

Category		Category		Category	
Adventure	28	German	17	Norwegian	4
African American	10	Greek	21	Novel	248
Architecture	2	Health	1	Novella	7
Arts	12	Historical	8	Outdoors	1
Austrian	2	History	32	Parenting	4
Autobiography	18	Holiday	5	Philosophy	18
Banned Books	33	Horror	11	Poetry	57
Biography	39	Humor	11	Politics	9
Book Samplers	9	In French	42	Psychology	8
Business	18	In German	11	Quotations	5
Children's	30	In Italian	3	Reference	6
Chinese	1	In Spanish	3	Religion	18
Christianity	11	Investing	4	Romance	14
Classics	604	Italian	7	Russian	15
Comedy	22	Khan Academy	19	Satire	13
Contemporary	107	Languages	4	Science Fiction	36
Cooking	7	Law	2	Self-Help	14
Crime	8	Lectures	1	Short Stories	122
Culture	19	Literary Criticism	2	Social Sciences	6
Diet	2	Management	9	Spanish	5
Drama	66	Math	9	Sports	3
Economics	8	Media	7	Swedish	6
Education	19	Medieval	1	Thriller	9
Entertainment	4	Memoir	5	Travel	6
Environmentalism	2	Men	50	War	5
Essay	8	Military	3	Wikipedia Tours	36
Fantasy	2	Motherhood	2	Women	43
Feminism	3	Mystery	36	Women's Fiction	18
Food and Drink	6	Nature	4		
French	70	Non-Fiction	68		

Figure 6.20

From here, selecting either the title or the author link sends you to a page of specific details, where you can sort your results by title, author, release date, popularity, and length. You can also view either basic or detailed levels of information for each book. On these same pages, note the option to view by genre, which is a nice addition (see Figure 6.20).

If you choose to use the categories option on DailyLit, as shown in Figure 6.20, you will get a numerical count of available titles on a wide selection of subjects. Ranging from common biographies to more esoteric subjects such as **Wikipedia Tours**, it's a great way for your patrons to look for something not so specific. Once you select a category, you are transported to a subcategory page, where you can sort results to include a basic or detailed view. You can also view links to the online member forums or see a list of newly added titles.

If you choose to directly search DailyLit via the site search option, you can input your query in a variety of methods, either by title, author, or keyword. Results are returned in a list showing title, author, and the number of parts the title has been divided up into that will be delivered either via email or RSS.

As you can see in Figure 6.21, an additional browsing option appears to the right of your search results, which if further searching is required can help you quickly drill down to a specific resource.

Figure 6.21

Other Tools and Features

DailyLit also contains other options and features that may interest you and your library. These include title reviews, user forums, and even a question of the week. While not directly related to the library, these offer you ways to interact with your patrons and ensure they are finding the information they are looking for while at the same time utilizing the resources available on the site. Users of DailyLit have full control over how their profiles appear, as seen in Figure 6.22, and if your library has an institutional account, you can share information via Twitter and Facebook, enabling titles that you have selected to show up on your page or feed. This ability to share information is a great way to emphasize particular library programming or just a certain part of your library's collection.

Figure 6.22

While this is just a short investigation of the DailyLit site, make sure to stop by and get acquainted with its many features and see if this might make a worthy addition to the electronic resources your library is already offering.

ManyBooks, ibiblio, and Others

Figure 6.23

From big to small and even in between, online book sites all employ different search options, different titles, and different delivery methods for connecting users with digital content. While it's virtually impossible to mention every site now available, a few more of these smaller and/or specialized sites that might be of interest to your library are worth mentioning. Let's take a specific look at the following: ManyBooks, ibiblio, and the Baen Free Library.

ManyBooks

Containing more than 29,000 free resources for use by your library and patrons, the ManyBooks site is a valuable addition to your portfolio of online book sites. Available at http://www.manybooks.net, the site contains a wide variety of titles that should fit nicely into your library's digital strategy. While not built on the same scale as Google Books or HathiTrust, this site contains many digital titles that are not easily found elsewhere, including magazines and audio links.

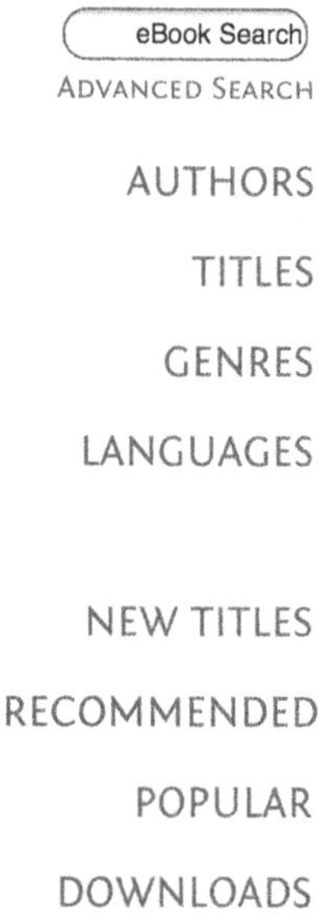

eBook Search
ADVANCED SEARCH
AUTHORS
TITLES
GENRES
LANGUAGES

NEW TITLES
RECOMMENDED
POPULAR
DOWNLOADS

Figure 6.24

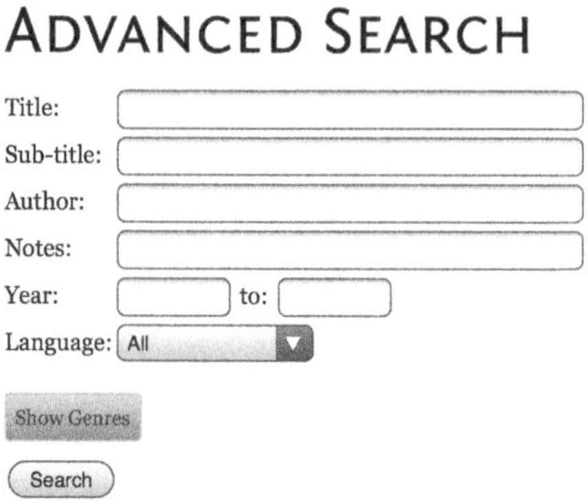

Searching

One of the strengths of the ManyBooks site lies in the different search options that are available. For quick basic searching, the search box on the left side of the site allows you to enter phrases, keywords, or other bits of information, as seen in Figure 6.24.

ADVANCED SEARCH

Title:
Sub-title:
Author:
Notes:
Year: [ ] to: [ ]
Language: [All ▼]

Show Genres
Search

Figure 6.25

As you can see in Figure 6.25, the advanced search options available on the site include title, author, notes, language, and even searching by year. You can stack your search qualifiers to get a more comprehensive and granular search, which is especially important if you are looking for a specific title. However, remember to use this option with discretion unless you are certain about the title or author. Sometimes I found searching too specifically resulted in zero results.

One compelling feature in the advanced search options is the ability to search via genre, as seen in Figure 6.26. This is a great way to find related materials or just something new to read. It's even possible to leave the search fields completely empty and just choose a particular category. Results will then include every title within the chosen category and will provide both the title and the author.

If you find something this way, you can quickly choose the specific book and go directly to its download page. Once there, you can find more specific details such as word count, download counts, the year it was added to the site, and even a thumbnail cover image if available. As discussed previously, this makes ManyBooks a great backup to your library's physical collection, giving you options to present to your patrons when their requested titles are checked out or otherwise unavailable for use.

Don't overlook some of the other tools available on ManyBooks, including **Book of the Week**, user recommendations, and even the reviews. The **Book of the Week** is great for introducing new titles, which you can then direct patrons to explore similar titles held at your library. User recommendations and reviews can help patrons who are undecided about reading a particular title, even if they've spotted it on your shelf in physical form.

Finally, one especially great feature is the cover browsing option. Available at http://www.manybooks.net/covers.php, this can breathe life into titles that your readers otherwise might not venture to try. Similar to browsing the new release shelves at your library, your patrons will find this option irresistible. If you pair this with your local physical collection, either via the library's website or by signage within the library, you can emphasize themes, authors, and even particular subjects that your patrons might find interesting.

ibiblio

While most of the sites profiled so far have emphasized a singular approach to digital materials, offering them via reading online or

GENRES

Browse Library of Congress Categories.

Adventure	Music
African-American Studies	Mystery/Detective
Art	Myth
Audiobook	Nature
Banned Books	Nautical
Biography	Non-fiction
Business	Occult
Canadian Literature	Periodical
Classic	Philosophy
Computers	Pirate Tales
Cooking	Poetry
Correspondence	Politics
Creative Commons	Post-1930
Criticism	Psychology
Drama	Pulp
Espionage	Random Selection
Essays	Reference
Etiquette	Religion
Fantasy	Romance
Fiction and Literature	Satire
Games	Science
Gay/Lesbian	Science Fiction
Ghost Stories	Sexuality
Gothic	Short Story
Government Publication	Short Story Collection
Harvard Classics	Thriller
Health	Travel

Figure 6.26

ibiblio

BROWSE SHARE SOFTWARE PROJECTS DONATE ABOUT HELP

Figure 6.27

downloading eBooks, ibiblio is different both in approach and types of materials that are available. Although offering eBooks and other digital titles, ibiblio also serves as the host site for other projects and software. Available at http://www.ibiblio .org/, ibiblio is currently maintained through a partnership between the School of Information and Library Science, the School of Journalism and Mass Communication, and Information Technology Services, all located at the University of North Carolina at Chapel Hill.

With origins dating back to 2000, the goals of the site as stated by ibiblio[14] are multi-fold and include advocacy of open source software, continuation and growth of digital materials and archives, and mentoring other open projects. Is there a role this online digital site can play in your library, especially considering the many larger sites we've discussed? Most importantly, is ibiblio really a site that you should be considering when looking for digital eBook content or online information for your patrons?

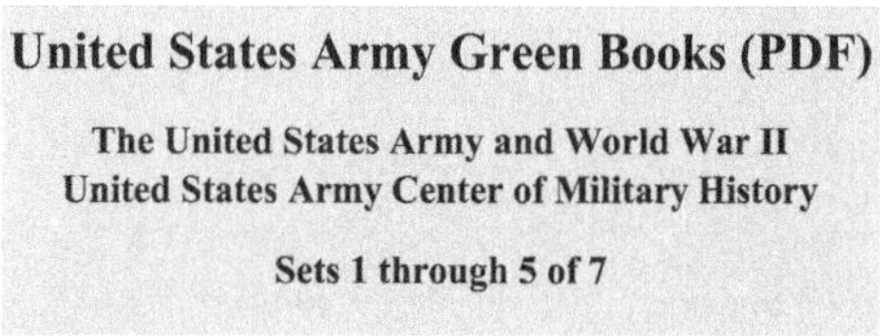

United States Army Green Books (PDF)

The United States Army and World War II
United States Army Center of Military History

Sets 1 through 5 of 7

Figure 6.28

What You Can Find

Concentrating on the digital materials contained within ibiblio, let's narrow the focus to get a better understanding of what we can find. As mentioned previously, the project hosts many different subprojects within the collections; it is not just a singular eBook depository. Examples of some of the materials you can find include the Online Burma/Myanmar Library,[15] the U.S. Army Green Books[16] (as noted in Figure 6.28), and even the website and other projects of the Norfolk Southern Railway Historical Society. This multi project approach may seem confusing at first, but it does give you and your patrons a fast way to burrow down to a very specific topic.

Searching ibiblio

So what's the best method for searching ibiblio? What techniques can you apply to help your patrons find the information they are looking for? To find out, let's visit the project's homepage and see what how the site is structured.

Figure 6.29

One of the first things you'll note is the toolbar across the top of the page. As seen in Figure 6.29, individual resources such as open source software and project information can be found in each section. You can also use the search box located on the top right of the page to look for specific keywords or subjects. On the right side of the page, you'll find an additional pane of information and links (see Figure 6.30).

Figure 6.30

Figure 6.32

However, the best method of looking for information and digital resources is to use the **Browse** option located on the top of the page. Clicking on that link brings you to the catalog page at http://www.ibiblio.org/catalog/, where you'll find a list of recently added items, as well as advanced search options and subject listings (see Figure 6.31). If you're looking for information and digital resources on specific subjects but do not see them on the list, check out the **More** option at the bottom of the **Popular Categories** column. Clicking on that brings you to a tag cloud of subject listing (see Figure 6.32).

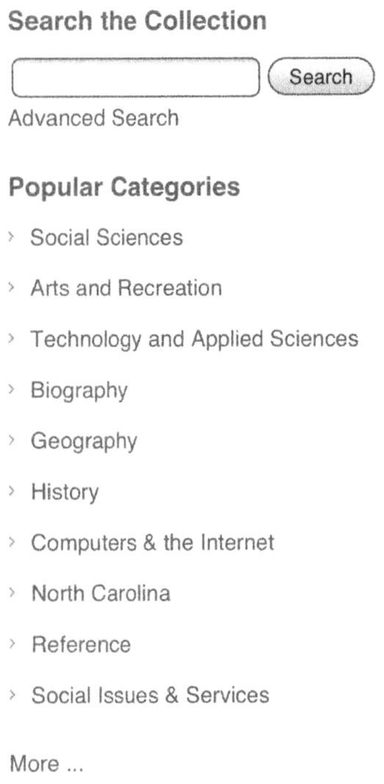

Note the advanced search option above the category listing. Clicking on that takes you to the following page: http://www.ibiblio.org/catalog/items/advanced-search.

Search the Collection

[   ] [Search]

Advanced Search

Popular Categories

> Social Sciences

> Arts and Recreation

> Technology and Applied Sciences

> Biography

> Geography

> History

> Computers & the Internet

> North Carolina

> Reference

> Social Issues & Services

More ...

Figure 6.31

As noted in Figures 6.33 and 6.34, there are many options on the advanced search page, including the ability to search by keywords, collections, types, and specific data fields. For now, let's do some sample searching so that you can learn more effectively how to use the site. Let's say you are working at the reference desk one day, and a patron asks for information on the CIA's involvement in the Korean War from the early 1950s. How can the ibiblio site help in this situation? There are many methods of searching ibiblio, but for this query, let's go to the advanced search page and try just a regular keyword

Advanced Search

Search for Keywords

[   ]

Narrow by Specific Fields

[Select Below ▼] [Select Below ▼] [   ]

[Add a Field]

Search by a range of ID#s (example: 1-4, 156, 79)

[   ]

Search By Collection

[Select Below ▼]

Search By Type

[Select Below ▼]

Search By Tags

[   ]

Featured/Non-Featured

[Select Below ▼]

[Search]

Figure 6.33

✓ **Select Below**
Dublin Core
   Contributor
   Coverage
   Creator
   Date
   Description
   Format
   Identifier
   Language
   Publisher
   Relation
   Rights
   Source
   Subject
   Title
   Type
Item Type Metadata
   BCC
   Bibliography
   Biographical Text
   Birth Date
   Birthplace
   Bit Rate/Frequency
   CC
   Compression
   Death Date
   Director
   Duration
   Email Body
   Event Type
   From
   Interviewee
   Interviewer

Figure 6.34

Browse Items (2 total)

› Browse All : Browse by Category ›

Korean War CIA Freedom of Information Act Release

Shadowed by WWII before it and the Vietnam war after, the Korean War is one of the least remembered conflicts of the 20th Century. The CIA recently released over 1,000 documents covering daily and weekly intelligence estimates as the war progressed.

...

Tags: Biography, Geography, History, History - American, History - Asian, Military, Social Sciences

Linux Focus

LinuxFocus is a free international magazine for Linux. It's a non profit organization and the magazine is managed by volunteers from all over the world. LinuxFocus provides free documentation for the Linux operating system. LinuxFocus is...

Tags: Computers & the Internet, Technology and Applied Sciences

Figure 6.35

Korean War CIA Freedom of Information Act Release

Shadowed by WWII before it and the Vietnam war after, the Korean War is one of the least remembered conflicts of the 20th Century. The CIA recently released over 1,000 documents covering daily and weekly intelligence estimates as the war progressed.

...

Tags: Biography, Geography, History, History - American, History - Asian, Military, Social Sciences

Figure 6.36

search using the terms **CIA Korean War**. What sort of results do you get?

Either looking through your own results or Figure 6.35, you should see two results. The first entry, **Korean War CIA Freedom of Information Act Release**, is probably going to help your patron quite a bit.

Clicking on this link brings you to another page, as shown in Figure 6.36, where you'll find a final page of information on the topic in question.[17] From this particular page, as noted in Figures 6.37 and 6.38, your patron will have access to a large amount of material to help in her research. These materials range from original documentation to reports, correspondence, and more.

As you can see, the results of your search reflect major differences between this site and other sites we've reviewed. It offers not just single titles, but digital collections and associated content that can be viewed on a wide variety of devices. This facet alone makes ibiblio an important component of your library's digital strategy. Collection sites of digital materials such as these are often found in many other online archives and museums. Often overlooked, these can contain many valuable resources for your patrons.

Because of this project/subproject approach taken by ibiblio, you should become familiar with the site before using it in your everyday reference work. In addition, navigation, searching, and using the materials do have the potential to be a bit more involved. Just knowing the basics isn't enough. Take some time and practice searching the site as well as viewing results of those searches. If you do staff training on online digital sites, be sure to include ibiblio in your classes.

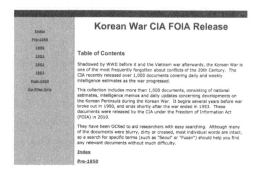

Figure 6.37

Baen Free Library

Most of the sites we've explored so far in this book have been aggregators of content across a broad spectrum of digital materials and not specific to a subject or resource. However, the Baen Free Library is based on a different concept that you should be aware of as another possible resource for your library. It's a hybrid of sorts, containing both free and nonfree titles devoted exclusively to a singular topic: science fiction and fantasy fiction published by Baen Books. A great way to find and explore fiction eBook titles at no or low cost, you will find popular authors such as Eric Flint and David Weber. The site was undergoing renovation and change in the early part of 2013. Navigate to the home page at http://www.baen.com/library to get started with this resource.

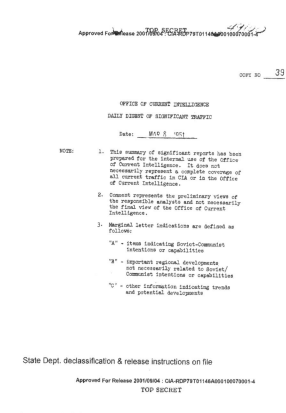

Figure 6.38

Using the site for the first time, you'll soon find a variety of ways to search for material. Links for authors, titles, and series are available on the left side of the library's home page and clicking on them will take you to the corresponding listings. From there, you can select an individual work, which gives you more information about the title, including reviews, author information, and a plot summary. On the same page (if available), you'll find download links in a wide variety of file options, including Kindle and older PalmPilot formats. Table 6.2 lists some that are currently on the site.

Table 6.2 Baen Free Library Popular eBook Format Options

Format Type
Kindle
Sony (lrf)
Nook (ePub)
Microsoft Reader (lit)
Word Processor (RTF)
Rocketbook (rb)

Beyond the free content, the Baen Free Library also offers a path to their paid eBook content, with Baen Ebooks (http://www.baenebooks.com/) serving as a portal to the content. Because you can search by author, category, publisher, and even custom search, this particular part of the site might be useful for your acquisitions department. One noteworthy aspect of the site is that readers with disabilities have free permanent electronic access to all published Baen Books, as noted at this link: http://www.baenebooks.com/t-disabled.aspx.

Important Points to Remember about the Other Sites

Now that you have had a chance to see how some of these other digital resource sites are organized and can be used (both from the patron's perspective as well as the library's point of view), you're likely amazed at the diversity of methods connecting readers with the content now available online. What follows are some points that you can use to help remember specifics as well as share with your staff and patrons.

There Are Many, Many More

- Many other digital eBook sites besides the bigger ones
- Quality, not necessarily quantity, emphasized
- Innovative viewing, usage, and methods of delivery

Project Gutenberg

- Public domain titles
- Classed by different categories; helpful in making the decision about what to read
- Mobile site, online bookshelves, and extensive catalog searching options
- Multiple formats available for each title listed on the site

DailyLit

- Innovative methods of delivery, including RSS and email
- User forums and book discussions
- Book reviews, ratings, and more
- Extensive searching and browsing options available on the site
- Books delivered in many parts, catering to busy patrons who might not have time to sit down and read for an extended length of time

ManyBooks, ibiblio, and Others

- ManyBooks search by author, title, genre, and languages
- ManyBooks contains both basic and advanced search capabilities
- ibiblio contains many different collections, not just a singular focus

- ibiblio contains both basic and advanced search capabilities but encourages browsing by categories

- Extensive category listings on ibiblio that include tagging options to help you locate needed information

- Baen Free Library includes current popular fiction

Questions for You to Try

One of the most important things to remember is that the smaller sites discussed in this chapter differ greatly in their approach to digital materials. Searching them can be challenging if you are not familiar with the basics of how each of them are structured and how they operate. The following questions will help test your knowledge of the sites discussed in this chapter. Remember that the answers are in the back of the book, but try to answer them as best you can before looking at proposed solutions.

Project Gutenberg

1. A history professor at the local college asks if you could help him find a wide variety of resources on music, especially music theory and music history. Using the resources on Project Gutenberg, what approach would you take to help him find these materials?

2. Although your library has placed a major emphasis on eBooks and other digital resources, many of your patrons have complained that their particular device does not support the popular OverDrive format. Using Project Gutenberg, what other formats could you find that might be acceptable for a variety of devices?

3. Your library is about to close for the night when a patron comes to the reference desk and asks for an electronic copy of the Gettysburg Address. Because the stack lights have been turned off, you naturally think of going to Project Gutenberg for your answer. What method would you use to find the speech? Why? Is there a quicker method of finding the speech?

DailyLit

1. You're working at the reference desk one Saturday morning when a patron comes to you, looking for stories by the popular author Cory Doctorow. However, she mentions she's looking for something that she can read with her smart phone on her lunch hour. Using DailyLit, how would you look for reading materials for this patron? How would you recommend she read the item in question?

2. On the DailyLit site, what's the best method of searching for classic fiction, and how would you find the top-rated books in this category? How are items rated on DailyLit?

ManyBooks

1. Using the search functions on the ManyBooks site, what's the best method of looking for spy novels from the early part of the twentieth century?

2. While you are working at the circulation desk one day, you realize that for the first time in your life, you actually have nothing to read at lunch! Using the ManyBooks site, find yourself something to read. What's the easiest method? Why?

ibiblio

1. You're doing a meet-and-greet at your library with a local community college class, telling them about digital book sites and other online archives. Amazingly, the students seem to really enjoy learning about these available resources. A few hours later, some students come to you asking for resources about press communications from the U.S. Navy during World War II. Using ibiblio, how would you find this information?

2. The advanced search options on ibiblio offer extensive lists of fields that you can search. On the other hand, ibiblio also offers extensive browsing capabilities for the digital materials offered on its site. Which method, in your opinion, works better for patrons? Why?

Baen Free Library

1. Using the Baen Free Library, what's the quickest method of finding series titles written by various authors?

2. Using the site, how many titles can you find by the author Eric Flint? What's the quickest method of doing so? What's the easiest method for your patrons to find out this same information?

Notes

1. Project Gutenberg, http://www.gutenberg.org/wiki/Main_Page.
2. Project Gutenberg, http://www.gutenberg.org/wiki/Gutenberg:Project_Gutenberg_Mission_Statement_by_Michael_Hart.
3. Project Gutenberg, http://www.gutenberg.org/wiki/Gutenberg:The_History_and_Philosophy_of_Project_Gutenberg_by_Michael_Hart.
4. Project Gutenberg, http://www.gutenberg.org/ebooks.

5. Project Gutenberg, http://www.gutenberg.org/wiki/Gutenberg:Offline_Catalogs.
6. MarcEdit, http://people.oregonstate.edu/~reeset/marcedit/html/index.php.
7. DailyLit, http://www.dailylit.com/about/.
8. DailyLit, http://www.dailylit.com/books/the-wisdom-of-steve-jobs.
9. DailyLit, http://www.dailylit.com/books/seth-godin-unboxed.
10. DailyLit, http://www.dailylit.com/books/with-a-little-help.
11. DailyLit, http://www.dailylit.com/books/3-short-reads-by-edgar-allan-poe.
12. DailyLit, http://www.dailylit.com/books/little-women.
13. DailyLit, http://www.dailylit.com/books/secret-adversary.
14. ibiblio, http://www.ibiblio.org/about.
15. ibiblio, http://www.burmalibrary.org/.
16. ibiblio, http://www.ibiblio.org/pha/USA-in-WWII/.
17. Ibiblio, http://www.ibiblio.org/korean-war-cia-foia-releases/.

Resources

With these sites, you've seen an incredible amount of content, including classic works as well as unique and hard-to-find titles. Adding depth and breadth to your digital resources as well as your local collection, these online sites and projects deserve a spot in your everyday reference work. What follows are links to news, reviews, and other information that may be helpful to you. Use these as a starting point for your own classes, presentations, or just information for your patrons.

Sites, News, and Information

About.com, "Discover Your Next Book at ManyBooks," http://websearch.about.com/b/2011/08/29/discover-your-next-book-at-manybooks.htm.

Fiction Writers Review, "Thursday Morning Candy: DailyLit," http://fictionwritersreview.com/blog/thursday-morning-candy-dailylit.

MakeUseOf, "6 Great Contemporary E-Books You Can Read by Email via DailyLit," http://www.makeuseof.com/tag/6-great-contemporary-ebooks-read-email-dailylit/.

Project Gutenberg, "The Audio Books Project," http://www.gutenberg.org/wiki/Gutenberg:The_Audio_Books_Project.

Project Gutenberg, "The History and Philosophy of Project Gutenberg by Michael Hart," http://www.gutenberg.org/wiki/Gutenberg:The_History_and_Philosophy_of_Project_Gutenberg_by_Michael_Hart.

Project Gutenberg, "The Sheet Music Project," http://www.gutenberg.org/wiki/Gutenberg:The_Sheet_Music_Project.

Chapter 7

Are There Any Safe Conclusions?

Figure 7.1

Figure 7.2

Millions of titles, lots of technology! You've learned about many sites in this book, from the Google Books project to HathiTrust, the Internet Archive, and the Open Library. And you've also explored some smaller sites as well, from Project Gutenberg to DailyLit, ManyBooks, and others. Along the way we've discussed how these sites work, as well as how you can use them to find eBook resources and all types of digital data.

Further, we've shown how you can integrate these sites into your library services and collections, using them on a daily basis as well as a starting point in your library's digital planning process. Finally, you've been given links, tips, and lots of practice questions to help you understand and get comfortable with these sites.

So are there any conclusions you can draw from the examination of these particular sites? What do these sites say about the future of our libraries, of our profession? What do your patrons think about these sites as they look up from their Kindles, Nooks, iPad Minis, smart phones, and

Figure 7.3

Figure 7.4

Figure 7.5

Figure 7.6

Figure 7.7

Figure 7.8

other mobile devices? Most importantly, how does your community view your library in the middle of this technology revolution that continues to reinvent everything we are familiar with?

Given the growth of mobile reading technology as well as these online digital book sites, our libraries, your library and mine, need to prepare for a future that is now taking hold but still unfolding, revealing itself a bit at a time. Specifically, there are three methods to consider when thinking about this future:

- Innovation
- Implementation
- Inspiration

While these are abstract concepts, let's look at them in light of all of this talk about digital change!

Innovation

Many of the sites we've covered have been forward thinking in terms of change and innovation, pursuing new ideas and methods of implementation. Were you surprised the first time you heard about the Google Books project? About millions of titles going online for free? While you may be used to this idea now, the initial concept was a game changer! Yet this innovation, this push forward by Google, has literally transformed how we view books today.

Consider the ongoing legal maneuvering over the issue of orphan works that the giants of Google, HathiTrust, and the Authors Guild are involved with. While things may be settling down somewhat, nothing is certain, and nothing has yet been decided. Look also at the astounding growth of eBooks and eBook readers. In this same sense of innovation, people's perceptions of our libraries have changed as well. Our patrons want in their library what they experience on a commercial level—the same instant information and the same novels, available anywhere and anytime.

So have we adapted? Have our libraries changed to meet this challenge of perception? Some have, but many have not. *We must change now*. The process of information gathering that we have become accustomed to is rapidly changing and is calling on us to innovate, be different, and take on the challenges of this new environment. All of us must meet our patrons' needs and shy away from old processes that no longer make sense.

Consider innovation on a practical level. Let's say your library is currently in a budget crisis, yet usage counts and circulation statistics continue to skyrocket. You know your library isn't meeting everyone's needs. What do you do? A traditional approach might be a levy, gathering money for a new library that would be able to support the increased circulation and patron traffic. However, what if your library's levy fails? What if it is rejected by voters who are already contending with increased taxes and higher unemployment? Would you abandon the idea of a library?

In times like this, you must innovate and change your mode of thinking. Does your town really need another physical library, or do your patrons need access to information? If it's information they need, it can be offered in many different ways. Create a virtual branch, using the digital resources we've spoken about in this work. Have your librarians work from home and allow patrons to communicate with them via Facebook, Google +, text message, or whatever other methods of communications that work. Change your library's website to include these new tools.

Take a chance and enhance your eBook collection, even if it means moving money away from your physical collections. By changing, innovating, doing something completely different, you can help meet at least some of your patrons' needs. Is this a perfect answer, a perfect solution? No, not by any means. But at least it's a start. If you can't achieve change by one method, then try another! Who knows how this might impact and motivate your community, your patrons, or even your staff?

Speaking of digital resources and innovation in libraries, I had the chance in putting this book together to talk to Sue Polanka, librarian, author of *No Shelf Required: E-Books in Libraries*[1] and moderator of the well-known blog **No Shelf Required.**[2] Well known in the library world as an advocate of eBooks, I asked her about this digital revolution and about ways that libraries can innovate, perhaps even creating their own digital resources based on local patron-created content such as genealogies and other sources.

Sue agreed that this would be a perfect application of both technology and service, mentioning eBook creation as well as the growing use of other innovative methods such as print on demand (POD), which can affect libraries in many positive ways, from children's programming to genealogy and more. She went on to discuss her response to the Chief Officers of State Library Agencies (COSLA) report, which addressed this very topic of eBooks, libraries, implementation, and the future. After reading this report and the other resources mentioned in this book, you'll see it's amazing what a little innovation can do for our libraries.

There are also forces outside our libraries that see these changes and are starting to push for the future as well. A great example of this is the continued massive growth of the Digital Public Library of America (DPLA). While still in the early stages, their website is active and future plans, people, and ideas are rapidly coalescing around it. Even now, librarians, academics, and others are today discussing how the DPLA will revolutionize information access in the years to come. Promising a great increase in access to digital material as well as a new approach to digital information, I hold out hope for the DPLA to be an information innovator.

For more background on the DPLA,[3] take a look at their website. If you are responsible for formulating any sort of strategic plan for digital access, you will find many interesting ideas to get your own creative forces going!

Implementation

Now consider implementation. How do you implement changes today to get ready for the future? While everyone's library is different to some extent, and all depend on the mission and budgets as well as staffing and other factors, implementation of digital resources in our libraries must be balanced against concerns such as budgets, internal training, and technology/vendors. Let's look at each one of these in detail as well as some practical explanations.

Budgets

As unpleasant as we all may find them, budgets are a necessary component of our discussion of resource implementation and planning processes. After all, our budgets help maintain salaries, collection materials, and even the physical aspects of the library itself. So how does considering your budget affect the integration of eBooks and other digital resources in your library? While most of the digital resources discussed in this book have no direct influence on your budget, indirect influences need to be considered, measured, and included as possible budget expenditures.

Look at it this way: If you plan to provide your patrons with support related to eBooks and eReaders of any sort, staff must be trained on the equipment, and they must also be available to interact with the patrons. This costs money. You will need to look at the training portion of your budget to see what you have and what you can afford. Likewise, if your library is offering eReader support, you will need to purchase a few devices, if only to get the staff up to speed on what is there and so that they will have the practical experience to be able to help your patrons. All of these factors depend on your budget, which in turn will affect your implementation.

So what if there is no budget for these things and no foreseeable increase in monies? It's a hard decision to make, and depending on how these digital resources are factored into your strategic plan, you might have to reduce the speed with which the changes take place or perhaps even seek out grants to help cover these expenditures. There are no easy answers when it comes to libraries and budgets. Just be aware that finance plays a tremendous factor in your library endeavors.

Internal Training

As mentioned previously, internal staff training is an important component of any successful digital resource implementation you may choose to pursue in your library. Your staff must be up to speed on the searching techniques, the file formats, and the technology specifics that each site has chosen to implement. Change cannot come through a handout or a small blurb in the weekly staff newsletter. Time must be set aside to answer staff questions about this process.

Too often this is overlooked. If you currently do not have staff training, what can you do to get a program started? Training doesn't need to be part of an extensive and formal program. It could just involve designating a colleague who is willing to do internal training. At the end of the day, you can't expect your patrons to embrace this digital change if your staff doesn't embrace it. For larger libraries, this is usually an easy decision. For smaller libraries, and sometimes even mid-size libraries, this is a larger hurdle to overcome.

Technology and Vendors

So far the focus has been on nonphysical items—planning, strategies, budgets, and so on. However, at the very bottom of any discussion related to implementation, you really need to consider the twin topics of technology and vendors. What sort of technology will you use to implement this digital future, these online digital sites, and these eBooks? It's hard to know what is right, if only because the market itself is not standardized. You need only look at the various DRM implementations and lack of eBook formats to see the truth in this.

In putting this book together, I had the opportunity to interview Paul Jones, the current director of **ibiblio**, one of the sites examined in Chapter 6. Speaking on the topic of technology as applied to digital resources, he made an excellent point, stating that "A good part of the problem—beyond rights management (both for authors and readers) and licenses—will be the technical means with which to provide enforcement . . . " Given this, and after doing my own research, I've found that technology is a key component of any digital strategy, and that the market has yet to decide on a clear-cut winner.

As you pursue any form of digital eBooks, you should realize that for many resources, local conversion is often an option. You don't necessarily have to rely on vendors for projects you want to pursue. For example, consider your local genealogy collection. If you're a public library, there's a good chance that you have at least a small genealogical collection related to your community. Today you have the tools to take that collection of papers, books, and other materials, and turn it into a digital resource for your patrons and the library. The barrier of "making" these types of items has been substantially lowered, bringing within reach the opportunities for libraries of all types and sizes to go digital!

Figure 7.9

There are other tools that you can use to help your staff address your patrons' eBook needs as well. A great example is Calibre,[4] a superb eBook software program that is free to use and can be implemented by your library to import, export, change format, and manage digital resources used in the collection. Although having a consumer-based orientation (as you can see in Figures 7.9 and 7.10), conversion, addition, and distribution of eBooks can be performed quite easily. What a great way to offer these resources to your patrons and help you in your daily library responsibilities!

Inspiration

Now consider inspiration. Given what you now know about digital sites, eBooks, your patrons' needs, and the ongoing tsunami of technology that seemingly never stops, what inspires you to change?

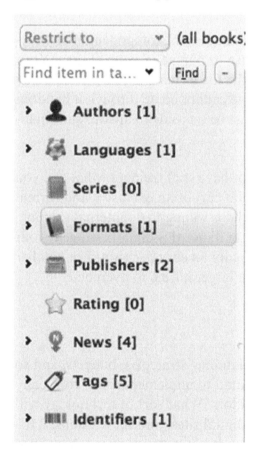

Figure 7.10

Digital sites such as Google Books, when used properly in your library, can inspire both you and your staff to dream up new ideas of how to get information to your patrons as well as how to provide services that currently are not being offered. Inspiration can be a powerful force if harnessed and directed toward the proper channels.

If you are a library administrator, you likely have seen your staff pick up new ideas and present them to you at meetings or other events. You might even have your own inspiration!

How you decide to use these digital book sites is up to you, but be bold! Use your ideas, see what works, and see what doesn't. While sometimes you might fail, many times you might not, and you will end up bringing an innovative new program to your patrons!

Final Notes

As you may have guessed by now, I'm completely biased in my approach and presentation. However, knowing this, I still believe that paper books, our analog collections, will be a part of our libraries for a long time. Books are part of the library experience and will continue to be so, but I feel the mixture of resources, both print and digital, will continue to increase. This leavening together of print and digital enhances your patrons' experiences, making your library even more valuable in the long run.

Using online digital book sites can have a transformative effect for your library. Given the uncertainty of the future we cannot see as well as the budgetary unknowns, integrating these sites into your everyday library processes of collection development and patron services can help your organization grow and prosper, becoming an essential part of your community, your college, or wherever you may be.

Notes

1. No Shelf Required 2, "Use and Management of Electronic Books," http://books.google.com/books?id=vNNdPX8K8ZEC.
2. No Shelf Required, http://www.libraries.wright.edu/noshelfrequired/.
3. Digital Public Library of America, http://www.dp.la.
4. Calibre, http://calibre-ebook.com/.

Answers to Chapter Questions

One of the best ways to learn any task is by doing. Using this approach, you learn the needed skills, but also become instantly aware of any potential pitfalls. We've all experienced this type of learning, and it may even be a technique you currently use. In Chapters 2 through 6, you had a chance to do exactly this as you answered questions about the online book sites.

In case you got stuck on any of the questions or are just curious about different techniques that could be employed to find the answers, this appendix presents possible solutions to each question. Use these as examples or possible alternatives to how you answered the questions. The importance here is not necessarily a correct or incorrect response but more of a "did you try this approach" sort of answer.

Chapter Two: Getting Started with the Google Books Project

Site Structure and Materials

1. You're working the reference desk and a teacher from the local high school pulls you aside for some special assistance. She is teaching British literature this semester and is concerned about having enough copies of

the books available for students to use. How can Google Books help, and what's the best method to help this teacher find what she needs?

For this scenario, Google Books is a great way to help students. Many classic British literature works are in the public domain and have been digitized by the project already. And while it does depend on the title, many of these works are freely downloadable or can be read on the screen through a web browser. To help students find the particular titles they need, run a regular search through Google Books on either author or title. For browsing, the Google Books project offers a Classics subject heading that lists many titles and can give students searching ideas if no particular title is needed.

2. Your director is planning a major eBook push for your library in the upcoming strategic plan to be presented at the next board meeting. What are some ways Google Books can be incorporated into the plan? Specifically, how can Google Books get eBooks to your patrons easily, quickly, and for free?

Any library's digital strategy obviously depends on its local situation. Theoretically, the Google Books project offers a great way to supplement your local on-shelf collection. When books you already own are checked out but are still available via the project, it is useful. Or if your library is closed, your patrons can go directly to the always-open Google Books project. It's also possible to embed book titles into your library's website using the Google API code or use the bookshelf option to keep your patrons up to date on new titles or collections. For public domain titles, the Google Books project offers downloads in a variety of formats, ranging from PDF to plain text and ePub. For your patrons with eReaders, this is a great method of finding new reading materials!

3. The children's librarian is going to be giving a talk to a local high school class next week about using Google Books to find articles for a persuasive essay. Considering the site and its structure, what's the best method for the students to browse for different subjects?

Given that these students are in high school, the quickest method would be to use the subject layout on the main Google Books page at http://books.google.com/books. Using this method to find a particular subject is both easy and fast. Once a particular title is found, it's then possible to find related titles by choosing the related books option within the selected books.

Searching Google Books

1. Your local genealogical society has expressed interest in learning more about various genealogical resources that might be available via the Google Books project. In particular,

they are looking for family histories. What sort of search strategy would you recommend for them and why?

The fastest method of searching for genealogy and related subjects on Google Books is obviously by family name. For common names such as Smith, this approach will not work as well, so in those cases, I would recommend an advanced search using a combination subject search on genealogy and the name in question. If too many results are returned, it's possible to also limit the search via year range and/or type of books.

2. It's science fair time at your library again, and as usual, all of your science books are checked out. How can the Google Book project help? How would you go about searching for supporting materials, and what sort of results might you find?

There are two solutions to this conundrum. The first is to conduct a generic search on Google Books with the term **Science Fair**. From here, it's possible to use individual books to supplement your own physical collection. Given the preview option in Google Books, recent titles can be useful, even if the entire title cannot be viewed or downloaded. The second solution involves using individual titles that are listed in your own catalog as a basis for searching within Google Books. Once a title is found, search the related books option to find more. It is also possible to find a particular title on the project and then jump to the **WorldCat** option within the project to find other libraries near yours that might have a particular title for borrowing.

3. You work at a small college library, and your director is looking to implement a digital book strategy for downloadable public domain titles. Using Google Books, find four or five resources that can be downloaded. Which do you find more of—PDF or ePub format?

Finding public domain titles should be easy via a specific title or author search. If these specifics are not known, an advanced search that limits the years to 1923 and earlier as well as the full view only option should return a list of public domain titles. Be sure to also mention that many of these same titles are listed under the Google Play option—but you can download these without having to use that particular selection. As to the types of formats available, in my experience, PDF is more common, but ePub is also a strong contender—and I've now started to see more titles with this particular format show up in my own search results.

Viewing Results

1. You've been helping a patron find more information on *Billboard* magazine from the 1950s. However, she is not quite sure what viewing options would work best. Knowing the multiplicity of views that are possible, which one would you recommend and why?

Viewing results will obviously depend on the patron and which technique will work best for her. However, in using the Google Books project, I've found the two-page layout to work best. In the case of looking for specific illustrations, the thumbnail viewing options are the most flexible and easy to use.

2. Look for public domain resources that are downloadable. How would you copy the text to a Word document? Which method is best?

When working with public domain titles, often you will find the option to copy text portions into your word processor of choice. Using the highlight tool, this is fast and easy. However, for larger portions, it's best to download either a PDF or ePub format then transform that to plain text via software such as Calibre (http://www.calibre-ebook.com) if possible. You can also screenshot the page(s) in question and then drop this into Word as a picture, although this can prove cumbersome if the selection is large.

Chapter Three: HathiTrust

HathiTrust Site and Structure

1. Given the many methods of searching, which method would you start with if you were asked to put together a library pathfinder of sources for the history of the Federal Reserve? What specific searching methods could you use to save time when creating this bibliography?

Using HathiTrust for this option, and tasked with quickly putting together a list of titles, the fastest method would be conducting a catalog search using the term **Federal Reserve**. When viewing an individual title and the searching links within it, it is possible to quickly pull up related titles and authors for the bibliography. You could also search the full text for related words or phrases if you were confident in your background knowledge of the Federal Reserve.

2. Name three types of materials (in addition to regular book volumes) that can be found on the site. Write down a few specific titles. What sorts of materials are **not** common to HathiTrust?

Formats other than books that are available in HathiTrust include audio files, maps, and videos. These alternative formats may or may not be full-text searchable (due to format type), but they can be found using the regular catalog search. Maps and other related non-book items are not as common.

Searching HathiTrust

1. You're working at the reference desk, and a patron comes to you looking for historical information on the World War II writer Ernie Pyle, specifically a quote from one of his

books about England during the war. The quote is: "Heroes are all the people ... " Given this information, how would you instruct the patron to begin her search? Can you find what title this quote is from, if any?

The fastest method of finding quotes or full-text phrases in the HathiTrust project is to use the full text search option. Using this method and quotations around the phrase in question you can find the title in question called ***Ernie Pyle in England***, which was published in 1941.

2. Do a regular catalog search on HathiTrust, focusing on titles about the American Civil War. How many results do you find that are available for full text use on the site? How many results are only catalog records? Now limit your search to the immediate postwar years of 1870–1890. How does this affect your results?

Using the regular catalog search in the project, this becomes a tricky question! Not using quotation marks around the phrase **American Civil War** returns many results. If you use the quotation marks and delineate a phrase search, the returned results are somewhat more manageable, but there are still many titles to search through. Of these, select the **full view only** option, and you end up with titles that can be viewed online. If you limit your search to the postwar years of 1880 to 1889, the list of results is narrowed quite a bit.

Viewing Results

1. Imagine you're working at the reference desk and a patron comes up looking for information on Charles Lindbergh. In particular, he's looking for some digital results that he can view on his Nook. How would you find materials for the patron? Name some titles that might fit his need, and explain how you would go about making these titles viewable on his reading device.

With the popularity of Charles Lindbergh in U.S. culture and history, this is an easy search, and it illustrates the many resources available to your patrons on HathiTrust. Do a regular catalog search with quotes around the name: **"Charles Lindbergh"**. Now perform the same search using the full-text search option. Notice the differences. In this case, the full-text option gives you much more detailed results. From here, you can examine the results or modify the search with additional terms to pull in more material.

Once a resource is found, you have many options for getting the materials onto the patron's Nook. The fastest would be to use the web browser on the Nook itself to view the material, but downloading a PDF is also an option. Image options and plain text work as well, but overall, the PDF is probably the way to go. Remember, however, that unless your patron has a library card with one of HathiTrust's member libraries, he is limited to downloading items a single page at a time, or sometimes in special cases, public domain documents can be downloaded in full.

2. HathiTrust makes source materials available in three primary formats. Name these formats and give examples of when each would be appropriate.

You can choose from plain text, images, or PDF. There are many formats available on HathiTrust, and it's sometimes hard to choose what is best. For regular reading, PDF best represents the page as presented in the book. Plain text loses the special formatting but does enable you to directly copy quotes into a document or other research paper. Images can be an option as well, particularly if you are using them for a presentation or talk.

3. Imagine you're working at the reference desk one afternoon and an older couple comes to you looking for a fast method for finding and using genealogy resources. Using the collections function in HathiTrust, what can you find on genealogy, and what options in the collection can help them quickly sort the titles?

In this particular scenario, the collections function on HathiTrust is a great choice. If you go to the main site and choosing the **Browse Collections** option, you will notice the search box on the right side of the page. Simply searching for the term **genealogy** will reveal multiple collections that your patrons can choose to begin viewing. Don't overlook the ability to search within a particular collection as well.

Chapter Four: The Internet Archive

Origins of the Internet Archive

1. Given the tremendous amount of materials available on the Internet Archive, which types of titles do you feel would be the easiest to integrate into your own library? Why? Which resource would be most difficult to use with patrons?

Much of any answer to this question ultimately depends on your library, your staff, your strategic plan, and most importantly, your patrons! To help you make your decision, plan on spending some time with the Internet Archive. View the many types of materials that are available and then compare what you've found to your library's current use of resources. Identify themes that will help to determine the materials you use most often. Identify and work with key staff members on this to get a broad cross-section of your information needs. Then work directly with them, bringing into focus the same types of materials currently available on the Internet Archive.

Site Structure, Materials, and Components

1. Given the site structure of the project, how would you recommend using the site for someone who has never used it before? Would you recommend a specific material type search over all the materials in the archive or only a few? Why?

For a patron or staff member who is new to the Internet Archive, a general overview of what is available as well as how to do basic searching is always a good starting point. From here, if you are working with a patron, conduct your standard reference interview, asking questions to pinpoint what they are looking for. Once this is known, selecting the types of materials to search for becomes easy. It's worth spending more time with staff members who perhaps will be instructing patrons on the site at some point. Perhaps give them sample questions such as these or a short training session to help them become more familiar with searching and using the materials on site.

Searching the Internet Archive

1. You're in charge of storytime one Wednesday morning and the parents of one of the children come up to you with a question. They're looking for a book of fairy tales written by Hans Christian Andersen. However, they're specifically looking for one story in the book: "Little Claus and Big Claus," and your library does not have a print copy of the tale. Using your knowledge of searching the Internet Archive, how would you find this story?

This search can be tricky, and the way you conduct it depends on what method works best for you. You could try the advanced search, using Hans Christian Andersen as the creator and using *Fairy Tales* as the title. However, doing the search this way **illustrates one of the biggest issues** with the Internet Archive—there are many titles by Hans Christian Andersen listed. One method is to quickly scan the list of results, pulling them up in the browser and looking at the stories listed in the table of contents of each work.

Another method that would possibly work is running your search against a general search engine or other reference point for Hans Christian Andersen, finding the date of publication of the individual story. Once this is done, an advanced search at the Internet Archive with the date range option would help you locate a specific published work that contains the story. Still, this is not an easy search and illustrates some of the issues related to relying solely on a single search point.

2. Given the advanced search functions of the project, name some of the custom fields available for searching. Which would be used most often? Which ones would not? Why?

Some of the advanced fields available for search include episode, number, title, creator, and description. The more common fields (e.g., title, creator, media type, date) would probably be the best way to conduct a quick search. Other more obscure fields (e.g., scanner, contributor, image count) are useful for involved searching but would not be practical in the everyday library environment. All of the fields are important; however, the less common fields are harder to use because you're probably not really sure who the scanner is, what the image count is, and so on.

Viewing and Using Your Results

1. You're working at the reference desk when a patron comes in with her Kindle. She wants to find comic books about the Lone Ranger for her device. Using the Internet Archive, how would you help her?

Start the search by navigating to main Internet Archive site at http://www.archive.org. Instead of searching first for texts, do a simple phrase search for Lone Ranger and view your results. To further narrow down to just comic books, limit your results with the mediatype option. From there, your patron could scan her results for Kindle formats such as AZW, image files, or PDF. If your patron has conversion software, it is possible to convert typical comic book formats (*.cbz and others) to a Kindle-capable format.

2. It's been a tough week, and just as you get ready to walk out the door, a patron comes up to you looking for information about 1930 census records from Florida. Because you really want to go home and relax, what's the fastest method to help your patron use the Internet Archive? Are the census records themselves searchable?

You could navigate to the texts section of the Internet Archive (http://www.archive.org/details/texts) and then do a quick phrase search for U.S. Census. However, doing so will give you many false hits. For faster results, go to http://www.archive.org/details/texts, search under Additional Collections, and then go to Genealogy. Once here, finding census records is a fairly easy process. The specific link to find is http://www.archive.org/details/us_census.

Special Tools for Libraries and Librarians

1. What are DAISY books? What extra tools does one need to be able to use them?

DAISY-formatted books can be considered digital equivalents of audiobooks for your patrons with vision impairment. Two types of DAISY titles are available on the Internet Archive: encrypted and unencrypted. For specific tools, try this link: http://www.archive.org/details/printdisabled.

2. What are some of the additional text collections that are available for use on the Internet Archive? Try two different collections. Do you think it is effective to have

these specialized collection notations, or would it be better to have a single large collection? Why?

One of the best features of the Internet Archive is the amazingly wide variety of texts that are available for use. Lists of the different collections can be found here: http://www.archive.org/details/texts. These specialized collections can help your patrons quickly find what they are looking for (e.g., genealogy or digitized microfilm).

Chapter Five: The Open Library

Site Structure and Materials

1. Considering the design of the Open Library website, what would be the best method of conducting a subject search for a patron looking for any sort of information on the Cuban Missile Crisis?

While many different options do exist, the quickest method is to go directly to the subject page of the Open Library (http://openlibrary.org/subjects) and search for the term **Cuban Missile Crisis**. Doing this enables to you to view many titles related to this time period and then expand your search to see what would work best with your patron's information needs.

2. One of the biggest strengths of the Open Library is the ability to have the Internet Archive provide many of the digital materials mentioned in its catalog. With this in mind, find two to three digital resource materials for a patron looking both for ePub and Amazon Kindle–based formats. Second, find a DAISY-formatted source. Why would or wouldn't your patrons be able to use this particular format if they wanted to?

As you search for your titles, remember the wide variety of file formats available at the Open Library. Did you have any success? What about failures? Remember that many DAISY-formatted titles are encrypted and do require specific software before you can use them. Try this link for more information: http://www.daisy.org/tools-services.

3. How are OverDrive and OCLC used within the Open Library and the Internet Archive? Do you think the inclusion of these commercial and nonprofit organizations helps or hinders the Open Library project? Does this influence how your patrons will search for and use titles they may find on the Open Library?

The Open Library is working with both of these outside organizations to provide links to other libraries that have necessary materials as well as options to borrow digital titles for checkout. Try this link for background and other detailed information: http://blog.openlibrary.org/2010/06/29/small-moves-open-library-integrates-digital-lending/.

Searching The Open Library

1. Using any combination of search techniques, find a list of titles from the author Evelyn C. White about the famous African American Pulitzer Prize winning author Alice Walker. How many did you find? Are there any special formats available?

You have many search options to consider, and one method you could employ is doing a simple search for the author Evelyn C. White, using the **More search options** link at the Open Library site. Your first search results should include multiple titles. Limiting these results by the other author name, Alice Walker, you'll find three separate editions available, one in DAISY format and the others available for searching on WorldCat.

2. You're working at the reference desk, and a student comes to you looking for download-able digital resources on oil spills. Your online journals database is not accessible, which leaves the Open Library as your sole source. How would you conduct the search and why?

An online database is the fastest route for conducting this search, but using the Open Library is also an option. A quick search on the phrase **oil spills** would be the first query to try, and from there, refine the search using the limit options on the right side of the results page. You could also try the specific subject searching page located here: http://openlibrary .org/subjects. Either option is a great place to start.

3. Using the **Search Inside** function of the Open Library, look for a list of titles about Judy Garland. Why do some titles turn out to be false hits? Is there a better method of using the **Search Inside** function for information on a particular topic?

Using the search terms **Judy** and **Garland** will return a large number of hits. Using the search phrase **Judy Garland** limits these results to a more manageable number. However, one of the biggest issues to be aware of is that even if the search phrase is used inside a title, that doesn't necessarily mean the title has anything to do with Judy Garland. It just indicates that those words are there.

For example, let's say you look through your initial search results and find a title with **Judy Garland**. However, once you examine the title, you see that the only mention of Judy Garland is that the main character is said to **"look like Judy Garland."** As a librarian, you may be familiar with this phenomenon, but many of your patrons are not. For a better method of using the **Search Inside** option, consider stacking your search queries using Boolean operators and adding more specific search terms. This could help you get around any false hits that show up.

4. In this chapter, you've learned about linking options within lists of records or individual results. These are clickable links to other resources that can help you either expand what

you're looking for or quickly zero in on a particular bit of information. Are these functions helpful? Give two examples you have found of these links being useful for you or a patron.

This is a great method of expanding your search, especially when you are not quite sure of the subject, spelling, or other details needed for the query. Using preformed links allows you to remove false hits and zero in on the titles that will be effective for your patron. A great example of this is our previously mentioned search for oil spills.

Viewing, Using, and Interpreting Your Results

1. Using your answers from question 1 in **Searching the Open Library**, how could you help a patron locate a copy to purchase?

Using your results, view the options within each edition and link out to various booksellers (including eBook sellers). From here, your patron can choose which site or vendor they are most familiar with or would like to use for some other reason.

2. Search for the *Iliad* on the Open Library. How many editions are available to read online or download? What if your patron wanted to read a copy on her Kindle—what's the best method of doing so from within the Open Library?

When you do a quick title search for the *Iliad* in the Open Library, you'll see many different editions in the results. Finding a Kindle-compatible format is as simple as picking one of these results, and from within the individual resource, using the **Send to Kindle** option.

3. Your patron comes to you just as your library is closing, looking for a particular title by Carl Sandburg. The only part of the title he remembers is "...*Slabs of the Sunburnt West.*" Find the title and then explain how you would show your patron he could read this title online through his web browser at home. Are there any other formats available that he could use?

Use the **Search Inside** link at http://openlibrary.org/search/inside, or the **More search options** link, and enter the phrase **Slabs of the Sunburnt West** in the title box. Doing so reveals a title by Sandburg. Clicking within that particular title, it's easy to read online through the web browser. Or you can choose a specific format such as PDF, plain text, or ePub.

Chapter Six: But What about the Others

Project Gutenberg

1. A history professor at the local college asks if you could help him find a wide variety of resources on music, especially music theory and music history. Using the resources on Project Gutenberg, what approach would you take to help him find these materials?

There are certainly many options to consider. But given the wide variety of subject materials, the best way to start would probably be to examine the bookshelves part of Project Gutenberg, where you will find an entry for music. Another option to consider is a subject search using the term **Music**. However, the bookshelves option, if available, can save you much research time. For quick reference, try this link: http://www.gutenberg.org/wiki/Category:Bookshelf.

2. Although your library has placed a major emphasis on eBooks and other digital resources, many of your patrons have complained that their particular device does not support the popular OverDrive format. Using Project Gutenberg, what other formats could you find that might be acceptable for a variety of devices?

One of the biggest advantages of Project Gutenberg is the wide variety of eBook formats that are available. From the Kindle-supported mobi format to the ePub format currently supported by a wide range of eReading devices such as the Kobo and Nook, options abound. For patrons who do not have these devices and are reading titles on their desktop or laptop computers, other formats such as HTML and plain text are also easy to get started with.

3. Your library is about to close for the night when a patron comes to the reference desk and asks for an electronic copy of the Gettysburg Address. Because the stack lights have been turned off, you naturally think of going to Project Gutenberg for your answer. What method would you use to find the speech? Why? Is there a quicker method of finding the speech?

The fastest method, and the one to start with first, is to search the book catalog for the phrase **Gettysburg Address**. Your results will include two selections that should be able to help your patron.

DailyLit

1. You're working at the reference desk one Saturday morning when a patron comes to you, looking for stories by the popular author, Cory Doctorow. However, she mentions she's looking for something that she can read with her smart phone on her lunch hour. Using DailyLit, how would you look for reading materials for this patron? How would you recommend she read the item in question?

Using the quick search box at the top of the page, simply enter the author's name, and you'll have many results for your patron to look through. Another option is to browse the author listings, but this would take a bit longer. Because the patron wants to read this particular item on her lunch hour, RSS might work best. But email reading would be fine as well.

2. On the DailyLit site, what's the best method of searching for classic fiction, and how would you find the top-rated books in this category? How are items rated on DailyLit?

Using the category search available at http://www.dailylit.com/tags, it's easy to find the classics category. Using the detailed views, it's possible to see current ratings for each title, or you could see if there are any comments posted in the forums section.

ManyBooks

1. Using the search functions on the ManyBooks site, what's the best method of looking for spy novels from the early part of the twentieth century?

Using the genre search at ManyBooks can give you a complete list of titles, but you will perhaps find too many to browse through. A better solution might be the advanced search, which shows the genre option. Then limit by years. Searching with this method will return a list of titles that might be appropriate.

2. While you are working at the circulation desk one day, you realize that for the first time in your life, you actually have nothing to read at lunch! Using the ManyBooks site, find yourself something to read. What's the easiest method of doing this. Why?

It's always possible to search for titles or authors you already are familiar with, and the Recommendations link at http://www.manybooks.net/eBook_recommendations.php offers a great way to find something new to read. This option might also work well for patrons who have already exhausted their favorite authors or titles.

ibiblio

1. You're doing a meet-and-greet at your library with a local community college class, telling them about digital book sites and other online archives. Amazingly, the students seem to really enjoy learning about these available resources. A few hours later, some students come to you asking for resources about press communications from the U.S. Navy during World War II. Using ibiblio, how would you find this information?

Using the browsing options available on the site to navigate to http://www.ibiblio.org/catalog/items/browse/tag/History would be a great start. But it will take longer to look through the results. For faster searching, try the advanced search options at http://www.ibiblio.org/catalog/items/advanced-search and look for information on the phrase **World War** or **Second World War**.

2. The advanced search options on ibiblio offer extensive lists of fields that you can search. On the other hand, ibiblio also offers extensive browsing capabilities for the digital

materials offered on its site. Which method, in your opinion, works better for patrons? Why?

Much of the answer to this particular question will obviously depend on what patrons are looking for as well as their experience in searching. Work with your patrons to determine their needs and then direct them to the appropriate parts of the ibiblio site. Spend some time searching and using ibiblio. Find what works and does not work and then build on that particular aspect.

Baen Free Library

1. Using the Baen Free Library, what's the quickest method of finding series titles written by various authors?

On the Baen Free Library website at http://www.baen.com/library/, the quickest method for finding series information is to click on the Series link on the left side of the website. Once you do this, you can find series information by author along with the specific titles, and other information.

2. Using the site, how many titles can you find by the author Eric Flint? What's the quickest method of doing so? What's the easiest method for your patrons to find out this same information?

Finding titles by author Eric Flint is as quick as trying the author link on the Baen Free Library, which can be found here: http://www.baen.com/library/authors.asp. Note that by selecting an author from this page, you will be directed to the list of both *free* and *paid* titles. This might be confusing for your patrons, especially if they are unfamiliar with the site.

Dictionary of Technical and eBook Terms

Keeping up with technology is not easy, especially in the context of eBooks, eReading devices, and online digital databases. The minute we understand one concept or technology term, it always seems two new ones show up! In light of this, in this section, you'll find an abbreviated dictionary of some of the terms and concepts used in this book. Each entry includes the word or phrase as well as a brief explanation to help you better understand each term. For more depth, I've also included additional online resources for more information. Finally, at the end of the section, you will find space to enter your own terms or concepts that you've encountered. You can use this as a model for your own learning or for staff training as needed.

AMOLED: Active matrix organic light-emitting diode. A specialized form of display found on many portable devices such as cell phones and tablets. More information/source:Android Authority, "How It Works: AMOLED Displays," http://www.androidauthority.com/amoled-display-how-it-works-91552/.

API: Application programming interface. Form of data communication that allows developers to query external websites and pull down data to a local application or server. Various forms of APIs are in use by the major digital book resources. More information/source: ReadWrite.com, "The New API Gold Rush," http://readwrite.com/2013/04/24/api-gold-rush.

AZW: The file extension that represents Amazon Kindle's primary eBook format. More information/source: About.com, "What is an AZW File?" http://pcsupport.about.com/od/fileextensions/f/azwfile.htm.

Amazon EC2: Also known as Amazon Elastic Compute Cloud and part of the larger service from Amazon known as Amazon Web Services. This service from Amazon allows you or your library to have a server "in the cloud," as well as provide for online storage, email, and more. Using this method, your library does not have to own or maintain the actual server hardware within your organization. This service is also used by various websites to help scale out their infrastructure, including Yelp and Netflix. More information/source: Amazon Web Services, "Amazon Elastic Compute Cloud (Amazon EC2),"http://aws.amazon.com/ec2/.

Boolean: Known under various terms from Boolean logic to Boolean algebra, this form of searching is utilized across the Internet and in the search engines profiled in this book. Allows you to quickly find needed concepts by using AND, OR, NOT operators and operations. More information/source: USC Beaufort Library, "Bare Bones Lesson 8: Searching With Boolean Logic And Proximity Operators," http://www.sc.edu/beaufort/library/pages/bones/lesson8.shtml.

CIC: Also known as the Committee on Institutional Cooperation, this consortium of colleges that includes the University of Chicago, The Ohio State University, and the University of Michigan is a major partner with digital book projects such as HathiTrust and the Google Books project. While CIC refers to the full group, CLI refers to the subproject Center for Library Initiatives, the part responsible for working with digital book projects. More information/source: Committee On Institutional Cooperation, "Center for Library Initiatives," http://www.cic.net/Home/Projects/Library/Home.aspx.

Cloud: As referred to in this book and in relation to modern computer technologies, cloud is a method of computing in which a majority of computing resources such as servers and software are maintained off site at another provider. Examples of this include Gmail and Dropbox. Not having the computing infrastructure on site frees a library from having to purchase and maintain expensive hardware and software as well as storage space. On the other hand, when using the cloud, the library is dependent on a high-speed Internet connection and the cloud provider to always be available and accessible. More information/source: IBM, "Navigating the IBM cloud, Part 1: A primer on cloud technologies." http://www.ibm.com/developerworks/websphere/techjournal/1206_dejesus/1206_dejesus.html

Calibre: eBook creation and management software used across a wide variety of platforms. Updated frequently and very popular, this tool is a great choice for libraries looking to get started with digital eBook management. Not an organizational piece of software, but more for use on an individual workstation or PC. More information/source: Calibre, "About calibre," http://calibre-ebook.com/about.

CARLI: Consortium of Academic and Research Libraries in Illinois. Includes online digital resources and other projects. Member of the Open Content Alliance (as profiled in our chapter on the Internet Archive). More information/source: Consortium of Academic and Research Libraries in Illinois, "About CARLI," http://www.carli.illinois.edu/about.html.

DRM: Abbreviation for digital rights management. Most often, DRM is used by vendors in electronic resources such as eBooks to prevent unauthorized copying. This can present a problem in some cases because DRM is platform specific and often depends on vendor implementation and support. More information/source: American Library Association, "Digital Rights Management (DRM) & Libraries," http://www.ala.org/ala/issuesad vocacy/copyright/digitalrights/index.cfm.

E-Ink: Specialized display found commonly in eReading devices such as the Kindle, Nook, and Kobo. Low power consumption makes this display technology a best choice for long battery life. More information/source: EInk, "Technology," http://www.eink.com/technology.html.

ePub: Another in the list of commonly encountered eBook file formats. Supported by a majority of eReader devices, ePub is known as an extension of sorts for XML (see definition) and has its origins in the Open eBook Forum of the International Digital Publishing Forum. The majority of the online digital resource sites mentioned in this book support this growing format. More information/source: MobileRead Wiki, "ePub," http://wiki .mobileread.com/wiki/EPub.

GOPHER: Along with the **Veronica** search engine, this early Internet protocol was used before the burgeoning popularity of the World Wide Web. Menu-based, this protocol was strictly text, as was the Internet before the advent of the modern web browser. More information/source: About.com, "Gopher," http://linux.about.com/cs/linux101/g/gopher.htm.

ILS: Integrated library system. The server-software combination that libraries use to check in, check out, catalog, and provide a publicly accessible web catalog. Examples of ILS vendors include Innovative Interfaces and Polaris. While most modern ILS systems are vendor supported and closed source, open-source ILS systems such as Evergreen and Koha are gaining both institutional users and popularity. More information/source: Library Technology Guides, "Key Resources in the Field of Library Automation," http://www.library technology.org/.

JSON: Noted by sites as JavaScript Object Notation, this text format is sometimes used in place of the ubiquitous XML format. Several of the major online digital book sites use

JSON for pulling records and information out of their databases. More information/source: Json.org, "Introducing JSON," http://www.json.org/.

Lyrasis: Membership-based library organization brought about by the mergers of the SOL-INET and PALINET library membership organizations. More information/source: Lyrasis, "About Us," http://www.lyrasis.org/membership/Pages/About-Us.aspx

MARC: Machine-readable cataloging. First developed in the 1960s, these standards are used by libraries worldwide to describe and catalog materials of all types. Individual elements consist of numerical fields followed by the data from each item such as title, author, and publisher. More information/source: Library of Congress, "Understanding MARC," http://www.loc.gov/marc/umb/.

Mobi: Shortened term for Mobipocket. Another eBook format popularized by Mobipocket SA.. More information/source: Mobipocket.com, "What is an ebook?" http://www.mobipocket.com/en/eBooks/whatisanebook.asp?Language=EN.

OGG VORBIS: Also known as Vorbis. Audio format is used most often as an alternative to the now ubiquitous MP3 format. It is supported by many devices but is not yet universal. More information/source: Vorbis.com, http://www.vorbis.com/faq/.

OCLC: Online Computer Library Center. This membership-based library organization helps libraries catalog their books and other items via shared records and several different software platforms and applications. This includes the **WorldCat** search engine and various software programs such as **Connexion** and the Internet-only **FirstSearch**. More information/source: Online Computer Library Center, "About OCLC," http://www.oclc.org/us/en/about/default.htm.

RSS: Really Simple Syndication. RSS is a method by which Internet-based sites can share updates in a single standard format. End users can use specialized RSS software such as Feedly to read RSS feeds of updated content. This option is used by several of the digital book sites covered in this book, including DailyLit and the Google Books project. More information/source: DailyLit, "FAQ: Table of Contents," http://www.dailylit.com/faq.

Rocketbook or Rocket eBook: One of the first eReading devices, the Rocketbook reader was about the size of a paperback book and included a liquid crystal display (LCD) screen and the ability to connect to your Windows-based PC to transfer purchased eBooks. Obsolete now, but was a precursor in size and application to today's eReading devices. More information/source: MobileRead Wiki, "Rocket eBook," http://wiki.mobileread.com/wiki/Rocket_eBook.

URL: Uniform Resource Locator. Unique Internet address used to access Internet websites and other online locations. For example, the URL to connect to the Google Books Project is http://books.google.com/books, with ""http" indicating a web browser–based request.

More information/source: Internet Engineering Task Force, "Uniform Resource Locators," http://www.ietf.org/rfc/rfc1738.txt.

Wildcard searching: A form of searching used in conjunction with advanced search options where symbols and/or punctuation are used to represent letters or numbers. An example of this would be the use of "**gol***" where the "*****" would represent several letters such as in golfing, going, gold, goliath. This is a great method to use when you are not sure exactly how a title, author, subject, or keyword is spelled. More information/source: Search Engine Journal, "HOW TO: Use Wildcard Search with Various Google Services," http://www.search enginejournal.com/how-to-use-wildcard-search-with-various-google-services/28911/.

WorldCat: Known as the "world's largest library catalog," this extensive catalog from **OCLC** helps bring together bibliographic information from member libraries' individual catalogs. WorldCat is also used by some of the digital book sites such as Google Books and HathiTrust More information/source: OCLC, "WorldCat," http://www.worldcat.org.

XML: Extensible Markup Language. XML is a method of encoding data in a consistent, particular format. Used often as an option by the online digital book sites we have spoken of, output in this format can be manipulated and used in the local library either via the ILS or specific software programs. Some of the larger online digital book sites offer API options with the XML format. More information/source: World Wide Web Consortium, "Extensible Markup Language," http://www.w3.org/XML/.

Here's space for you to add your own terms and definitions as you come across them.

Term:

Description:

Sources:

Term:

Description:

Sources:

Term:

Description:

Sources:

Term:

Description:

Sources:

Term:

Description:

Sources:

Bibliography

In putting together this book, one of the biggest tasks was sifting through the many resources, from traditional publishing outlets as well as personal blog posts, reviews, websites, and many other access points. In light of this, what follows is a detailed list that you can use either for background knowledge or when you want to look for specific information on the topic of eBooks, usage in libraries, and integration into the everyday library world.

Some are newer than others, but I've left the older resources to provide insight on the vast change that has occurred over the past few years. I've also included some of the sources already mentioned in the chapters. Use these as a starting point for your own reference or just finding out more about each site.

ALA TechSource. "Coming to Terms with Mobile." http://www.alatech source.org/blog/2010/04/coming-to-terms-with-mobile.html.

About.com. "Discover Your Next Book at ManyBooks." http://websearch. about.com/b/2011/08/29/discover-your-next-book-at-manybooks.htm.

Albanese, Andrew Richard. "Brewster's Millions." *Publishers Weekly* 258, no. 22 (May 30, 2011): 33. MasterFILE Premier, EBSCOhost.

Albanese, Andrew. "HathiTrust Is Launched." *Library Journal* 133, no. 18 (November 2008): 13. Academic Search Premier, EBSCOhost.

American Libraries. "England's Libraries and the Funding Crisis." http:// americanlibrariesmagazine.org/news/09072011/england-s-libraries-and -funding-crisis.

"An Elephant Backs Up Google's Library." *New York Times.* http://bits. blogs.nytimes.com/2008/10/13/an-elephant-backs-up-googles-library/? ref=technology.

The Atlantic. "The Fight over the Future of Digital Books." http://www.theatlantic.com/technology/archive/2011/09/the-fight-over-the-future-of-digital-books/245577/.

The Atlantic. "Moving Towards a Physical Archive of the World's Books." http://www.theatlantic.com/technology/archive/2011/06/moving-towards-a-physical-archive-of-the-worlds-books/240045/.

"Backed by Internet Archive, Entrepreneur Takes on OCLC." *American Libraries* 39, no. 4 (April 2008): 27. MasterFILE Premier, EBSCOhost.

Ben, Mook. "Project Gutenberg: Your Homely Key To Free, Classic Books Online." *Daily Record* (Baltimore, MD) Regional Business News, EBSCOhost.

Benny, Evangelista. "His Mission: Preserve Our Fleeting Digital Past." *San Francisco Chronicle*, October 14, 2012, A1. Newspaper Source, EBSCOhost.

Block, Melissa. "Judge Rejects Google Books Deal." *All Things Considered* (NPR). Newspaper Source, EBSCOhost.

Booth, Char, Heather Christenson, and Paul Fogel. "Unlocking HathiTrust." *Library Journal* 136, no. 12 (July 2011): 34–35. Academic Search Premier, EBSCOhost.

Carter, Lauren. "Make Time to Read the Classics in a Novel Way." *Writer* 121, no. 5 (May 2008): 10. Academic Search Premier, EBSCOhost.

Chief Officers of State Library Agencies. "COSLA: eBook Feasibility Study for Public Libraries, Final Report." http://www.cosla.org/documents/COSLA2270_Report_Final1.pdf.

Chief Officers of State Library Agencies. "Spring Meeting and E-Book Session COSLA's Role in Providing E-Book Access" (report presented at the National Press Club May 11, 2011). http://www.cosla.org/documents/COSLA_Ebook_Report_3.pdf.

Christenson, Heather. "HathiTrust: A Research Library at Web Scale." *Library Resources and Technical Services* 55, no. 2 (2011): 93–102. Academic Search Premier, EBSCOhost.

Coombs, Karen. "Opening Up to Open Library." *Library Journal* 133, (Spring 2008): 28. MasterFILE Premier, EBSCOhost.

"Dartmouth, TRLN Sign on with HathiTrust." *Library Journal* 135, no. 18 (November 2010): 17. Academic Search Premier, EBSCOhost.

"Digital Bookmobile Displays Latest Library Technology." *Roanoke Star-Sentinel.* http://news roanoke.com/?p=13237.

"E-Content: Informing the Transformation of Libraries." *E-Content.* http://americanlibraries magazine.org/e-content.

Education-Portal.com. "Libraries in Crisis: What Budget Cuts Mean for CA Libraries." http://education-portal.com/articles/Libraries_in_Crisis_What_Budget_Cuts_Mean_for_CA_Libraries.html.

Emanuel, Jenny, and M. Kathleen Kern. "Next Generation Catalogs: What Do They Do and Why Should We Care?" *Reference and User Services Quarterly* 49, no. 2 (2009): 117–120. Academic Search Premier, EBSCOhost.

ENews Park Forest, "Internet Archive Reaches 3 Million Items with Rare Galileo Texts from the University of Toronto Libraries." http://www.enewspf.com/latest-news/science-a-environmental/27312-internet-archive-reaches-3-million-items-with-rare-galileo-texts-from-the-university-of-toronto-libraries.html.

Enis, Matt, and Meredith Schwartz. "AAP/Google Announce Settlement Agreement." *Library Journal* 137, no. 18 (November 2012): 18–20. Academic Search Premier, EBSCOhost.

Enis, Matt. "OverDrive, Baker & Taylor Streamline Ebook Checkout." Library Journal 138, no. 9 (May 2013): 20. Academic Search Premier, EBSCOhost.

Fialkoff, Francine. "Too Many Ebook Cooks." *Library Journal* 137, no. 13 (August 2012): 8. Academic Search Premier, EBSCOhost.

Fiction Writers Review. "Thursday Morning Candy: DailyLit." http://fictionwritersreview.com/blog/thursday-morning-candy-dailylit.

Google. "1.5 Million Books in Your Pocket." http://booksearch.blogspot.com/2009/02/15-million-books-in-your-pocket.html.

Google. "About the Google Books Project." http://books.google.com/googlebooks/about.html.

Google. "Basic Search Help." http://www.google.com/support/websearch/bin/answer.py?hl=en&answer=134479.

"Google Books Shrinks Its Ambitions." *Information World Review*, no. 261 (December 2009): 2. MasterFILE Premier, EBSCOhost.

Google. "Discover More Than 3 Million Google eBooks from Your Choice of Booksellers and Devices." http://googleblog.blogspot.com/2010/12/discover-more-than-3-million-google.html.

Google. "Find Out What's in a Word, or Five, with the Google Books Ngram Viewer." http://booksearch.blogspot.com/2010/12/find-out-whats-in-word-or-five-with.html.

Google. "Google Books Family API." http://code.google.com/apis/books/docs/getting-started.html.

Google. "LIFE Magazine Now Available on Google Books." http://booksearch.blogspot.com/2009/09/life-magazine-now-available-on-google.html.

Google. "The Point of Google Print." http://googleblog.blogspot.com/2005/10/point-of-google-print.html.

Gray, Naomi Jane. "Fair or Foul? Mass Digitization and the Fair Use Doctrine." *Licensing Journal* 32, no.6 (June 2012): 6–15. Business Source Premier, EBSCOhost.

Greenwalt, R. Toby. "Developing an E-Book Strategy." *Public Libraries* 51, no. 1 (January 2012): 22–24. Library Literature and Information Science Full Text (H. W. Wilson), EBSCOhost.

Grimes, William. "Michael Hart, a Pioneer of E-Books, Dies at 64." *New York Times*, September 9, 2011, p.21. Academic Search Premier, EBSCOhost.

Hadro, Josh. "After Kindle Lending, the Deluge." *Library Journal* 136, no. 9 (2011): 12. Academic Search Premier, EBSCOhost.

Hadro, Josh. "Summon/HathiTrust Deal Ups Access to In-Copyright Works." *Library Journal* 136, no. 8 (May 2011): 17. Academic Search Premier, EBSCOhost.

Hadro, Josh. "The Tech behind the HathiTrust." *Library Journal* 134, no. 2 (February 2009): 19. Academic Search Premier, EBSCOhost.

Hane, Paula J. "Ebooks and Libraries: Time for Library Renewal." *Internet@Schools* 18, no. 2 (2011): 8. Academic Search Premier, EBSCOhost.

Harper, Eliot. "You've Got Literature! Publishing Books in E-Installments." *Seybold Report: Analyzing Publishing Technologies* 8, no. 23 (December 4, 2008): 10. MasterFILE Premier, EBSCOhost.

"HathiTrust's Copyright Detectives." *Library Journal* 135, no. 19 (November 2010): 15–16. Academic Search Premier, EBSCOhost.

"HathiTrust Digital Library Gets Searchable." *Library Journal* 134, no. 10 (June 2009): 17. Academic Search Premier, EBSCOhost.

HathiTrust News, Presentations and Information about the Project: http://www.hathitrust.org/papers_and_presentations.

HathiTrust. "Our Partnership." http://www.hathitrust.org/partnership.

HathiTrust. "Statistics and Visualizations." http://www.hathitrust.org/statistics_visualizations.

"HathiTrust Research Center to Open Corpus to Research." *Library Journal* 136, no. 10 (June 2011): 21. Business Source Premier, EBSCOhost.

HathiTrust. "Technological Profile." http://www.hathitrust.org/technology.

Howard, Jennifer. "Reader Choice, Not Vendor Influence, Reshapes Library Collections." *Chronicle of Higher Education* 57, no. 12 (2010): A11–A12. Academic Search Premier, EBSCOhost.

Howard, Jennifer. "With No Google Books Deal, Libraries Push New Plans for Digital Access." *Chronicle of Higher Education* 57, no. 30 (April 2011): A12. MasterFILE Premier, EBSCOhost.

Inside Higher Ed. "Abuse of Trust?" http://www.insidehighered.com/news/2011/09/19/michigan_admits_flaws_in_hathitrust_system_for_identifying_orphan_works.

Internet Archive. "FAQ's." http://www.archive.org/about/faqs.php.

Internet Archive Blogs. "Book Scan Wizard Software Now Supports Internet Archive Uploads!" http://blog.archive.org/2011/03/14/book-scan-wizard-software-now-supports -internet-archive-uploads/.

Internet Archive Blogs. "How Archive.org Items Are Structured." http://blog.archive.org/2011/ 03/31/how-archive-org-items-are-structured/.

"Internet Archive Raises Copyright Concerns." *InsideCounsel* 16, no. 175 (June 2006): 73. MasterFILE Premier, EBSCOhost.

"Internet Archive Unveils New Physical Archive." *Library Journal* 136, no. 12 (July 2011): 18. Academic Search Premier, EBSCOhost.

Jones, Edgar. "Google Books as a General Research Collection." *Library Resources and Technical Services* 54, no. 2 (April 2010): 77–89. Academic Search Premier, EBSCOhost.

Kahle, Brewster, and Rick Prelinger. "Many Libraries." *Technology Review* 115, no. 3 (June 2012): 10–11. Computer Source, EBSCOhost.

Kelley, Michael. "DPLA Steering Group Adds Public Library Directors." *Library Journal* 136, no. 10 (June 2011): 14. Academic Search Premier, EBSCOhost.

"Kindle eBooks Available around Clock at Library." *Blade* (Toledo, OH), September 26, 2011. Newspaper Source, EBSCOhost.

Langer, Emily. "Digital library 'legend' invented the eBook in '71." *Washington Post*, September 2011. Newspaper Source, EBSCOhost.

Language Log. "Google Books: A Metadata Train Wreck." http://languagelog.ldc.upenn.edu/ nll/?p=1701.

Levy, Steven. *In the Plex: How Google Thinks, Works, and Shapes Our Lives.* New York: Simon & Schuster, 2011.

LibConf.com. "CIL Opening Keynote Panel." http://www.libconf.com/2011/03/21/cil-opening -keynote-panel/.

"Libraries at Webscale." Online Computer Library Center (OCLC). http://www.oclc.org/ reports/webscale/default.htm.

LibraryJournal.com. "DAISY Formatted Books for the Vision Impaired." http://www .libraryjournal.com/article/CA6728034.html.

LibraryJournal.com. "IDPF Digital Book 2011: The Internet Archive's Potential 'Library Option.'" http://blog.libraryjournal.com/ljinsider/2011/05/24/idpf-digital-book-2011-the -internet-archives-potential-library-option/.

LibraryJournal.com. "Internet Archive Offers One Million Works for the Blind and Print Impaired." http://www.libraryjournal.com/article/CA6728034.html.

LibraryJournal.com. "The Open Library Is Opening Room for Debate." http://www
.libraryjournal.com/lj/newsletters/newsletterbucketacademicnewswire/885595-440/the_open
_library_is_opening.html.csp.

LibraryJournal.com. "Periodicals Price Survey 2011: Under Pressure, Times Are Changing."
http://www.libraryjournal.com/lj/ljinprintcurrentissue/890009-403/periodicals_price_survey
_2011_.html.csp.

LibraryJournal.com. "University of Michigan Project to Identify Orphan Works in HathiTrust
Collection." http://www.libraryjournal.com/lj/home/890712-264/university_of_michigan
_project.html.csp.

LibraryJournal.com. "The Voices of Librarians and the DPLA." http://www.libraryjournal
.com/lj/home/889797-264/the_voices_of_librarians_and.html.csp.

Literary Tourist. "Brewster Kahl Talks about the Open Library Project." http://literarytourist
.com/2006/02/brewster-kahl-talks-about-the-open-library-project/.

MakeUseOf. "6 Great Contemporary E-Books You Can Read by Email via DailyLit." http://
www.makeuseof.com/tag/6-great-contemporary-ebooks-read-email-dailylit/.

Milliot, Jim. "DailyLit to Zip Books via E-mail." *Publishers Weekly* 254, no. 21 (May 21,
2007): 6. MasterFILE Premier, EBSCOhost.

Mobileread. "Google Books Offers ePub Downloads of Free Books." http://www.mobileread
.com/forums/showthread.php?t=55071.

Musto, Ronald G. "Google Books Mutilates the Printed Past." *Chronicle of Higher
Education* 55, no. 39 (June 2009): B4. MasterFILE Premier, EBSCOhost.

National Public Radio. "The Secret of Google's Book Scanning Machine Revealed." http://
www.npr.org/blogs/library/2009/04/the_granting_of_patent_7508978.html.

No Shelf Required. "ALA Launches new E-content Blog," October 6, 2011. http://www.
libraries.wright.edu/noshelfrequired/2011/10/06/ala-launches
-new-e-content-blog/.

Nunberg, Geoffrey. "Counting on Google Books." *Chronicle of Higher Education* 57, no. 18
(2011): B11. MasterFILE Premier, EBSCOhost.

"NYPL Joins HathiTrust, as Repository Brands." *Library Journal* 135, no. 12 (July 2010):
20. Academic Search Premier, EBSCOhost.

"OCLC, HathiTrust Unveil Prototype Interface." *Library Journal* 136, no. 3 (February 2011):
21. Academic Search Premier, EBSCOhost.

O'Leary, Mick. "Open Library and the Gatekeepers." *Information Today* 28, no. 9
(October 2011): 22–23. Academic Search Premier, EBSCOhost.

Open. "British Library Encloses the Public Domain." http://opendotdotdot.blogspot.com/
2011/06/british-library-encloses-public-domain.html.

Openlibrary.org. "In Library Lending." http://openlibrary.org/subjects/in_library#ebooks =true.

Open Library Blog. "New BookReader." http://blog.openlibrary.org/2010/12/09/new -bookreader/.

Openmoko. "WikiReader Can Now Deliver Over 33,000 Digital Books from Project Gutenberg." *Business Wire* (English), (December 2012). Regional Business News, EBSCOhost.

OverDrive.com. "About." http://www.overdrive.com/About/.

"OverDrive Unveils Project Gutenberg eBook Downloads." *Library Journal* 135, no. 15 (September 2010): 18. Academic Search Premier, EBSCOhost.

Palfrey, John. "What Is The DPLA?" Library Journal 138, no. 7 (April 2013): 38. Academic Search Premier, EBSCOhost.

Parry, Marc. "The Humanities Go Google." *Chronicle of Higher Education* 56, no. 37 (June 2010): A1. Academic Search Premier, EBSCOhost.

"Perceptions of Libraries, 2010: Context and Community." Online Computer Library Center (OCLC). http://www.oclc.org/reports/2010perceptions.htm.

Pew Research Center. "E-Book Reading Jumps: Print Book Reading Declines." http://libraries .pewinternet.org/2012/12/27/e-book-reading-jumps-print-book-reading-declines/.

Pew Research Center. "Mobile Connections to Libraries." http://libraries.pewinternet.org/ 2012/12/31/mobile-connections-to-libraries.

Pew Research Center. "E-Reader Ownership Doubles in Six Months." http://pewinternet.org/ Reports/2011/E-readers-and-tablets.aspx.

Pike, George H. "Divide and Conquer: Update on the Google Books Lawsuit." *Information Today* 29, no. 2 (February 2012): 1–34. Academic Search Premier, EBSCOhost.

Polanka, Sue. "An Ebook Primer." *Library Journal* 137, no. 7 (April 15, 2012): 42–44. Academic Search Premier, EBSCOhost.

Poudre River Public Library District (via TeleRead and InfoDocket). "eBooks and eReaders in Public and Academic Libraries." http://www.poudrelibraries.org/about/pdf/ereader -report-2011extended.pdf.

Project Gutenberg. "The Audio Books Project." http://www.gutenberg.org/wiki/Gutenberg: The_Audio_Books_Project.

Project Gutenberg. "The History and Philosophy of Project Gutenberg by Michael Hart." http://www.gutenberg.org/wiki/Gutenberg:The_History_and_Philosophy_of_Project _Gutenberg_by_Michael_Hart.

Project Gutenberg. "The Sheet Music Project." http://www.gutenberg.org/wiki/Gutenberg: The_Sheet_Music_Project.

Rapp, David. "DPLA Gets Real at Plenary Meeting." *Library Journal* 136, no. 19 (November 15, 2011): 16. Biography Reference Bank (H. W. Wilson), EBSCOhost.

ReadWrite. "Will Your Local Library Lend E-Books (Or Can They?)" http://readwrite.com/2010/11/10/will_your_local_library_lend_e-books_or_can_they.

"Scan This Book." *New York Times Magazine.* http://www.nytimes.com/2006/05/14/magazine/14publishing.html.

"Shoot First, Get Copyright Later." *New Atlantis: A Journal of Technology and Society* 28, 134. Academic Search Premier, EBSCOhost.

"State of America's Libraries: A Report from the American Library Association." American Library Association. http://www.ala.org/ala/newspresscenter/mediapresscenter/americaslibraries2011/index.cfm.

Swiss Army Librarian. "Linking from the Catalog to Google Books." http://www.swissarmylibrarian.net/2011/05/24/linking-from-the-catalog-to-google-books/.

TechCrunch. "That Was Fast: Amazon's Kindle Ebook Sales Surpass Print (It Only Took Four Years)." http://techcrunch.com/2011/05/19/that-was-fast-amazons-kindle-ebook-sales-surpass-print-it-only-took-four-years/.

TeleRead.com. "Internet Archive Launches In-Library Ebook Lending Program." http://www.teleread.com/library/internet-archive-launches-in-library-ebook-lending-program/.

"University of California Joins Google Library Protect." *American Libraries* 37, no. 8 (September 2006): 16–17. Academic Search Premier, EBSCOhost.

University of Michigan Library via *The Charleston Advisor.* "An Interview with John P. Wilkin, Executive Director of HathiTrust." http://www.lib.umich.edu/media/news/interview-john-p-wilkin-executive-director-hathitrust.

University of Texas Libraries. "Electronic Books." http://www.lib.utexas.edu/books/etext.html.

Walker, Diane Parr. "HathiTrust: Transforming the Library Landscape." *Indiana Libraries* 31, no. 1 (January 2012): 58–64. Library Literature and Information Science Full Text (H. W. Wilson), EBSCOhost.

Warburton, Bob et al. "HathiTrust Verdict Aids Access for the Blind." *Library Journal* 137, no. 20 (December 2012): 12–14. Academic Search Premier, EBSCOhost.

Weinberger, David. "DPLA: A Good Idea That Has a Shot." *KM World* 20, no. 6 (June 2011): 1–26. Business Source Premiere, EBSCOhost.

Wesleyan University. "Google Books and Hathi Trust." http://ptully.blogs.wesleyan.edu/2011/03/25/google-books-what-is-the-fuss-about/Background information on both the Google Books project and HathiTrust.

Wilcox, Amanda. "Library Patrons Granted Access to More Than 200,000 Free E-Books." *Daily News* (Jacksonville, NC), July 5, 2012. Newspaper Source, EBSCOhost.

Wilkins, John. "BackTalk: HathiTrust and the Google Deal." http://www.libraryjournal.com/article/CA6625155.html.

Wired.com. "Africa's Past Landscapes Revealed in Historical Travel Accounts." http://www.wired.com/wiredscience/2011/09/travel-writing-conservation/?pid=2064&pageid=72411.

Woyke, Elizabeth. "Kobo CEO on the Future of E-Readers and Google Books." Forbes.com. July 12, 2011. Business Source Premier, EBSCOhost.

Index

About the Author

Librarian, technologist, and history enthusiast, H. ANTHONY BANDY is a graduate of the University of Kentucky School of Library and Information Science. He currently works with libraries on training and technology issues via his company, Library Knowledge, which can be found online at www.library knowledge.com. You can find him on Twitter posting fresh updates about the library and technology world at twitter.com/libknowledge.

Bandy is also a published freelance writer for *Family Tree* magazine (UK), Moorshead Magazines, and others, and can often be found writing about all types of American history at his personal blog, found at Adventures in History, history.writingwithtony.com.

CPSIA information can be obtained at www.ICGtesting.com
Printed in the USA
LVOW03s0522110614

389483LV00015B/187/P